"At the outset of this book George Marsden makes the simple but profound observation that the United States is 'both remarkably religious and remarkably profane.' This organizing principle helps make his *Religion and American Culture* an astute, accessible, and wonderful introduction to the fascinating puzzle of American religious history."

— Thomas S. Kidd
Baylor University

"In this highly readable volume Marsden provides a sweeping overview of religion in American history. He not only sketches the landscape with enviable clarity but also offers an interpretive frame for understanding the relationship of American religion and culture—and ultimately for comprehending a nation that is 'both remarkably religious and remarkably profane.' "

— Kristin Du Mez
Calvin College

"Any list of the most influential American historians of the past half-century would undoubtedly include George Marsden. His *Religion and American Culture* is a careful, balanced assessment not only of Christianity's complex role in American history but also of American culture's influence on Christianity. No better brief yet profound treatment of Christianity's 400 years in the United States exists than this volume."

— Rick Ostrander
Council for Christian
Colleges & Universities

"In this survey of the religious (and, paradoxically, secular) forces that have shaped American life over the past four centuries, Marsden masterfully weaves colorful insight and incisive analysis into an accessible narrative that readers of all levels will find highly instructive. This is a must-read, invaluable resource for anyone interested in making sense of past and current trends in American religious culture."

— Darren Dochuk
University of Notre Dame

"With measured prose Marsden's *Religion and American Culture* deftly illuminates the consistently central role of people of faith in our country's history. Often dealing with matters that have been overheated by insistent polemics, Marsden broad-mindedly lets the chips fall where they may, allowing churches their role in sowing seeds both evil and good. The book is especially innovative when showing the role of Protestantism, Catholicism, and Judaism in elite political and intellectual circles from the 1870s to the 1970s."

— RICK KENNEDY
Point Loma Nazarene University

"I am thrilled that Marsden's *Religion and American Culture* is back in print. While the text certainly stands alone as an introductory survey by one of our generation's greatest American religious historians, it will also serve as a supplementary textbook for teachers and professors who want to bring religious developments to bear on US history survey courses."

— JOHN FEA
Messiah College

Religion and American Culture

A Brief History

• •

THIRD EDITION

George M. Marsden

WILLIAM B. EERDMANS PUBLISHING COMPANY

GRAND RAPIDS, MICHIGAN

Wm. B. Eerdmans Publishing Co.
4035 Park East Court SE, Grand Rapids, Michigan 49546
www.eerdmans.com

First edition 1990
Second edition 2001
Third edition 2018
Printed in the United States of America

27 26 25 24 23 22 21 20 19 18   1 2 3 4 5 6 7 8 9 10

ISBN 978-0-8028-7539-6

Library of Congress Cataloging-in-Publication Data

Names: Marsden, George M., 1939- author.
Title: Religion and American culture : a brief history / George M. Marsden.
Description: Third edition. | Grand Rapids : Eerdmans Publishing Co., 2018. |
    Includes bibliographical references and index.
Identifiers: LCCN 2018018271 | ISBN 9780802875396 (pbk. : alk. paper)
Subjects: LCSH: Religion and culture—United States. | United
    States—Religion. | United States—Civilization.
Classification: LCC BL2525 .M36 2018 | DDC 200.973—dc23
    LC record available at https://lccn.loc.gov/2018018271

To my students, who are continuing to enrich this history

Contents

Preface

Throughout American history, religious beliefs and practices have interacted with other aspects of the culture in many fascinating ways. I have designed this account of those interactions to be a useful guide for anyone seeking to make sense of religious expressions in the United States. In offering these narratives and observations, I draw on what I have learned from more than a half century of teaching and studying this topic. I wrote the initial version in mid-career to serve primarily as a textbook, then simply titled *Religion and American Culture.* Even at that time, however, I wrote in part with the intention to provide general readers, as well as students, an accessible overview of this intriguing history. As it turned out, it reached only the textbook market. The initial version, appearing in 1990, was successful enough to warrant an updated and revised second edition that came out in 2001. After that, the original publishing company was absorbed in a series of mergers and the book seems to have been all but lost in the shuffle. Now the rights have reverted to me so that I am pleased to present a revised and updated version that is clearly as much addressed to a general audience as it is to students.

With such an audience in mind, I have also strengthened its interpretive dimensions. So, even though the basic narrative remains much the same, I now see this work as a full offering of the best interpretive insights that I have accumulated in considering these topics. I would be pleased, of course, if teachers discovered or rediscovered it as a useful overview of the topic for students. But now the design and format are more clearly tailored, as well, for general readers who wish better to understand the ways in which religious faith has influenced American culture and how American culture has shaped the most prominent American faiths.

This history differs from most texts on American religion in that it has relatively little to do with religious institutions but is primarily a cultural history, trying to understand the reciprocal roles of American religions and American culture in shaping each other. It includes a good bit of what I used to teach as "American Intellectual History" and later as "American History through Beliefs and Values," which explored the changing shapes of dominant and subdominant values and assumptions that people take for granted. Also, unlike some accounts of religion in American life, this book is weighted more toward modern eras since the Civil War, rather than toward the colonial era, because the more recent eras are the ones in which religious dimensions have been most often neglected in general American histories. Also, I suspect that most readers wish to understand the roles of religion in more recent America to better understand their own religious practices, as well as those of their neighbors and fellow citizens.

Acknowledgments

Since this book has evolved, many of my debts go back quite a way. A generous grant from the Pew Charitable Trusts for the study of "The Religious and the Secular in Modern America" initially gave me time to work on this volume. I am also grateful to the Divinity School of Duke University and to Dennis Campbell, its dean at that time, for release from some duties while I worked on this project. I also want to thank the University of Notre Dame, the Francis A. McAnaney Chair, and the McAnaney family for their long-standing and always gracious support.

I also owe substantial debts to those who read the first draft and provided valuable commentaries on it. These include Diana Butler Bass, Tony Jenkins, Paul Kemeny, Evelyn Kirkley, Brad Longfield, Bruce Mullin, Jeff Trexler, and Grant Wacker. I am especially grateful to Paul Kemeny, who, in addition to making extensive comments on the manuscript, served as research assistant in preparing the notes and checking many details. For work on the second edition, I thank Brian Bademan, Kristin Kobes DuMez, and John Turner for their comments and suggestions and Darren Dochuk for his research help. I am also grateful for the help of the outside reviewers in preparation for the second edition: Maxie B. Burch, Grand Canyon University; Barry Hankins, Baylor University; and Stephen M. Johnson, Montclair State University.

In a work of this sort, one is dependent on many colleagues in the field who have provided research and insights that are appropriated into a larger synthesis. I have attempted to acknowledge any direct dependency, but since one's understanding grows over the years and is shaped by a community of scholars, there are contributions whose sources are not easy to identify but for which I wish to express my gratitude.

I would like also to acknowledge the fine support I have received from the William B. Eerdmans Publishing Company, especially the excellent editorial support and advice I received from executive editor David Bratt and from Linda Bieze, who served as project editor and copy editor. I am also happy to thank my granddaughter, Anneke Roberts, for her good work in updating the index.

My dedication reflects my gratitude to the many wonderful students I have had the privilege of teaching over the years. Quite a few continue to enrich our understanding of these subjects in their own teaching and in what is collectively a formidable array of publications. These, as well as many others of my former students, have also added to the history through their participation as citizens who contribute to the welfare of their communities in countless ways. As always, my deepest gratitude is to my wife Lucie, who offers untiring friendship and love.

GEORGE M. MARSDEN

Introduction

> In the United States the sovereign authority is religious, and conse-
> quently hypocrisy must be common; but there is no country in the
> world where the Christian religion retains a greater influence over
> the souls of men than in America.
>
> Alexis de Tocqueville, *Democracy in America* (1835)

The United States is both remarkably religious and remarkably profane. Observers since at least the time of Tocqueville have noticed the pervasive religious expression in much of America. Even in the twenty-first century, something like 90 percent of Americans profess to believe in God. Over half say that religious belief is "very important" in their lives and another quarter that it is "somewhat important." Over 70 percent say they believe in heaven and well over half believe in hell. Over a third claim to attend religious services at least once a week.[1] These figures far exceed those of other highly industrialized regions such Great Britain or Europe. Yet as professedly religious as many Americans have appeared to be since the nation's early days, the dominant American culture that developed during that same era and was eventually exported to much of the world was, along with lots of good things, notoriously materialistic, self-indulgent, sensual, and profane.

The central purpose of this book is to explore the interactions of re-
ligious faiths with other dimensions of American culture that have led to such striking paradoxes. It addresses these two parallel questions: What do American religious beliefs and practices tell us about American culture? What does American culture tell us about American religions? In other words, in what ways have American religions shaped American morality,

1

value systems, beliefs about priorities, and views about themselves, other humans, their families, their government, the nation, and the nation's role in the world? At the same time, to what extent has the American experience transformed traditional religious beliefs and practices?

Integrating Religion into Understanding American History

In the Western world, the prevailing interpretations of human behavior have long emphasized nonreligious factors. So despite the conspicuous mixtures of the religious and the profane in American culture, the overwhelming tendency of historians was, at least until recently, to emphasize only non-religious forces. Such conventions became especially strong during the first half of the twentieth century when many sophisticated interpreters came to believe that traditional religion, like primitive medicine or the horse-drawn plow, would inevitably disappear as modern culture and education advanced. Hence it became common practice to assume that religion would not have to be taken seriously in order to understand the modern world.

Since the latter decades of the twentieth century, it has become more widely apparent that such dismissals of the religious factors in modern cultures have been a mistake—sometimes a costly mistake when shaping foreign policy. Traditional religions are not going away. In the United States itself, religions with many traditional, supernaturalist features, though often mixed with some very modern expressions, continue to flourish. In particular, the explicit political alliances that some religious groups have made in recent decades have forced historians to take religious influences more seriously. Study of religious history has become a leading subfield in American historical scholarship. Even so, most general accounts of American history do not do a good job of integrating the religious elements into the rest of the story. Jon Butler, in a widely cited address to the Organization of American Historians, spoke of the phenomenon of "Jack-in-the-Box faith" to characterize the way religion is treated in most American histories. Typically, historians have noted that religious faith had a formative role in colonial America, but in accounts of later eras, especially since about 1870, it only occasionally "pops up," soon to disappear again with little or no reflection on its roots or lasting influences.[2] Here I attempt to supply what is missing by offering a sustained account of the major roles that various religions have played in relation to the cultural mainstream.

At the same time, giving religion its due in American history has to be done without overstating the case and falling into the error opposite of that made by overly secular histories. That error has been especially prominent among conservative, white Protestants who claim that America was originally a "Christian" nation and that it needs to be restored to its Christian roots. The mistake arises both from exaggerating the degree to which religious influences shaped the founding of the United States and from jumping from that exaggeration to speaking of the nation as having been "Christian" in a normative sense, as though earlier America provided a model of what a truly Christian culture would look like.

Protestants on Center Stage

One quick way to strike the needed balance is to say that the early United States and its colonial antecedents were a lot more Protestant than they were "Christian." A major thesis of this volume is that a key to understanding American culture is to appreciate the degree to which Protestantism has left its imprints on many of that culture's distinctive features. At the same time, as this book also emphasizes, many other forces were shaping both the culture and its religions. These include social, ethnic, racial, economic, political, and personal forces. Sometimes Protestant or other religious influences reshaped these to a greater or lesser degree. Just as often, however, such forces reshaped religion or led to co-opting or using religion to serve values determined mostly by these other interests. Take, for example, views on slavery among white, colonial American Protestants. Protestantism was surely a significant factor in shaping the North American versions of slaveholding. Doubtless the religious piety of some slave owners led them to treat their slaves better than they might have otherwise. But whatever those genuine blessings of personal concerns and kindnesses might have been, they were mixed with religious justifications of a system of race-based and often cruel oppression that, in retrospect, appears extraordinarily unjust.

So even though certain sorts of culturally dominant Protestants are often on center stage during America's formative years, that does not necessarily imply a positive evaluation of them. Depending on one's point of view, one may find the dominance of such white, Anglo-Saxon, male Protestants reprehensible, laudable, or paradoxical.

That being acknowledged, one cannot understand the formative influences shaping American culture without understanding Protestants and Protestantism. With few exceptions, the people who had the most decisive impact in shaping just about every aspect of American life until well into the twentieth century were Protestant either in practice or by recent heritage. Just one example of that fact is that, as late as the 1950s, Unitarians, members of a small, liberal, Protestant denomination centered mostly in eastern New England, had more of their number listed in *Who's Who in America* than did Catholics, who had *several hundred times* more adherents.[3] In the centuries up to then, not all of the Protestants who ran almost everything were active in their faith. Probably most were not. But many were secular in ways that were mixed with inherited Protestant attitudes regarding liberty of conscience, the value of individual choice, a work ethic, moral responsibility, and some degree of tolerance in a pluralistic setting.

So even though Protestantism provides the dominant religious influences, it needs to be immediately added that the United States is not simply one culture, just as it is not based on one religion. Rather, it is an amalgamation of many subcultures and of many religious influences. Particularly important to note is that because Protestantism itself came in so many varieties, Protestants had to learn to tolerate and get along with each other. And such tolerance became a model, however imperfect, for accepting people of other faiths or of no faith. So from the time of the nation's founding, the United States included among its citizens not only many varieties of Protestants, but Roman Catholics, avowed secularists, some Jews, and those of other faiths.

One helpful way to understand the formative influences shaping American culture is to see the history as an interaction between insiders, who have disproportional influence, and outsiders, who have less influence. For the first several centuries, almost all of the insiders were of white, Protestant, British, or northern European heritage. But even in those eras, many other Protestants from smaller sects, popular revival movements, and minority ethnic groups were outsiders. Enslaved African Americans, regardless of whether they accepted Protestant faith, remained the ultimate outsiders. By the mid-nineteenth century, massive immigration from Catholic nations and elsewhere resulted in an America that included many strong ethnoreligious subcommunities. Religion remained an important factor shaping identity in most of these outsider groups. Yet for acceptance in the mainstream, they had to accommodate to some of the ways of the dominant culture. The histories of ethnoreligious immigrant communities typically involved negotiations and exchanges with the insider culture. That dominant culture promoted assimilation of diverse cultures and good citizenship through public schools and the mainstream press and literature. Until about the era of the Civil War, schools and publications included some specifically Protestant traits and teaching. Later, the identifiably Protestant elements faded but did not disappear. The project of assimilation and good citizenship, for instance, involved promoting reverence for the American nation and its ideals as expressed with generic religious language of a sort of cultural Protestantism. With some notable exceptions, most immigrant communities eventually blended into the mainstream.

Eventually, especially beginning in the twentieth century, many people from outsider cultures themselves became cultural insiders and introduced some of the distinctive concerns drawn from their heritages. In the meantime, the dominant insider culture was being steadily transformed by secularizing forces including modernized beliefs, new technologies and lifestyles, and new economic and social forces. So whatever (always mixed) religious influences there ever were in the cultural mainstream became increasingly diluted both by growing diversity and overt turning away from religious considerations.

A Theme and Three Sub-Themes

The United States has always been simultaneously a very religious and a very secularized nation,[4] but the ways in which this paradoxical main theme plays itself out have changed over the centuries. These changes suggest three sub-themes that help shape the way this story is told: (1) Religions have played major roles in the struggles, just mentioned, between insiders, who aspire both to dominate and to provide moral leadership for the culture, and outsiders, who wish to live free from that domination and follow their own moral vision. (2) Closely related to this is the transition, especially since the Civil War, from an era when Protestant Christianity was at the center of American public life to the present, when it is on the periphery. That transition left in its wake some major cultural tensions that remain unresolved into the twenty-first century. (3) Finally, the relatively high degree of religious interest of many Americans has been sustained in the context of an unprecedented expansion of a scientific and technological culture that disenchanted nature and effectively removed vast areas of people's lives from explicit spiritual considerations. Much of American religion adapted effectively to these modern circumstances, so in the long run, religious expression grew. For religious people themselves, the most interesting question that such remarkable developments raises is, Which of the adaptations came at the expense of the quality or authenticity of religious expressions?

Many people assume that American religious history is simply the story of a transition from the more religious era of colonial times to the more secularized era of recent times. That story is too simple. Rather, what we find is a repositioning of the religious and the secularized. In colonial times, public life, such as government, education, and the media, were indeed much more often tied formally to religion than they are today. However, partly because Protestant Christianity was an official aspect of public life, private resistance to church participation may have been more widespread than today. In any case, in recent generations, the percentages of Americans active in religious communities have been far higher than in the colonial era. But the trade-off is that in modernized America, the huge enterprises of high-tech business, government, and the military allow little room for real religious influences in large areas of life. Moreover, today's opinion-forming centers of the culture—public education, most of higher education, and the major media—are vastly more secularized than they were in earlier times. The paradox is that, in the American setting, voluntary religious expression seems to flourish in the face of these secularizing influences. And that paradox is the more remarkable because the American experience contrasts to its British and European counterparts, where Christianity has faded as the societies have become more technological and secularized. So the history of the American interactions of religion and culture offers some good questions regarding how we should understand those differences.

A Word on Point of View

Since the late nineteenth century, most authors of histories have written as though they were neutral and objective observers. Thoughtful readers know there is no such thing. So it has become their task to figure out an author's point of view so they may take that into account. As an author, I think it is more helpful if I frankly identify my point of view. In that way, readers can take it into account and more easily assess my evaluations from their own perspectives. Not every reader may be interested in such reflections, and those who are not should feel free to jump ahead to the main narrative.

While I share many contemporary evaluative concerns, this history is also embedded in a long Christian tradition of reflection on the interrelations between faith and culture. That tradition goes back to St. Augustine, the fourth- and fifth-century theologian and church leader. The Augustinian perspective has the merit of being one of the longest-lasting ongoing traditions of interpretation of both the relationship of God to individual humans and the relationship of Christianity to the civic order. As in all traditions, the Augustinian perspective comes with many variations.

One characteristic of an Augustinian outlook that is especially relevant to the study of history is its starting premise that humans as children of God are supremely valuable but also inherently selfish and sinful. So, despite wonderful accomplishments, they are also inevitably prone to evil. One might suppose that today there is so much evidence of human evil in recent human history that something like human depravity would be a standard interpretive category. One need think only of all the genocides, wars, and other mind-boggling violence and injustices of modern times, which have occurred even as civilizations were supposed to be reaching advanced states. Yet the prevailing secular views that shape most historical interpretation seem to be based on the assumption that humans are naturally good, and that social, economic, political, psychological, or religious circumstances are usually responsible for leading them astray. In an Augustinian view, by contrast, a mixture of inherent human good and inherent human evil is just what one would expect. Moreover, and very importantly for our purposes, Christians are not exempted from human depravity. Even though they regard themselves as redeemed in Jesus Christ and as those who by grace try to follow a divinely given ethical imperative to love one's neighbor as oneself, they recognize that they often fall short of that ideal and need to ask for the further grace of forgiveness. Sometimes such propensities lead to the most striking contradictions. As Blaise Pascal, an Augustinian Catholic and great observer of the human condition, remarked in the seventeenth century, "[People] never do evil so cheerfully and completely as when they do it from religious conviction."[5] Pascal was a devout Christian who also deeply believed that religious faith could be the source of some of the highest acts of human virtue and self-giving. The twentieth-century American theologian Reinhold Niebuhr, from whom we shall hear more in these pages, was particularly acute at articulating these ironic interactions of good and evil in religious history.

In his classic work, *The City of God*, Augustine provides a template for understanding why such paradoxes are often manifested in Christians' relationships to the civic order. Augustine describes two "cities," or two sorts of civilization. The first is the City of God, which is the ideal community made up of those who are united to each other and dedicated to the highest good because of their common love for the one Triune God. But Christians, along with everyone else, also live in the civilizations of the world. Those civilizations, rather than being based on "loving one's neighbor as oneself," are dedicated ultimately to protecting their own self-interests. Augustine points out that every human civilization has been established by violent conquest from without or violent revolution from within that forced some former regime from power. Continuing violence or the threat of violence is an essential means for maintaining human civic order and protecting it from internal and external threats.[6]

Given such basic realities that Augustine identified, one valuable way for historical observers to understand differences among various types of Christians (and persons of other religious traditions also manifest similar variations) is to look at how they relate their religious faith to the dominant culture of their time. Such relationships of faith to dominant culture will, of course, vary a great deal with the character of the dominant culture. If the dominant culture is shaped substantially by a particular religious faith, then issues in relating faith to culture will be much different than if the dominant culture is hostile to that faith. At the time of the American colonial settlements, for instance, all the European powers involved had official state churches. So the issues regarding church and civilization were very different for early settlers than they are for religious believers in twenty-first-century America. But among colonial settlers there were also vast differences in the ways that various types of Christians related to the dominant culture. Those who belonged to the established state church of a region would probably enjoy a privileged position in society and might be comfortable with the dominant civil order and expected beliefs, values, and practices. Others in an established church might have hopes to reform and improve the current order. Christians who were not part of the established church of a region would come in many more varieties. Roman Catholics in Protestant regions often had limited rights. Enslaved Africans had almost no rights, even if they became part of the established church. Women in every group were in most ways subordinated to men. Some Protestants from outside the established church might want to reform the society and might even hope their group would someday become dominant. Others might fight for their rights and oppose any established church and become champions of religious freedom. Others might be Christian in name only and not think about such issues. Still others (the Amish would be the best known example today) would believe that it was the duty of Christians to separate themselves from the dominant civic and social order.

In sum, in reading this history, one should be alert to a number of issues regarding the relationships of religious people to their surrounding cultures. Such relationships vary over time, according to religious affiliation, race, ethnicity, gender, and other factors. Furthermore, the dominant cultures with which religious people have to interact have to do not only with the public status of their religion but also the most common beliefs, ideals, practices, and values of their time. These are the values that are taken for granted in a given era, taught in the schools, and promoted in media and the entertainment industry. For readers who are themselves religious believers, reflecting on the various ways believers of the past have related to their mainstream culture might help spark reflections on their own beliefs and practices in relation to their cultural setting. For readers who are not religious, such perspectives should help them appreciate that religious people relate to their surrounding civilization in many ways. Even adherents to one type of religion vary greatly in the ways they interact with their host civilizations. Seeing how that has been true historically should help avoid simplistic generalizations about how members of a certain religious group will act.

As a historian who is both an American and a participant in one of the groups whose history I am writing, I inevitably have an interested point of view on such matters. I am a Protestant writing a history in which Protestants are overwhelmingly the dominant actors. Further, I am part of the Reformed (or Calvinistic) wing of Protestantism that has had an especially large role in trying to shape mainstream American culture. I am especially intrigued by the strengths and the failures of my own tradition. In fact, that is one of the main reasons I have dedicated myself to the study of American religious history for these many decades. Building on the Augustinian starting point regarding the tensions arising from loyalties to the two "cities," I have been alert to how religious faiths, especially culturally influential faiths, have a way of becoming mixed up with social, political, economic, ideological, ethnic, and other cultural or personal forces that their adherents can, at best, only partially control. While the faith can sometimes temper the cultural forces that are most antithetical to its principal teachings, often the faith instead becomes reshaped by those very forces. One contribution of historians is to help identify these interactions so that people of various faiths can better sort out what outlooks are essential to their heritage and what seem inauthentic mixtures of the sacred and the profane.

Since I am both sympathetic and critical concerning the roles played by Christians in this history, I hope that my perspectives may be helpful not only to other self-critical Christians but also to persons of other religious faiths or of no religious faith who wish to make fair assessments of Christians' cultural roles. My intention is to treat each of the players in the story fairly and according to the same principles that I apply to the heritages closest to my own. If anything, I am more comfortable in critically evaluating religious outlooks similar to my own than I am regarding those of others.

CHAPTER 1

Christendom and American Origins

For this end we must be knit together in this work as one man, we must entertain each other in brotherly affection, we must be willing to abridge ourselves of our superfluities for the supply of others' necessities, we must uphold a familiar commerce together in all meekness, gentleness, patience, and liberality, we must delight in each other, make others' conditions our own, rejoice together, mourn together, labor and suffer together, always having before our eyes our commission and community in the work, our community as members of the same body. . . . For we must consider that we shall be as a city upon a hill, the eyes of all people are upon us.

John Winthrop, "A Model of Christian Charity" (1630)

To understand the role of religion in American history, we must recognize the immense importance of the ideal of "Christian civilization." The Europeans who settled the Americas throughout the colonial era simply took for granted that they represented Christendom. This was as much a part of their identity as being Spanish or French or English.

Christendom, however, was bitterly divided. The Eastern Orthodox Church and the Western church under Rome had separated early in the Middle Ages so that Eastern Orthodoxy was a distant reality to most Western Europeans. Central to the Western European experience, though, was the split in the Church of Rome brought about by the Protestant Reformation. The Reformation, triggered by Martin Luther in 1517, shattered European unity and dominated Western politics for the next century. This coincided almost exactly with New World explorations and early settlements. The Protestant reforms, though motivated primarily by deep disagreements over religious issues, had immense political implications. Europeans in the sixteenth century assumed, as they had through the Middle Ages, that a country's ruler would not only determine its religion but also would suppress heresies and false worship. "One state, one religion" was the rule.

The Cold War

The success of the Reformation depended not only on persuading the population about Protestant doctrines; it hinged as much or more on converting rulers to the cause. As a result, existing political divisions and monarchical rivalries in Europe were vastly deepened by fierce ideological-religious struggles for political control of the ruling houses. The closest counterpart to this situation in recent times would be the lengthy cold war through much of the twentieth century between Marxists and anti-Marxists. Sixteenth-century Europe was similarly divided between two contending ideologies both vying for the hearts of people and political control. As in the communist or anti-communist fervor of the twentieth century, each side vilified the other. Each was sure God was on their side and that it was God's will that the other side be stopped by any means possible. Each saw the other as literally of the Devil.

The largest group of early Protestants were Lutherans, followers of Martin Luther (1483–1546), whose churches became state churches in many German provinces and in Scandinavia. By the second generation of the Reformation, the most aggressive major Protestant group pushing for political-religious revolutions was the Calvinists. Calvinists followed theologian John Calvin (1509–64), who had established a model for Christian rule in the independent city of Geneva, Switzerland. Because Calvinists had a disproportional influence in shaping the future culture of the United States, their teachings should be given due attention.

Calvin attempted to build a thoroughgoing Reformation theology based on the Protestant principle of "the Bible alone" as religious authority. This principle challenged the institutional authority of the Catholic Church. Catholics believed that God had ordained the institutional church, ruled on earth by the pope, to interpret biblical revelation and especially to provide the sacramental means through which people could receive the grace of God necessary for their eternal salvation. Protestants claimed the church had become a corrupt human institution. It needed to be reformed, they asserted, by testing its claims against the Bible alone.

Calvinists attempted to carry as far as possible the principle that one should rely entirely upon God and not on humanity in religious matters. God, they emphasized, was the absolute sovereign ruler of all creation. Nothing happened outside God's ultimate control. Humans, accordingly, could do nothing to promote their salvation. They were corrupted, sinful beings whose only hope of redemption was through the grace of God. Yet that was a wonderful hope. Through the sacrificial death of Christ, God graciously provided salvation from sin for those whom he would save. The Bible alone and the sovereignty of God were thus the two organizing principles of Calvinist Christianity.

For most of the sixteenth century, Protestants battled Catholics for control of a number of European countries, with Calvinists often taking the lead in pressing for further expansion. Catholics fought back ardently, especially under the influence of the new Jesuit order. The Jesuits were instrumental in countering the Reformation, sending out missionaries, and securing centers of Catholic influence.

The New World was of strategic importance to the Catholic powers, especially to the Spanish, who dominated European advances in South and Central America throughout the 1500s. Exploitation of New World wealth provided the chief practical motive for European conquests, but what seemed a God-given opportunity to expand Christendom provided a higher justification. As always had been the case when political power and economic interests were closely related to religious rationales, remarkable paradoxes resulted. Providing opportunity for Catholic missions was one of the rationales for military conquest. Yet the conquests were accomplished with much cruelty toward the native peoples, vastly increasing the difficulties of effective mission work. Even so, dedicated Catholic missionaries brought with them Christian moral principles that mitigated some of the exploitation. Bartolomé de Las Casas (1474–1566), a Dominican priest, was especially notable among the early missionaries in insisting that the Indians be treated as fellow humans. Eventually, most of the natives decided to live peacefully with the new arrivals, and many were Christianized. So most of the Western Hemisphere was at least officially Catholic long before Protestants were on the scene.

In the 1600s, French Catholics became another force in settling and evangelizing substantial territories in the New World, particularly what are now eastern Canada and the American Midwest. During the 1500s, it had not been clear whether France would become Protestant or Catholic, and the nation had been divided by a bloody civil war over that issue. Once that issue was settled in favor of Catholicism, France emerged in the 1600s as a major international power with New World aspirations. In the more sparsely settled, largely wooded regions of French influence, missionaries played a leading role in the quest for evangelizing Native Americans. Missionary explorers, most notably the Jesuit Father Jacques Marquette (1637–75), penetrated the Mississippi valley, into the areas that are now Michigan, Illinois, Wisconsin, and Iowa (where place names such as Eau Claire, Des Plaines, Fond du Lac, and Des Moines still exist). The French, especially the Jesuits, were probably the most effective European missionaries in the New World. They usually had the advantage over their Spanish or English counterparts of not being either preceded by conquests or accompanied by large numbers of settlers who wished to displace the native peoples from their territories. They were thus able to preach the gospel message without the encumbrances of the political dimensions of Christendom. By the 1700s, nevertheless, their missionary efforts had helped secure for France many Indian allies who were then drawn into Christendom's rivalries and wars.

The English Reformation

The English settlements on the eastern coast of what is now the United States should be understood in the context of the religious conflicts between Protestants and Catholics. International rivalries, especially with Spain, and quests for economic and imperial expansion were essential motives. Still, when the English established their first permanent settlement, one in Jamestown in 1607, it was not lost on them that they were establishing a very small beachhead in a largely Catholic hemisphere. Throughout American colonial history, struggles between Protestants and Catholics were crucial factors in defining British-American identities.

The English had a peculiar role in the ongoing Protestant-Catholic struggles. England had more or less backed into the Reformation. In the early years of Luther's revolt, the English had been in the Catholic camp. By the late 1520s, however, Henry VIII (1491–1547) wanted to change wives, and when the pope refused to grant a divorce, Henry decided to change churches. In 1534, he severed the English church from the leadership of the pope in Rome and declared himself the sovereign over English church affairs. This opened the door for Protestantism in England. The issue was far from settled, however.

Henry's first wife, Catherine of Aragon, was Spanish and Catholic.

When their daughter Mary (1516–58) became queen of England in 1553, she reinstituted Catholicism, putting to death many Protestant leaders. Others of these leaders escaped to the continent; some went to Geneva, where John Calvin presided. When Mary died in 1558, Elizabeth (1533–1603), Henry's Protestant daughter by his second marriage, acceded to the throne, and England went back to the Protestant fold. Elizabeth forged a compromise for the Church of England, retaining the Episcopal form of government (leadership by bishops) and much of traditional Catholic ritual but instituting Protestant doctrine. This "Elizabethan compromise," although it placed England solidly in the Protestant camp, did not please all Protestants, especially some of those exiled under Mary to Calvin's Geneva and now returning, who wanted to press the Protestant principle of "the Bible alone" as the guide for the church. The church, they contended, should have only practices explicitly commanded in Scripture. Hence, they argued, the Episcopal hierarchy, lavish ecclesiastical adornments, and formal rituals of Anglican worship should go. This Calvinist party within the Church of England, who wanted to further purify the church, became known as Puritans.

Protestant England under Elizabeth emerged as a leading naval power and successfully challenged the dominance of Catholic Spain. The turning point was the defeat of the Spanish Armada by the English fleet in 1588, an event that, for centuries after, English-speaking Protestants viewed as evidence of God's providential intervention on their side. The defeat of the Spanish Armada gave England sufficient security on the seas to begin North American settlements.

The Religious and the Secular

Despite the prominence of religion in such national conflicts, it is difficult to tell how deeply religious motives figured for those who settled the colonies. In the rhetoric of early Virginia, for instance, the first settlers boldly proclaimed themselves, as John Rolfe (of Pocahontas fame) put it, "a peculiar people, marked and chosen by the finger of God, to possess it, for undoubtedly he is with us."[1] Establishing Protestant outposts in the New World to counter what they regarded as the evils of Roman Catholic influences seemed to many English men and women to be a God-given duty. They also had hopes to convert the Indians, although these soon foundered. The early colonial authorities strictly maintained the religious formalities of the day, including laws requiring church attendance. Yet in reality, the Virginia colony in its earliest decades soon became more like a company town, perhaps like a mining outpost in later times in the distant reaches of Alaska.

Anglican England, from which the settlers came, was, like every nation, a mix of religious practices with secular forces that had little to do with religion. This was, after all, the age of William Shakespeare, whose plays reflected the sophisticated, Renaissance, this-worldly humanism of the day. People in Shakespeare's plays were motivated by rivalries, ambitions, greed, loves, hatreds, and much more in human nature that seldom seemed connected to any discernible religious considerations. So it is hardly surprising that a motley assortment of English men and women from Shakespeare's time transplanted to the New World would be driven by a similar assortment of concerns. For some, these perennial human traits would be refracted through strong religious commitments. For most, the purely secular would predominate. In fact, in the Virginia colony, formal Anglican Christianity depended largely on government authority and custom and tended to languish in the frontier setting. What worked in a settled Anglican parish in England would be hard to sustain in the rugged open spaces of the American continent.

The Puritan Heritage

At the same time, some very intense Protestantism, especially through the Puritan movement, soon influenced British-American colonies. When Elizabeth I died in 1603, she was succeeded by one of her cousins, King James VI of Scotland, who as king of England (r. 1603–25) was known as James I. James's Stuart family in Scotland had been forced, reluctantly, to accept a Calvinist Presbyterian Church. James and his Stuart successors, who ruled England for most of the 1600s, accordingly disliked English Puritans intensely. The feelings were mutual. A small group of more extreme Puritans felt they must leave the Church of England and hence England itself. Eventually, this group founded the Plymouth Colony in 1620, famed largely for its early struggles and for the first Thanksgiving celebration. When James's son, Charles I (1600–49), came to the throne in 1625, the tension in England became so severe even for moderate Puritans that a substantial number of these Puritans were willing to brave the high seas and the wilderness to found an alternative society based on Puritan principles. This society, the Massachusetts Bay Colony, would be, as Governor John Winthrop put it in 1630, "a city upon a hill," a model Christian state that all the world could imitate.

The Puritans in the Massachusetts Bay Colony were convinced that they had been commissioned by God to play a major role in world history. Their rule for life was the fundamental Protestant principle that the Bible alone should be their supreme guide. For a model society, they looked to the Old Testament, which described God's governance of Israel. Surely, they reasoned, these God-given principles should apply to nations even in their time.

Central to the Old Testament view of the nation was the covenant, which defined the relationship between God and a nation as a contract whose terms were the law of God. By far the most crucial factor determining the success or failure of a nation was its relationship to God. If a nation kept the law of God, that nation would be blessed. If it broke God's law, it would be punished. Morality, based on biblical law, was the key to success.

The seventeenth-century Puritans were by far the most articulate and best educated of North America's early settlers and so had an immense and disproportional influence on the later American culture. One of the first things that the Massachusetts Puritans did was to found Harvard College in 1638. Through the next three centuries their New England heirs were often the leading educators in the new nation. As particularly intense Protestants in overwhelmingly Protestant British North America, they offered a language that many later Americans used for talking about the religious dimensions of their nation's heritage.

The Thanksgiving holiday is the best-known example. The Pilgrims of the fledgling Plymouth Colony held a feast of Thanksgiving in 1621 in gratitude to God for the harvest and other blessings. At least ninety Native Americans were their guests in an event lasting three days. Occasional Thanksgivings became a common practice in Puritan New England. These celebrations had Old Testament precedent and fit well with the idea that their society was under a covenant with God, who would bless them for faithfulness and punish them for misdeeds. So they had not only Thanksgiving feast days but also fast days for collective repentance. When the United States was founded, it adopted similar practices. Presidents would occasionally call for days of thanksgiving or of fasting. But during the Civil War, President Abraham Lincoln (1809–65) declared Thanksgiving to be a national holiday. He also declared days of fasting. Eventually days of fasting became rare, but Thanksgiving became a regular holiday. Even though there had been many sorts of thanksgiving celebration in North America before 1621, the colorful story of the Pilgrims became the standard national story. That fit with trends, especially in the nineteenth-century North, to emphasize the Puritan role in the foundation of the nation as a whole. Furthermore, the persistent image in the popular lore was that the Pilgrims and Puritans came to America as champions of freedom.[2] These ardent Protestants did indeed cross the ocean seeking a refuge where they would be free to practice their religion. But they were not interested in other people's religious freedom. Rather, they saw it as their God-given duty to banish those whose religious teachings differed substantially from their own.

The influences of the Puritan covenantal heritage on later American national self-understanding are a good example of the mixed benefits of the Protestant religious heritage. On the positive side, it was one among a number of influences that helped define the nation not simply in terms of protecting its own interests but as having moral obligations. That emphasis fit, for instance, with later republican ideas that the success of a nation depended on the virtue of its citizens. Such emphases on morality and virtue helped create a sense of civic responsibility among the citizenry—clearly an important ingredient in a successful republic. Most citizens will play by the rules, for instance, accepting election results that they strongly oppose. Moreover, such moral emphases have fostered countless reform efforts at home and humanitarian concerns both at home and abroad.

Ironically, such a sense of the importance of virtue, which the Puritan heritage helped provide, can lead to an arrogant moral superiority that transgresses the very rights of others that the moral system claims to protect. For instance, when the new nation was founded, Americans saw themselves, with some justification, as beacons to the world demonstrating the virtues of a republic. When the new nation was formed, Americans readily accepted covenant talk about being blessed by God or in danger of God's judgments. Americans liked to think of themselves as having a special mission. They readily spoke, almost as the Puritans had, of the United States as a new Israel chosen by God to play a leading role in a new era of the world's redemption. That helped inspire a moral idealism and a willingness to be open to helping the stranger. As the plaque on the Statue of Liberty reads: "Give me your tired, your poor, your huddled masses yearning to breathe free." Yet that same moral idealism, combined with a sense of being a chosen nation, a new Israel, heightened nineteenth-century Americans' sense of mission, or "manifest destiny," in becoming a transcontinental power. Americans took vast tracts of land from native peoples and from Mexico, partly on the grounds of the United States's supposed moral superiority. In the twentieth century, when America became a world power, the chosen-nation ideal and American sense of virtue were important rationales in American foreign policy, sometimes for the good, but also sometimes for overreaching.

As we will be see in the history that follows, defining one's nation's uniqueness in terms of its virtues has involved many ironies. The alternative, defining a nation's mission without reference to morality, seems clearly worse, however. The problem involved is not uniquely American or something that can be blamed on the Puritan heritage. Rather, it is a human problem. Essential to the human condition is that we are all self-centered. So we all think of ourselves more highly than we ought. Christian beliefs and practices may temper such tendencies. They might help people to have a perspective on themselves so that they might cultivate more selfless virtues and be able to be more generous to those different from them. But being convinced that one is following God's will is also likely to give one a sense of moral superiority that may undermine such generous attitudes.[3] So the trick is to cultivate genuine virtues but to be sure they include those that emphasize self-giving and humility. As any honest history will show, that very challenging goal is more likely to be approached by individuals and religious communities that lack political power than it is by those who are closely tied to political power.

Here, again, is an irony and a dilemma for Christians. Civil governments have the legitimate task of protecting their communities' interests and have the authority to use force or violence to do so. Christians will want their government to be constrained by moral considerations. If they are in a position to influence the government, or to participate in it, they will hope to promote what is morally best for all concerned. Yet having political influence works both ways. The more a religious group is identified with political power, the more it will be shaped by concerns to preserve that power and to protect collective self-interest. For Christians, that creates a tension with the ethic in which selflessness is a supreme virtue and one is to love not only one's immediate neighbors but also the stranger and even one's enemies. Governments necessarily treat citizens differently from non-citizens and enemies. Christians (and everyone else, for that matter) seem simply to have to live with such civic practices that fall short of an ethic of perfect equality. More importantly, they have to recognize that even the best governments, in their zeal to protect their self-interests, will often act unjustly. If history teaches anything, it teaches that. So the important practical point seems to be that Christians *recognize* they should never make a simple equation of their religious faith with the program of their nation, political regime, or party.

These inevitable tensions and contradictions involved in the close identification of Christianity with a civil government are well illustrated in the history of Puritan New England itself. For instance, the Puritans regarded their settlement of New England as a God-directed mission to bring true Christianity, based on the Bible alone, to the New World. They believed that God had given them this land in a way analogous to God's giving the ancient Israelites the land of Israel. And as New Testament believers, they also believed in evangelism of all peoples. So one rationale for settling in New England was that it would open up opportunities to bring the gospel to Native Americans. The Puritans made some real efforts to befriend and evangelize the Indians. Nonetheless, the reality was that as the English settlements expanded, their settlements were displacing the Indians. Misunderstandings were inevitable. The Indians themselves were divided into rival tribes, some allied with the English, adding to the probabilities of violent outbreaks. In the first such disaster, the Pequot War, the colonists and their Indian allies virtually eliminated the Pequot tribe, which had been trying to expand its influence. Not only did they brutally destroy Pequot villages, and eventually kill their fighting men, but they also captured and sold many of the women and children into slavery in the West Indies. A generation later saw an even more disastrous conflict, King Phillip's War. The Indian leader Metacom (1639–76) was known to the English as King Philip and his father, Massasoit (1580–1661), had been friendly to the Pilgrims at Plymouth and even participated in their first thanksgiving. A suspected murder of a Christian Indian rival of Metacom and Puritan retaliation by executing three of Metacom's associates led to devastating Indian attacks on many English settlements during 1675 and early 1676. After fierce struggles, the English, with some Indian allies, gained the upper hand and Metacom was defeated and killed in the summer of 1676, thus ending the worst of the fighting. Both sides had destroyed civilian settlements with little restraint, and eventually the Indians who had allied with Metacom were left decimated. The Puritans believed they were fighting for justice, self-defense, and survival. That led them to justify in the name of Christianity whatever brutality, including killing women and children or selling them into slavery, it took to survive. Those retaliatory actions of their "Christian" civil society thus subverted their other Christian goals of loving their Indian neighbors and bringing them to know the Christian God. They were left, then, with bitter relations to many of the remaining Indians whom they had hoped to convert. For much of the next century, New England villages were subject to devastating raids by displaced Indians. Most of New England's well-meant mission efforts languished.

The Puritans of seventeenth-century New England were a Christian society in a formal sense, and they indeed manifested many admirable traits. They sought to follow God's will and to obey God's laws. Yet as a human society with all the human limitations of blind spots, self-interest, and sin, they inevitably often identified God's will with questionable practices. As Protestant Christians they were also limited by their assumptions regarding how the Bible was to be regarded as their highest authority in all of life. Like most Europeans, they took for granted that in Christendom church and state should work hand in hand. As Protestants, they assumed that the Bible should provide a model for how such a Christian society should act. So they assumed that Old Testament Israel should be their model. As a result of the combination of their own human flaws and these questionable assumptions, they maintained a Christian society in name, intent, and in some very admirable practices. Yet as a whole, it hardly seems to be normatively Christian or to provide a model that we should imitate.

Christians as Outsiders

Not all of the Protestants who settled the American colonies were happy with the close fusion of church and society assumed by the Anglican established state church in the South or in the Puritans' vision of themselves as a new Israel. Throughout Christian history, some of the faithful have believed that it is not the role of the church to run society; rather, they see society as simply "the world," the domain of Satan, and believe the church should be a separate community. This outsider version of Christianity prevailed for centuries in the ancient church before Christians had any prospects of power in the Roman Empire. After the emperor Constantine (AD 272–337) was converted to Christianity in AD 312, the vision of a Christian society predominated. The older ideal—Christians literally giving up the world—survived, however, especially in monastic movements.

At the time of the Reformation, the outsider version of Christianity appeared among Protestants in the radical Anabaptist movement. Anabaptists insisted that Christians must form "gathered" churches made up of believers only. To symbolize separation of true Christians from the world, they baptized only professed believers, rebaptizing those who had been baptized as infants in the Catholic Church. The name "Anabaptist" means to baptize again. Many Anabaptists expressed their separation from the world by forming their own communities. They believed firmly in the separation of church and state, and most Anabaptist sects were pacifist. In Europe they were often cruelly persecuted by both other Protestants and Catholics, thus increasing their sense that to be a true Christian meant to be separate from the mainstream society. The best-known Anabaptist groups to settle in America were the Mennonites and Amish.

The Baptists were a more influential group in later American society. Early Baptists appearing in England after 1600 were a degree less radical than the Anabaptists (though considerably more radical than most of their Baptist heirs today). Growing from the Puritan movement, but influenced by Anabaptists, Baptists carried the Puritan emphasis on conversion a step further by insisting that baptism of adults symbolized spiritual separation from the world. Interested above all in the spiritual purity of the church, early Baptists believed in separation from the state Church of England, rather than working for reform from within, as most Puritans believed. For the Baptists, the separation was a spiritual concern primarily of individuals. Unlike most Anabaptists, they did not insist on withdrawing into separate communities or on pacifism.

In early seventeenth-century England, the Baptist movement—as a church outside of the Church of England—was illegal. Not surprisingly, Baptists were from the outset champions of religious liberty and of the rights of individual conscience.

In Puritan Massachusetts, one of the first clergymen, Roger Williams (d. 1683), soon adopted radical views much like the Baptists. Williams, who became Baptist for a brief time, challenged the Puritan notion that their society represented a new Israel. For instance, he argued that Puritans had no right to take land from the Indians as though they were ancient Israelites taking over the Promised Land. All political arrangements, Williams thought, were corrupt. Therefore, Christians should not claim they were building Christian societies. Only the separated church, said the dissident Puritan, could be Christian. The church must be a purely spiritual entity, not corrupted by aspirations to run the state or by the need to depend on it for support.

Williams thus championed the separation of church and state, but not for the same reason that later Enlightenment thinkers, such as Thomas Jefferson (1743–1826), did. Jefferson was concerned that the church would corrupt the state; Williams feared that the state would corrupt the church.

Williams was exiled for his views. The Puritans may have sought freedom to practice their own religion in the New World, but they did not believe in religious freedom as a general principle. Williams fled to Rhode Island, where he set up a colony that became a refuge for religious dissenters. On the whole, he maintained better relations with the local Indians than did most of the Puritans. But near the end of his life, Rhode Island was drawn into the all-out war with Metacom.

Spiritual Sources of Equality

Because the Baptists were radical, Williams and the early Baptists anticipated a number of principles that in the next century were popularized in secular as well as religious terms. Separation of church and state and civil rights based on individual conscience are the best-known principles. Just as important were the twin emphases on the role of individuals and equality within the church. For Baptists, the individual was the basic unit of the church. This was reflected in the emphasis on conversion experience as the test of church membership. The church was not primarily a hierarchical institution but a gathering of spiritual individuals. Baptists and most American Puritans had a congregational system of church government, giving the male members of the local church the supreme governing authority. Such churches were thus more egalitarian than most of the institutions of the era.

Moreover, the doctrine of conversion was a radically leveling doctrine. Anyone, even the poorest person in society, could become the spiritual equal of anyone else and the spiritual superior of those unconverted who held power and prestige in the world. Such definitions of men and women in terms of individual spiritual qualities instead of solely by group status planted seeds for later demands for social equality.

Early New England experienced a foretaste of how doctrines of spiritual equality could influence views of gender when Anne Hutchinson (1591–1643) emerged as one of the most effective spiritual leaders and teachers in the Massachusetts colony. Due to her gifts, she had been given latitude as a religious teacher at house meetings that included some men. Because the Puritans encouraged universal literacy, a few talented women found outlets for their creativity in writing. Anne Bradstreet (1612–72) became the most outstanding Puritan poet. And later, Mary Rowlandson (c.1637–1711) wrote a highly regarded account of her captivity during King Philip's War. But these were rare exceptions in a society that permitted only males in public offices of church and society or in college education and left little record of most women's activities. In Anne Hutchinson's case, she crossed a line when she began to challenge the authority of some of the clergy by saying they did not measure up to what she saw as a higher spirituality. She was brought to trial and might have sustained her case if she had confined herself to her sophisticated theological arguments, which were shared by a faction of the clergy. But she shocked her Puritan interrogators by claiming a higher authority than they themselves had: a direct voice from the Holy Spirit. That claim challenged the Puritan principle of reliance on the Bible alone.

Sentenced into exile, she died at the hands of Indians in 1643. Her example, however, remained an illustration of the leveling potential of a Christianity that emphasized a conversion experience.

More Radicalism: The English Civil War

In England, such more radical Protestant views suddenly gained a sizable following with the outbreak of the Civil War in 1642. More than any other event in English history during the colonial era, the war is central to understanding the role of religion in the later American experience. Indeed, the war is crucial to understanding American culture generally.

While some leading Puritans left for the colonies in the 1630s, others remained in England to contend with Charles I and the hostile archbishop of the Anglican Church, William Laud (1573–1645). Civil war broke out, with the Puritans, Parliament, and the Scottish Presbyterians (who were Calvinists much like the Puritans) on one side, and the king, most of the nobility, and anti-Puritan Anglicans on the other. The revolutionary parliamentary party won, executed Archbishop Laud, and called the Westminster Assembly of Divines, which drew up a Confession of Faith for what was at first to be an established Presbyterian Church, as the one church of the nation. The war, however, released more radical sentiments. Oliver Cromwell (1599–1658), a Puritan general with much popular support, rose to power, oversaw the execution of Charles I in 1649, declared England a "commonwealth" or a republic, and allowed religious toleration of Dissenters.

The Puritan execution of Charles I was one of the great turning points in the transition toward the modern era. It anticipated the later age of revolutions, especially in becoming an important precedent for the American Revolution. Declaring the king an outlaw, the Puritans forcefully asserted on religious grounds that kings were subject to a higher law.

The Puritan revolution, however, was short-lived. Cromwell himself became the virtual dictator of the new Commonwealth. Soon after his death in 1658, Puritan rule came to an end with the "Restoration" of the monarchy in 1660, when Charles II (1630–85), son of the executed king, came to power. Puritans and other dissenting groups were then repressed.

Tensions in New England

The Restoration of the anti-Puritan Stuart kings in 1660 left the future of the Puritan colonies in New England uncertain. The colonies became a place of refuge for some of the Puritans who fled England after the Restoration. Due simply to their distance from England, they retained their virtual independence.

Then in 1685, James II (1633–1701), a Catholic, succeeded to the English throne. The crown reorganized New England as the Dominion of New England under a royal governor, thus involving them with some direct oversight from England for the first time. The Puritans felt oppressed, and they especially feared that James might lead England back into the hands of their most dreaded enemy, Roman Catholicism.

These fears were relieved by the news of the success of "The Glorious Revolution," as ardent Protestants viewed it, when in 1688 James II was driven from the throne and succeeded by his daughter Mary (1661–94) and her husband, the Protestant prince William of Orange (1650–1702). Even so, the new charter that Massachusetts obtained in 1691 still provided that the crown would appoint the governors.

The Witch Trials

About this time, the most bizarre incident in New England history occurred. In early 1692, in Salem Village, Massachusetts, a group of girls in their early teens began experiencing hysterical fits. Upon questioning, they blamed various people in their village for afflicting them through the practices of witchcraft. When some arrests were made, the hysteria and the accusations spread further. Eventually, more than a hundred people in the region were arrested on charges of practicing witchcraft, sometimes simply on the claim that a neighbor had seen them as an apparition. Nineteen people—fourteen women and five men—were tried and put to death. Once the accusations spread to some highly respected citizens, some of the ministers intervened, and the royal governor brought the trials to an end.

Several things need to be understood in order to put this incident into context. First, in the 1600s, most Europeans interpreted witchcraft as involving a pact with the Devil and, hence, saw the practice as a threat both to true religion and to society. Puritans believed the Devil to be a real person and viewed such a pact as an evil parody of the covenant between a believer and

God. Second, during the seventeenth century, executions for witchcraft were less common in New England than they were in many parts of Europe. Third, the casting of spells and other magical arts were practiced in New England, as they have been throughout American history. So there probably were actual witchcraft and occult practices that helped trigger the hysteria. Fourth, once the accusations and trials started, they brought out all the pent-up tensions of the time and region and led to mass hysteria—a fairly common human phenomenon against which any society should be warned. The older New England ways were coming to an end as the society adjusted to royal rule. The people of Salem were also suffering from devastating Indian attacks in nearby Maine. So for a time, even responsible leaders interpreted the mysterious outbreaks as part of Satan's concerted attack on their society. Finally, soon after the trials, most of the New England leadership recognized that there had been a serious miscarriage of justice. They were appalled at the excesses that they had permitted or encouraged, and witchcraft quickly disappeared as a legal issue in New England.

The Quakers

For American history, the most significant of the groups to grow out of the turbulent era of the Puritan revolution of the 1640s and 1650s was the Society of Friends, popularly called "Quakers," founded by George Fox (1624–91). Of all the seventeenth-century religious movements, the Quakers illustrated best that principles of equality and liberty, so important to modernity, first took a spiritual form.

The Quakers went beyond the potentially equalizing doctrine of conversion and beyond most of the Christian tradition by emphasizing that all persons had an innate "Inward Light" of the Holy Spirit. Quakers saw themselves as leaders of a new age of the Spirit that would be socially revolutionary. Their social revolution, however, was to be effected by purely spiritual means. Quakers were pacifists and insisted on a strict puritanical lifestyle, which included simplicity as opposed to materialism. Like some later revolutionaries, they rejected any social deference to nobility and insisted on addressing everyone as "brother" or "sister."

In this new age, women were to be the spiritual equals of men. Quakers accordingly instituted the revolutionary practice of allowing women to preach. Earlier Puritans had taught spiritual equality, but believed that male leadership in the church was required by Scripture. A telling example of the attraction of Quaker teaching to former Puritans is that of Mary Dyer, who had been a close friend of Anne Hutchinson in Massachusetts. After spending some time in Rhode Island, Dyer went back to Cromwell's England in 1651 and there became a Quaker. Later she returned to Massachusetts as a Quaker missionary, determined to show them the new way of the Inward Light of the Holy Spirit for all. After repeated warnings, punishments, exiles, and returns to the colony, she was executed in 1660.

Hutchinson, Dyer, and the Quakers illustrated the potentially revolutionary implications of the doctrine that every believer could have direct experience of the Holy Spirit. Women and others who did not have access to higher education or formal channels of religious authority could nonetheless claim spiritual equality. Throughout American history, Christian groups who have emphasized personal experience of the Holy Spirit have made important contributions to broader cultural ideals of the equality of all classes of people.

Quakers eventually found a New World refuge where they could practice their principles in William Penn's "Holy Experiment," the colony of Pennsylvania, founded in 1681. Penn (1644–1718) was the son of a prominent English admiral. He gave up an aristocratic lifestyle to identify with the persecuted and mostly poor Quakers. After spending some time in prison himself, he eventually used his wealth and elite connections to establish a colony for the oppressed Quakers. Once in America, the radical Quaker movement was in an anomalous position. In England they had been radical outsiders. In Pennsylvania they had access to political power and eventually to wealth. Such worldly success created some tensions within the movement. Nonetheless, by the mid-1700s, Quaker spiritual values helped create a society in Pennsylvania that anticipated many of the egalitarian ideals of later America. Similar to Roger Williams's Rhode Island, Pennsylvania was one of the first places in the Western world to have no established church, and hence the Pennsylvania colony was remarkably open to religious, and ethnic, tolerance.[4]

The Eighteenth Century

In eighteenth-century British-American colonies, such radicalism was the exception. Most Americans had a more conventional religious heritage; for the majority, religion was probably a largely formal affair. Many were Anglican, especially in the South, where the Church of England was firmly established as the state church. New England was still overwhelmingly Calvinist and the most intensely religious region of the colonies. Congregational churches were established by law, though the Congregational heirs to the Puritans now had to tolerate Anglicans and a few others.

The middle colonies were a religious mix. Dutch Reformed ("Reformed" refers to Calvinists) were prominent in New York, while Maryland was still home to most of the few Catholics in the colonies. In Pennsylvania, the tolerant Quaker policies opened the doors for German immigration, including mostly Lutherans but also such sects as the Mennonites. The most influential new religious group in the middle colonies was the Presbyterians, strict Calvinists who were mostly Scots and Scotch-Irish (Scots whose forebears had earlier moved to Northern Ireland). But in the middle colonies, and probably even more so in the South, relatively few inhabitants were active in a church.

In the early decades of the eighteenth century, the British colonies in North America were distant from each other and far from unified culturally. During that century, however, the American nation took shape and a discernible American culture appeared. Undoubtedly, the events surrounding the American Revolution were the major factors in shaping this new identity. Preceding the Revolution, however, was another intercolonial set of events, less often remembered, which anticipated many of the American traits since associated with the Revolution.

The Great Awakening

The Great Awakening, like the American Revolution, was a series of events. The first sparks were revivals in the 1720s among the Dutch Reformed in New Jersey. It continued in the 1730s in local awakenings among Presbyterians in the middle colonies and among some Congregationalists in western Massachusetts. What we now call the Great Awakening took shape in 1739 and 1740 when a young Calvinist evangelist from England, George Whitefield (1714-70), conducted a spectacularly popular preaching tour through the colonies. Whitefield stoked the local fires of religious interest into what became for a time a "great and general" conflagration. Whitefield journeyed up and down the East Coast, preaching to large gatherings wherever he went, in what was one of the first truly inter-colonial events. We might say that Whitefield was the first media star in American history. His medium was the pulpit, and he had immense skill as a dramatist using the spoken word. His tour anticipated a pattern in American culture: lacking long-established traditions and rituals, Americans have been susceptible to waves of popular enthusiasm for people who are stars. This pattern had its beginnings in revivalism and remains a prominent dimension of American cultural and religious life.

The American Great Awakening was part of a broader pietist revival throughout the Protestant world, beginning in Germany in the late 1600s. Pietist groups, such as the German Moravians, came to the New World to settle and evangelize. These groups attempted to renew churches by emphasizing the individual's personal relationship with God, a devotional life, a strict discipline of moral piety, and vigorous evangelizing about the necessity of being converted, or "born again," based on the atoning work of Christ's sacrifice on the cross. These emphases (today usually known as "evangelical") found fertile soil in eighteenth-century America. Puritanism, with its emphasis on individual conversions, helped pave the way, as did some of the smaller Baptist groups. The Awakening brought many versions of such emphases to the colonies on a large scale.

In England the most influential of the new evangelicals was John Wesley (1703–91), who organized the popular Methodist movement. Wesley had been influenced early in his career by the intense piety of the Moravians. When Methodism first took shape in the late 1730s as a renewal movement within the Church of England, Wesley's good friend, George Whitefield, was part of the movement. Both brought revivals to large crowds through popular preaching. By the early 1740s the friends broke with each other over doctrinal difference. Whitefield was an evangelical Calvinist, but Wesley's theology put more emphasis on individuals' God-given freedom to choose. Wesley also promoted rigorous moral discipline among his followers and taught that they should be able to attain a sort of perfection. Charles Wesley (1707–88), John's younger brother, was his closest ally and played an inestimable role in the success of the movement. Charles was a great hymn-writer and did more than anyone to give accessible music a prominent place in popular evangelism. Methodism remained a movement within the Church of England during John Wesley's lifetime but then became a separate denomination. The Methodist movement did not have much direct impact in America until after the Revolution.

In the meantime, beginning with the spectacular awakenings of 1739 and 1740, George Whitefield's style of evangelism sparked ongoing so-called new light revivals in America. These revivals were revolutionary in that most of them challenged established authority by appealing directly to the people. In most of British North America, preaching had been reserved for a highly educated elite who were expert in theology and in Hebrew, Greek, and Latin. Traveling or "itinerant" preachers such as Whitefield upset this pattern of social authority. The traveler could challenge local authority in the name of God and then move on. Moreover, Whitefield used a more popular style of preaching, dropping the elaborate expositions and arguments of elite clergy. Whitefield and his imitators frankly appealed to the emotions of their listeners, a practice often seen as shocking in an "enlightened" age when rationality was so highly valued both within and outside the churches. More alarmingly, Whitefield and his successors suggested that many church people were unconverted because the clergy themselves had not been truly born again: the blind were leading the blind. Such challenges to the authority of established clergy often brought divisions in American churches between new lights and antirevivalist "old lights."

Jonathan Edwards

Deeply involved in this debate was Jonathan Edwards (1703–58). Spending almost his whole life in small towns near the Massachusetts frontier, Edwards was both a leading preacher of the Awakening and an incisive analyst of the current religious questions. He also is considered to have been America's one truly world-class Christian theologian and is still studied for insights that speak to contemporary Christianity.

Edwards was deeply faithful to New England Calvinism but understood better than his contemporaries the threats it would face in the modern era. Calvinism was built around the sovereignty of God. Calvinists emphasized that humans were inherently sinful, or depraved, and could do nothing to save themselves. God's grace in Christ was their only hope.

Edwards identified threats to this God-centered outlook coming from two directions. On the one hand, threats could come from religious liberals who adopted eighteenth-century enlightened views that denied humans' total depravity and trusted more in human rational abilities and natural moral sense. On the other hand, complete trust in God could be undermined by the Awakening itself. To an extent, the liberal champions of reasonable Christianity were right. It was possible, at least, that sensational preachers could simply excite people's passions and so simulate religious conversions, which really would be human-generated self-delusion rather than acts of God's grace.

Edwards defended God-centeredness against these two threats by describing God's relationship to creation as an ongoing expression of God's love. If the essence of God is love, then God must be constantly communicating that love to created beings. When the Bible says, "The heavens declare the glory of God" (Ps. 19:1), it means that created reality is, in a sense, the language of God. Though sin and hate obscure that language, ultimately it points to the highest beauty imaginable, God's own loving sacrifice through the death of Jesus Christ on the cross on behalf of hatefully rebellious creatures. While creation can give people glimpses of the beauty of God's love, that beauty can be fully appreciated only through the revelation of Jesus Christ in Scripture. The role of those who preach the good news is to be a means through which the Holy Spirit awakens people to see and feel the "divine and supernatural light" of God's love. If any have eyes opened by the Spirit, they will glimpse that absolute beauty of the love of Christ and so be drawn to it. The power of that beauty will draw them from being preoccupied with love of self toward loving God and what God loves. This experience, said Edwards, was like receiving a "sixth sense," a spiritual sense to see, and so to love, the beauty of God's love.

So in answer to the religious liberals of the day, Edwards maintained that humans are naturally too self-centered to be open to seeing the full beauty of the love of God on their own. They need, rather, the full revelation of God's love in Christ as found in Scripture, as well as the Holy Spirit to awaken them to their natural selfish blindness and sin and to open their eyes to the beauty of that love. And in response to concerns about the emotional excesses of the awakenings, Edwards answered that extravagant emotional outbursts might well be appropriate responses to a genuine experience of God's overwhelming love. But at the same time, it was possible that similarly extravagant emotions might be generated by sensational and artificial means or even by Satan. So highly emotional expressions were not in themselves evidence one way or the other of whether a religious experience was true. Rather, as Edwards argued in his great work on *Religious Affections,* one must test religious experiences on the basis of whether they lead to the sort of balanced and humble life of service as taught in Scripture.[5]

The Awakening and Missions

Jonathan Edwards spent most of his last years in the 1750s as a missionary to the Indians in a tiny village on the western Massachusetts frontier and was there at the outbreak of the French and Indian wars. That a theologian of such magnitude should dedicate himself to such dangerous missionary work reveals a major dimension of American colonial life that is often forgotten. British colonials were acutely aware of living at the intersection of three cultures: their own, Catholic European, and Indian. For people today, who know the outcome, it may seem inevitable that British America would survive. At the time, however, it was not so obvious. If the French and their Indian allies had won the colonial wars of the eighteenth century, at least parts of the British settlements might have ended up mirroring what happened to the province of Quebec (which after 1763 became a Catholic-French enclave in a British-Protestant domain).

Missionary work to the Indians was one of the great British colonial failures. French-Catholic missionaries had been more successful. In the early decades of New England, for instance, a few missionaries had made strenuous efforts in converting the Indians. Most notable of the missionaries was John Eliot (1604–90), who translated the Bible into Algonkian and succeeded in establishing some villages of "praying Indians." Nevertheless, the inescapable fact was that the English were taking over territory that had once been controlled by native peoples. Attempts to claim that the British settlements were establishing a Christian commonwealth were always undercut by the reality that the English were taking from the people who already lived in these territories. In New England, the terrible tensions growing out of this anomaly had blown up in King Philip's War during the 1670s, virtually destroying Eliot's accomplishments.

Two generations later, in Edwards's time, New England was only just recovering from this disaster. Leaders of the Awakening hoped the movement would not only make the British truly Christian but also that it would spread the gospel to all nations, including the Indians. The American Awakening was the outpost of an international Protestant movement, which had strong centers in Scotland, England, and among pietists in Europe. The larger vision of the missionaries was for building a truly evangelical (gospel-based) Protestant civilization. One dimension of this enterprise was to renew their efforts to evangelize the Indians. Even so, few of the missionaries to the Indians had much success. The Moravians, a German pietist group in Pennsylvania, were the most effective at converting the Indians. Yet the realities of imperialism and the aggressiveness of many settlers who expanded the frontiers were difficult for missionaries to overcome.

The Continuing Awakening

While the Awakening was strong among Congregationalists in New England and Presbyterians and pietists in the middle colonies, its most lasting direct impact was in the spectacular burgeoning of Baptists. Many of the ardent new lights came to believe that baptism was valid only for adults who could testify to a conversion experience. Moreover, this Baptist doctrine appealed especially to non-elites. Anyone might experience the saving work of the Holy Spirit, so a conversion-oriented gospel had a socially leveling effect. Baptists encouraged ordinary people without theological education or ordination to testify and preach. This radical departure from most Protestant traditions helped the movement to spread quickly. Baptist preachers crisscrossed the colonies, preaching a message that resonated with other ordinary folk. By the end of the century, Baptists had become the largest religious group in the country.

The thunder of the Awakening thus continued to reverberate throughout the colonies long after Whitefield's famous tour. In the South particularly, this ongoing religious enthusiasm effected a remarkable cultural transformation. Prior to the Awakening, the religious life of the South was largely monopolized by an established Anglican Church—the official state church—supported by taxes. Having an established church was closely tied to the assumption that, as in England, the culture would be controlled by gentry who enjoyed God-given social authority. The Awakening marked the beginning of a process that eventually gave Southern culture an entirely new character. First, in the 1750s Presbyterian revivalists in the backcountry inspired new religious enthusiasm. The Presbyterians were soon followed and surpassed by the Baptists. These non-Anglicans, or "Dissenters" as they were known, were largely the ordinary people rather than the gentry.

No dimension of this revolution was more momentous in the long run than its impact on the enslaved. Up to this time, enslaved Africans had only begun to be evangelized and had not shown great interest in Christianity. After the mid-1700s, many of them found that because the enthusiastic and intense revivalist forms of Christianity were more congenial to their African religious heritage, they could appropriate them as their own. Evangelical Christianity offered them a new standard of values that asserted the superiority of the spiritual over the merely temporal, and it promised that the last should be made first. Baptist worship was informal, allowing for individual expression, and often was open to both blacks and whites. Almost immediately, blacks were contributing to new styles of worship that influenced both whites and blacks. Soon, blacks, both in the North and the South, free as well as enslaved, were developing their own semi-independent religious cultures that included some of their own preachers, based especially on Baptist and Methodist models.

One beneficiary of the awakenings was the African-American poet Phillis Wheatley (d. 1784). Freed by her Boston owners and given an education, she published her first poem as a memorial to George Whitefield. She praised Whitefield for proclaiming:

> Take him, ye Africans, he longs for you,
> Impartial Saviour in his title due;
> Washed in the fountain of redeeming blood,
> You shall be sons and kings, and Priests of God.[6]

The awakenings not only were vitally important in reshaping the lives of many women, but they also contributed to some opportunities for leadership. Throughout the eighteenth century, women constituted the majority of church members in the colonies. Nonetheless, the legal status of colonial women was severely limited, and in formal church activities they were expected to play only secondary roles. By contrast, the revivals proclaimed that the worth of the spiritual individual transcended social or ecclesiastical status. In conversion-oriented Christianity women could find spiritual and moral equality to men and even superiority to unconverted men. Women, whose overwhelming domestic vocations were arduous, whose lives were often at risk in childbirth, and who suffered the most intense agonies from high death rates among children, often found in these values a basis for self-fulfillment. The more radical awakenings encouraged ordinary people to testify and to preach, and in more radical groups it was not unusual for women to take up such roles. Typically, as such groups became more mainstream, the formal roles for women diminished. But through the era of awakenings and in many evangelical settings, talented women became informal spiritual leaders, even if not officially allowed to preach. One such woman of whom we have a good record was Sarah Osborn (1714–96) of Newport, Rhode Island. In the years just before the Revolution, although a Calvinist in a church not open to women preachers, she led a remarkable revival through meetings in her home attended by hundreds each week.

The awakenings would become a major American cultural force providing a partial counter to some largely secularizing trends. British colonial America was not an especially religious place. Rather, it had the rough and often violent features that we associate with the later American western frontier. Much of its development was driven by characteristic human ambition and greed along with some higher motives such as the wish to build healthy communities. Transplanting the church institutions that supported the ideals of Christendom had proven especially challenging. Outside of New England, the state churches were weak. Settlers came from a variety of nations and an even greater variety of religious or nominally religious backgrounds. In such a setting, the awakenings introduced what would become a highly significant religious counterforce. Conversionist-oriented Protestantism offered grassroots religion that could take hold and spread from the ground up, rather than being promoted from the top down as in Old World state churches. Like the American economy, it would grow through free enterprise and competition. Such evangelical religion would come in many varieties. Some was populist and anti-intellectual, some learned and traditional. Its influences would be similarly varied. Often, even as evangelical churches and movements were contributing to reshaping some aspects of American life, they were also being shaped by the characteristic biases of the various audiences they were trying to reach. Playing many roles in helping to fashion most American communities, such conversionary Protestantism would become one of the characteristic features of the American landscape.

CHAPTER 2

Religion and the American Revolution

Thus was human nature chained fast for ages in a cruel, shameful, and deplorable servitude to him [the pope], and his subordinate tyrants, who it was foretold, would exalt himself above all that was called God, and that was worshipped.

From the time of the Reformation to the first settlement of America, knowledge gradually spread in Europe, but especially in England; and in proportion as that increased and spread among the people, ecclesiastical and civil tyranny . . . seem to have lost their strength and weight.

John Adams, "A Dissertation on the
Canon and the Civil Law" (1765)

A Protestant Tradition of Dissent

The overturning of social values implicit in the Awakening was a portent signaling a new age of social change. In the American Revolution, which followed on the heels of the Awakening, the impact of the new cultural style was especially evident. While the Awakening did not cause the Revolution, it did anticipate many of its attitudes, especially the assertion of the rights of those from lower ranks in society to challenge established authority.

More important than the Awakening as a direct influence in shaping the American Revolution was an older tradition of Protestant dissent. The potentially revolutionary aspect of this tradition went back to Cromwell's Puritan Commonwealth in the 1650s. The American colonies were populated largely by people—especially New England Congregationalists and Scotch-Irish Presbyterians—who thought of themselves as heirs to that heritage. They were "Dissenters" rather than part of the powerful Anglican establishment. The Awakening, without itself involving any direct political program, intensified the dissenting traditions in America and increased their numbers. When the Revolution came, Congregationalists, Presbyterians, and Baptists were almost invariably on its side.

One often-overlooked dimension of early America is its almost tribal ethnoreligious diversities. Politically, the most significant tribe was the Scotch-Irish. Beginning in the Elizabethan age, these Scots migrated to Ulster in northern Ireland. As Scots, they disliked the English, and as Presbyterians, they despised the Anglican establishment. In the eighteenth century, they moved in large numbers to the colonies, constituting about one-fourth of the population of Pennsylvania and the inland regions to the south. In Pennsylvania, they developed a strong animosity to the ruling Quakers, who were English and whose pacifist principles the gun-toting Scotch-Irish thought cowardly. Eventually, the Scotch-Irish brought to an end the Quaker rule. Their even stronger hostility toward Anglican English, who controlled the imperial government, was an important ingredient in the Revolution. Rough-hewn back-country Scotch-Irish ethnic loyalties, sometimes mixed with religious fervor and opposed to strong central government, set the tone for a persistent type of white ethnic subculture.

In the American Revolution itself, as is often the case, religion was a significant factor but not an isolated variable in political events. Rather, the resurgence of dissenting religious heritages in the eighteenth-century American awakenings reinforced other ethnic and regional loyalties that contributed to revolution.

A Secular Society

While the role of religion is often neglected in accounts of the shaping of the nation, it should not be exaggerated either. As is always true, at least in modern Western societies, a great deal that went on in eighteenth-century America had little to do directly with traditional organized religion. Although most white Americans thought of themselves as part of Protestant Christendom, their society was Christian largely in a formal sense. A good many people, especially those touched by revivals, were intensely religious. Many more, most of the population, in fact, were religious only occasionally or ignored religious services entirely. Some also trusted in minor folk magic that had little to do with their traditional Christian connections.

In certain areas of eighteenth-century life, such as warfare or commerce, traditional religion seldom played more than a small, supporting role. The society took violence for granted, cruelly oppressed other races, and gave in to many vices attractive to human nature. Alcohol provided a chief entertainment, and indeed, one would have found much of eighteenth-century America thoroughly profane. Such tendencies appeared more often in the South before the awakenings and in frontier areas, where traditional religious organizations were not strong.

The overall trends in Western civilization seemed to favor the expansion of areas of life that religion would not touch. England and her colonies both had become considerably more secular by the mid-eighteenth century than they had been in the mid-seventeenth. A combination of forces favored such developments. Perhaps most important were the technological and scientific revolutions. Although these had not yet transformed everyday life, they were terrifically exciting to educated eighteenth-century people because they seemed to promise that many new areas of life could be improved by using practical, scientific reason. It seemed to such people that they were in the midst of a vast human breakthrough, not simply in better understanding their physical environment, but also in applying the same rational principles to mastering most other problems. They therefore thought they ought to be able to discover universally valid scientific principles for questions of morality, politics, and (for some) even of religion itself.

A Scientific Age

Basic to this set of attitudes, usually associated with the Enlightenment, was the belief that humanity no longer had to depend on tradition for its surest authority. Until that time, almost everyone in Western civilization assumed that the older a belief was, the more likely it was to be true. In the eighteenth century, enlightened thinkers were claiming there was no need to depend on the past. The human race could solve their problems if they started over, following the scientific method. They should begin with no prior assumptions or superstitions inherited from tradition.

By the end of the eighteenth century, such views became widespread among both educated and uneducated Americans. The American Revolution came just at the time when the vogue of such ideas was at its height, so the popular definitions of the new nation were undeniably shaped by these ideas. Leading American revolutionaries, such as Thomas Jefferson and Benjamin Franklin (1706–90), endorsed these views in their purest form. Both were practical philosophers; each was responsible for a long list of inventions. Practical scientific reason, they assumed, was the key to solving many of humanity's longstanding problems, whether they concerned how to make life more comfortable or how to build a better society. Such an outlook—that most of the important questions of life have a technical solution—has had an immeasurable impact on shaping American society.

Jefferson and Franklin and some of the other leading revolutionaries were Deists who believed in what they viewed as "rational Christianity." They abandoned those parts of Christian heritage that they thought were not based on reason, yet they retained faith in a creator deity since they believed it was unreasonable to think that the wonderful machine of the universe appeared without a designer. They also believed in a created moral order, reflecting the wisdom of the Supreme Being and necessary for the practical ordering of society. They admired the moral teachings of Jesus but did not consider him to be God incarnate.

One might suppose that the nation Jefferson, Franklin, and their Deist friends helped create would become a very secular place, accelerating the forces in the society away from the impact of traditional Christianity. The relationship of American culture to such secular trends, however, has always been far from simple and has been marked by paradoxes and contradictions. One gets a sense of this deep mix of the Christian and the secular by looking at the central event that shaped American society, the American Revolution itself.

A Moral Age

Consider first the Declaration of Independence. Why were Americans willing to fight and die to separate themselves from what in retrospect looks like a rather mild British rule? Although there were many practical reasons to want independence, these reasons would have seemed hardly sufficient to justify a dangerous armed rebellion if the Revolution had not been regarded as based on moral principles of some cosmic significance. Jefferson—when drafting the Declaration of Independence—stated in Enlightenment language the moral factors on which most Americans could agree.

While there were many sources for Jefferson's thought, the most direct parallel is to the views of John Locke (1632–1704). Locke was a figure of the earlier English Enlightenment who attempted to do for politics and morality what his contemporary Isaac Newton did for physics. He tried to discover universal moral laws based on reason alone. When Jefferson proclaimed in the Declaration that rights to life and liberty were beyond doubt, or "self-evident," he was summarizing views of Locke that had become commonplace in eighteenth-century political thought.

Jefferson also followed Locke in building a theory of revolution based on these foundations. If the government constantly violates fundamental moral laws, for instance, by arbitrarily taking away its people's life, liberty, or property (taxation without representation), then the supposed governors become, literally, outlaws. Therefore, people have a right and a duty to alter or abolish such a corrupt government and to set up a proper government that honors the moral law.

Locke and the Puritans

From the standpoint of American religious history, the striking aspect of this familiar Lockean-Jeffersonian formula is its similarity to the Puritan view of the covenant. In each, the nation and its rulers are bound together by a contract, the terms of which are divinely ordained moral law. If the governors break the contract by systematically breaking the laws, then the contract is dissolved. Yet while the Puritans emphasized that one's certainty about the moral law came from the Bible (though it might be confirmed by reason), Locke and Jefferson grounded their certainty on human reason alone (though they agreed that the Bible said the same thing). All parties agreed that the Bible and reason concurred on fundamental moral principles. For instance, the biblical commandment "Thou shalt not steal" and the self-evident "right to property" were two ways of stating the same truth.

This similarity of the two views was not accidental. With the execution of Charles I in 1649, the English Puritans became the first modern revolutionaries. As we have seen, many of the modern principles for redefining human relationships were anticipated in the religious radicalism of England in the mid-seventeenth century. John Locke lived during the next generation, brought about when, in the bloodless revolution of 1688–89, William and Mary displaced the Catholic king, James II. Locke developed his political views and his justification of revolution in this context. Though his most influential arguments for revolution were based on self-evident principles of reason, rather than on Scripture, the influence of the Puritan model was substantial.

The connection between Lockean and Puritan thought illustrates the important point that most eighteenth-century Americans perceived no conflict between scientific or rational "Enlightenment" ways of looking at things and their Christian heritage. The strengths of their Christian commitments, of course, varied widely, and for many, perhaps for most, their Christian heritage had only a vague impact on their beliefs. Nonetheless, even when Christian commitments were strong, as they were for many of the heirs to the Puritans in New England, Christian and scientific Enlightenment beliefs were almost always seen not as contradictory but as complementary. This was especially true for those Americans who supported the Revolution and hence had the most to do with shaping the characteristic outlook of the new nation.

Both the Puritan emphasis on covenant and later enlightenment formulations reinforced and helped consolidate one of the most valuable principles that long had been developing in the British heritage and that became a foundational principle for the American republic: that nations must be governed by the rule of law. Government is not based simply on the arbitrary authority of persons, with the result that rulers and others with power are not supposed to stand above the law. They are not supposed to govern simply on the basis of patronage, power, bribery, and whim, as had been so common throughout most of history and still is the effective norm in much of the world today. Even though its principles have been violated countless times in American history, the rule of law nonetheless remains the national norm to which those seeking justice can hope to appeal.

A Land of Dissenters

The connections between religious heritage and the American Revolution were often direct. British North America, as has been seen, was largely a land of Dissenters. Many of the supporters of the Revolution were at least nominally connected with Dissenter denominations such as the Congregationalists, Presbyterians, or Baptists. One very significant aspect of these heritages was that, because of their histories of opposition to the Anglican establishment in England, they had fostered a tradition of political thought. And that tradition helped shape the thinking of almost all of the American revolutionaries. Developed first in the 1720s, this tradition of English Dissenter thought has been variously known as the Real Whig or Common-wealth tradition. The Commonwealth referred to the earlier days of Puritan rule in England in the 1660s. The eighteenth-century Commonwealth men were heirs to this heritage in that they belonged to nonconformist or Dissenter denominations.

It is very important for understanding American culture and the role of religion in the Revolution to recognize the political implications in England of having an established church. Reflecting the very old practices of Christendom, the Church of England was practically a department of the state. Political power was tied to church membership. In the eighteenth century, other denominations were tolerated, but the memory of the Puritan takeover was recent enough that Anglicans were not ready to give up their political and social control. Throughout the 1700s in England, if one were to hold public office or even to attend the major universities, Oxford and Cambridge, one had to belong to the Church of England.

The Course of Empires

For the Dissenters, such discrimination sharpened their awareness of political tyranny. By the 1720s, they were producing a body of political thought that linked political and ecclesiastical tyranny with the accumulation of executive power around the monarch. Citing the precedents of ancient Athens and Rome, they pointed out that republican governments tend to be subverted if the republic acquires an empire. Massive colonial administration would then bring accumulation of power around an executive, and corruption would soon set in. There would be buying and selling of offices and privileges. This is what the Dissenters saw happening to England. Its mixed government of monarchy and parliament was losing its balance of powers in the direction of growing executive power and growing arbitrary privilege. The privileged Church of England was on the side of this executive power. Dissenters were not usually as strict in their theology as were their Puritan forebears, yet they shared with the Puritans the belief that high-handed monarchical power is always supported by ecclesiastical privilege. Therefore, the Commonwealth men championed both the inalienable rights of humanity to life, liberty, and property in the tradition of John Locke and the inalienable rights of conscience in the traditions of English religious dissent.

One could hardly overstate the importance of this Commonwealth heritage in shaping American revolutionary political thought. Most Americans were Dissenters, and even many of those who were Anglicans, such as the Virginia gentry, were outsiders to the political privilege surrounding the crown. Most of those who held local political or social power in America stood only to lose if the full-fledged English system were exported to the colonies. So, when England, after 1763, began to take an interest in reorganizing her newly expanded North American empire, many colonists grew alarmed. They stated their alarm in the terms of Commonwealth or Real Whig heritage. This dissenting tradition became the base for the republican outlook that long dominated American political thought.

An American Bishop

The most striking evidence of the religious Dissenting factor in colonial alarms about the Anglicization of the colonies was the great fear over the prospect of an Anglican bishop for the colonies. The Church of England required the direct laying on of hands by a bishop for the ordination of clergy. That made it a great inconvenience for American Anglicans to have no resident bishop in the colonies. However, the same republican Americans, including many Anglicans, who opposed the new taxes for the empire were dead set against such an otherwise sensible proposal to appoint an American bishop. They saw it as a major step toward imposing on the colonies the entire English hierarchical model for governing society.

Catholicism and Monarchy

Such fears were compounded by the militant anti-Catholic sentiments of many American revolutionaries. Ironically, movements that champion freedom do not extend that freedom to those whom they consider their mortal enemies. The Catholic population, mostly in the middle colonies, was small. They were often discriminated against but were generally tolerated. They were not the problem. Some Catholics, such as the influential Carroll family in Maryland, supported the Revolution and even hoped to make the American Catholic Church more republican. The problem was that the English colonies were still Protestant enclaves in a largely Catholic hemisphere, so the cold-war mentality lingered. This was especially true in New England. A number of times during the eighteenth century, amid much religious fanfare, New Englanders mobilized for military action against French Catholics in Canada. In 1763, at the conclusion of the French and Indian War, they rejoiced that Canada was finally in British and Protestant hands. Soon, however, they were chagrined that in the Quebec Act of 1774 the British administration of Canada allowed for continued tax support for the Catholic Church and allowed for the continued spread of Catholicism in what is now the US upper Midwest.

Most of the American revolutionaries took for granted a Real Whig or republican view of history that grew out of the British religious and political experience. They associated tyranny with the Middle Ages and the marriage of ecclesiastical and royal power. "Thus," as John Adams put it, "was human nature chained fast for ages in a cruel, shameful, and deplorable servitude to [the pope] and his subordinate tyrants." As the longer quotation at the beginning of this chapter suggests, revolutionaries like Adams saw Protestantism as crucial to the rise of freedom. According to the Whig view, Protestantism opened the door for reason or common sense to challenge superstition and privilege. Once again, one can see that dissenting Protestant views and Enlightenment views would blend far more than they would disagree. Both saw superstition as the problem and common-sense reason as the solution. Both regarded Catholicism (and some Anglicanism that resembled Catholicism) as defending monarchy and the authoritarianism of the Middle Ages. Dissenting Protestantism, they believed, was on the side of liberty.

A Republic of Virtue

These revolutionary traditions also agreed that virtue was essential to the American republican enterprise. This point was central also in classical Greek and Roman thought. Classical models, as we can still see in the neoclassical "colonial" architecture of the eighteenth century, were immensely important to those who were shaping the new republic. In the republican blend of dissenting Protestant, classical, and enlightened thinking, all authorities agreed with the fundamental moral maxim, "Power corrupts." Americans, who were far from the centers of power, saw themselves as on the side of virtue.

It is this definition of their cause as a matter of virtue, as evidenced in the Declaration of Independence of 1776, that could rally Americans to risk dying for independence. This lens through which the revolutionaries viewed their cause accounts for what, from the British point of view, must have looked like a colossal misperception. Even from a modern perspective, it is difficult to understand how the British rule was quite as tyrannical as the Declaration describes. The British Empire, despite some administrative faults, was one of the relatively more enlightened regimes in world history. It seems a far cry from the tyranny of ancient Roman rule and not even in the ballpark with the more advanced twentieth- and twenty-first-century tyrannies, such as those of Hitler, Stalin, Pol Pot, Kim Jong-il, or many others. The British, quite sensibly, were attempting to reorganize their empire and have the colonists help pay for it. How could so many Americans see this as an extreme case of despotism that called for revolution?

This puzzling question can be answered by understanding that the Americans viewed these events through the lens of their Whig blend of dissenting Protestant, classical, and Enlightenment ideologies. In that view, there was a history of repeated tyrannies associated with Catholicism, Catholic-leaning Anglicanism, monarchy, and the corrupting development of empires. Protestantism, republicanism, common-sense reason, and freedom were reputedly locked in a centuries-long struggle against repressive forces. The American revolutionaries thought they had to save their heritage before they were overwhelmed by these forces of tyranny.[1]

The New Order for the Ages

Given this perception of the larger historical issues at stake in the Revolution, it is not surprising that American preachers often raised the cause of liberty to sacred status. The minions of the Antichrist, said Samuel West of Dartmouth, Massachusetts, in an annual election sermon before the legislature in 1776, "better be understood as political rather than ecclesiastical tyrants." Turning to the book of Revelation, West suggested that the "horrible wild beast" ascending from the bottomless pit could refer to the British army. Therefore, West announced, "We must beat our plowshares into swords, and our pruning hooks into spears."[2]

Understanding such rhetoric coming from the nation's most respected public speakers calls for some knowledge of the cosmic view of history that the dissenting clergy typically tied to their republican sentiments.

During the Great Awakening, some of the new light preachers successfully popularized the notion that the earth was near the dawn of a new era. The Bible, which was widely regarded as an absolute authority on all subjects, spoke of a "millennial" age, or thousand-year reign of Christ. By the mid-1700s, the most common interpretation of this prophecy by American revivalists was that it symbolically foretold the culminating era in history when the Spirit of Christ, or the Holy Spirit, would reign on earth. The Awakening itself was seen as the chief evidence of the beginning of this age, which would witness massive conversions to the gospel.

Inevitably, such prophecies took on political connotations. In order for the millennium to come, according to these interpretations of Scripture, Christ must defeat the Antichrist. In Protestant thought, the Antichrist traditionally referred to the papacy. Therefore, reasoned the American Dissenters, any political defeat of Catholic countries was a step toward the dawning of the millennium. The French and Indian Wars of 1756 and 1763 fit this model exactly. For instance, the famed Presbyterian evangelist Samuel Davies described the British efforts against France as "the commencement of this grand decisive conflict between the Lamb and the beast." A British victory, he proclaimed, would help bring "a new heaven and a new earth."[3]

When the victory of 1763 brought not a grand new age, but the reorganization of the British Empire, it took some rhetorical gymnastics for the Dissenter preachers to put Protestant England into the columns of the pope. Their Puritan-Whig traditions, the fears of a bishop, and the Quebec Act of 1774 that continued the Catholic establishment in Canada, however, all contributed to this reading of the conflict. Simply by virtue of lining up on the side of tyranny against the colonists, reasoned the pious revolutionaries, England had signaled its betrayal of the *true* cause of Protestant civilization. Reverend Alexander MacWhorter, chaplain to Washington's troops at Valley Forge, described the enemy as "Papist Highland barbarians"—even though most of them were actually fellow Presbyterians.[4]

Important as it was to have the respected clergy of America's popular religions providing the Revolution with such cosmic historical significance, this dimension of the origin of American identity should not be pushed too far. As we have seen, the revolutionaries welcomed the Catholics who would join their cause, and the new nation would be committed to legal tolerance of Catholics. Moreover, the American Revolution also provides a dramatic illustration of the limits of religious rhetoric. When Catholic France took an interest in supporting the American cause against the British and the very survival of the new American nation depended on that French support, few raised any objections to the convenient alliance with Catholics. One clear lesson of history is that people are seldom consistent. Rather, they are remarkably capable of holding contradictory opinions at the same time. Furthermore, religious people are often resourceful in adjusting their principles in times of need. And especially during wartime they are ready to accept whatever it takes to survive.

A Paradoxical Heritage

The Dissenter rhetoric allowed many in the dominant white, Anglo-Saxon, Protestant population to do what they always had done since the Puritans— view their civilizing efforts as a divine mission.

Americans today tend to talk about this propensity as either wholly good or wholly bad. On the positive side, this sense of national calling certainly has contributed to the vitality and success of American civilization. It has also provided a moral idealism and sense of civic and national responsibility. The American nation, when it was founded, became a beacon for liberty and order in an age when that combination was rare. Peoples of every race and nationality have rallied under the standard of these moral ideals, finding in them expressions of the best in their own traditions. Much of whatever one regards as successful in America must be attributed to such ideals.

There is a negative side, however, that is just as undeniable. Critics, including sympathetic critics, point out that the very virtues of this American tradition often become its vices. High moral idealism and a sense of divine calling to spread the ideals of liberty and justice, as one conceives them, can easily lead to injustice. This is particularly true of those who combine these ideals with power. Once in power, champions of liberty and order often use the rhetoric of liberty to impose an order that favors themselves. Groups out of favor may be excluded from the liberties. In the case of the new nation, the most disturbing example of this inequity was the failure of white Protestants to apply the moral ideals of the Revolution to enslaved people. Moreover, moral idealism, just because of the important virtues it self-evidently stands for, can lead to an overestimation of the nation's rights toward other peoples. In the new nation, liberty and justice were seldom applied toward relations with Indians. Moreover, the United States developed a questionable sense of "manifest destiny" in spreading its ideals from coast to coast and eventually around the world. Sometimes lofty moral ideals were true motivating forces in American foreign policy, but they were often used in the self-interest of the powerful and the ambitious.[5]

On balance, and compared to most of the alternatives, the American experiment has been attractive to many people in part because of its traditions of the high moral ideals of liberty and justice. Expressions of high ideals, however, make groups particularly vulnerable to criticisms for failure to apply such ideals equally to all.

Civil Religion

America's religious heritage also contributed to a sort of deification of the national enterprise. In recent generations, this tendency, first seen during the American Revolution, has been tagged "civil religion." Civil religion attributes a sacred character to the nation itself. Throughout history, rulers had claimed divine sanction either by saying that they themselves were divine (as Roman emperors did) or that they were chosen by God or the gods of the nation. Typically, national loyalty was focused on loyalty to the person of the monarch. In eighteenth-century France, for instance, the kings claimed to rule by divine right and the person of the king was considered a sacred object.

The Puritans in America and England challenged such claims in important ways. In America, as we have seen, the early Puritans claimed divine sanction for their enterprise by viewing themselves as a new Israel. God would bless the colonies only if they were explicitly Christian and obeyed God's laws. In England at the time of the Revolution of 1649, that Puritan principle was extended to say that God's law stood above even the king, who could be declared an outlaw. From the Puritan-Presbyterian outlook, loyalty was directed not toward the person of the ruler, but toward a set of principles. In eighteenth-century England, questions of loyalty to principle or person were still hotly contested. In America, however, loyalty to principle triumphed. The revolutionary Thomas Paine (1737–1809) put it best in his immensely popular pamphlet of 1776, *Common Sense*: "in America, *the law is king.*"

However, Americans had a problem. How could they claim religious approval for their nation? Thomas Paine, for instance, was a notorious infidel. After the Revolution, he authored scathing attacks on Christianity. With leading citizens such as Paine and the Deist Jefferson, clearly the nation could not officially claim a traditional Christian sanction.

Americans resolved this problem by three primary means, all aspects of civil religion. First, Deist leaders of the Jeffersonian sort argued that the natural laws on which American rights were founded demonstrably originated with the Creator. Thus, as illustrated in the Declaration of Independence, Americans, whether Christian or not, could appeal to the Creator who stood above all sects. Accordingly, official references to God in American life, such as "In God we trust" or "so help me God," could have this vague meaning.

Second, American civil and political leaders informally continued to speak of the nation as though it were a Christian nation, or at least a biblical nation. Politicians as well as clergy often referred to America as though it were the new Israel and Americans were a chosen people. For instance, in the twentieth century it became common in presidential and other patriotic addresses to speak of the United States as a "city on a hill," using the term first enunciated by Puritan governor John Winthrop in 1630.

Finally, the United States was the first modern nation systematically to shift public veneration of the government from reverence toward persons to reverence for the nation and its principles. The United States developed a set of rituals and symbols that bore a striking resemblance to traditional Christian rites and symbols but in which the nation itself was the object of worship. The flag, like the cross in Catholic churches, was a sacred object. Elaborate rules developed as to when and how it could be handled. The act of pledging allegiance to the flag arguably played the role of crossing oneself in a church. And the pledge one recited was like a creed. The nation developed holidays (holy days) and its own brand of saints. George Washington, for instance, soon took on mythical qualities. National architecture and shrines provided centers for pilgrimages and worship. Some people have pointed out that three of the most popular shrines in Washington, DC—those to Washington, Lincoln, and Kennedy—have designs that would be appropriate symbols for each of the three members of the Christian Trinity (the transcendent obelisk of the Washington Monument for the father, the personal presence in the Lincoln Memorial of the martyred champion of national reconciliation and charity, and the eternal flame at Kennedy's grave for the spirit of service to country).[6]

Such specific analogies should not be pushed too far, but the crucial practical test of a functional religion is ultimacy. Here the United States, the model of the modern nation-state, qualifies. This nation, like all modern nations, demands unswerving allegiance from its citizens. It is the nation for which one is expected to make the supreme sacrifice. Therefore in American wars, national loyalty has always been demanded above church loyalty. Presbyterians killed Presbyterians during the Revolution; Anglicans killed Anglicans. In the Civil War, Baptists killed countless Baptists, Methodists countless Methodists, Catholics and Jews killed fellow Catholics and Jews, and so forth. This has been the practice in every war.

The major exceptions, of course, were pacifists such as Quakers, Mennonites, Amish, and Moravians. Loyalty to Christ's principles of love, they maintained, must stand before loyalty to nation. Pacifists often suffered for this radical stance. Pennsylvania Mennonites and Quakers, for instance, sometimes had their property confiscated by patriots for failing to pay taxes for the Revolutionary War. Other citizens felt these pacifists neglected their civic responsibilities and aided the enemy by refusing to fight in a good cause.

Except for the pacifists, almost all American religious groups saw their national loyalties not in conflict with their traditional religion but simply as an extension of their religion. Throughout the nation's history, Americans overwhelmingly have insisted that loyalty to God and nation go hand in hand.

A Secular Constitution

Recognition of the roles played by Dissenter Protestantism and civil religion should balance the more familiar accounts of the secular origins of the American republic. Enlightenment and classical categories did dominate the political discourse of the new nation, but Christians did not see these as conflicting with Christian principles. God was author of both Scripture and nature and so truth was a unified whole. Accordingly, Christians were convinced they had nothing to fear from practical principles derived from scientific reasoning. True principles of governments, they reasoned, were as universal as the laws of physics.

Dissenter Protestantism and Enlightenment thought combined to guarantee separation of church and state in the new national government. This alliance, which emerged before the Revolution in the fears of an Anglican bishop, led to the momentous effort in disestablishing the deeply-entrenched Anglican church in Virginia after the war. Thomas Jefferson saw his role in the adoption of the Virginia "Act for Establishing Freedom of Religion" in 1786 as one of the three great accomplishments in his life, along with authoring the Declaration of Independence and founding the University of Virginia. Crucial to the success of this effort was the vigorous support of Virginia Baptists and other Dissenters.

The Virginia law, which forbade an established state religion, was a precedent for the US Constitution, authored in part by James Madison (1751–1836), Jefferson's right-hand man in the Virginia disestablishment. On the other hand, the connection cannot be pressed too far, since the Constitution is very different from the Virginia law. It neither establishes nor disestablishes religion. In fact, this is precisely how the policy was stated when the First Amendment was added: "Congress shall make no law respecting an establishment of religion, or prohibiting the free exercise thereof." Established

Congregational churches, supported by taxes, remained in New England into the early nineteenth century. The Constitution assumed that the federal government would not touch traditional religious practices. At the same time, the US government and the army had Protestant chaplains; legislative sessions were still opened with prayer; and Protestant theology was standard fare in most state-supported schools.

In fact, the best explanation of the Constitution's stance on religion is very simple. The Constitution stays away, almost entirely, from the subject of religion. The only thing it says is that "no religious test shall ever be required" for public office. As historian John F. Wilson explains, the framers of the Constitution were political realists. They knew that getting the new document ratified was going to be a very close call. In the religiously divided tribal United States, nothing could kill the proposal more quickly than to take a stand on religion. The framers, therefore, said as little as possible about the subject, not even invoking any pious language.[7]

The assumption at the time certainly was that religion, and especially Christianity, should be able to flourish in the republic without interference from the state. Though the federal government was not going to take any new steps in promoting religion, neither was there a strict " wall of separation" between church and state, as Jefferson later described it. The new Constitution was indeed conspicuously revolutionary in creating the first major government in Christendom that was not officially Christian and did not have a state church. At the same time the Constitution did not interfere with Christianity as a dominant and privileged force in the culture and even in public life.

Was the Early United States a Christian Nation?

As should be apparent already, any fully honest history will have to say that neither the United States nor any other nation has been Christian in more than a limited sense. Even the American Puritans, as we have seen, whose governments were officially Christian, who tried to make their laws conform to biblical teaching, and whose leaders were strongly professing Christians, failed to create a society that was normatively Christian in the sense that it was a model society that Christians today should want to imitate. Despite some very admirable Christian features, their society was also sometimes harsh and oppressive toward those who differed from themselves, and it had what most people today would consider serious blind spots regarding the rights of Indians, toleration of religious minorities and dissenters, cruel punishments, roles of women, and acceptance of African enslavement. Even at the time, some Puritans, most notably Roger Williams, questioned the assumption, inherited from Christendom, that the civil government should promote one official state religion.

More than a century later, the early United States was already far more secular and pluralistic than were the early Puritan colonies. Although most citizens were nominally Christian, a large majority of them were not active in churches. Protestant revivalists often complained bitterly about how profane and dissolute the population was. Many of the most influential founders of the nation were more inclined toward Deism or liberal Christianity than toward traditional Christianity. The federal government was not officially Christian and the US Constitution not only avoided any establishment of religion, but it was conspicuous among governing documents of the time in that it nowhere invoked the authority of God. And as in every society, despite efforts to promote justice, many blatant injustices remained, in this case most manifestly regarding enslavement of Africans. So if Puritan New England falls short of being a model Christian society that Christians today should want to imitate, the early United States was also too flawed to come up to that standard.

It is worth taking note of one striking paradox in this discussion. Puritan New England is subject to criticism for being too officially Christian, for having a state church, for being intolerant, and even for acting unjustly toward other Christians who differed from themselves. The early United States, by becoming *less* Christian in an official sense, represents an improvement so far as justice is concerned. If civil societies should be dedicated to promoting justice, then they ought to tolerate varieties of religious beliefs. Especially in a nation that includes many sorts of immigrants, the government ought to be dedicated to promoting pluralism, attempting to maximize protections of the rights of minorities to hold peculiar beliefs. So there is an irony involved in that being less Christian in a formal sense may be more consistent with some principles of justice that Christians and others ought to support.

The question is further complicated by the fact that, even though the early United States did not have an established church, it still had an informal religious establishment. Protestant Christianity was favored in many ways. The same First Amendment that prevented a federal establishment of religion also left in place not only established churches in some states but all sorts of inherited Christian privileges. Protestant Christianity remained standard fare in government ceremonies, such as in prayers of invocation, or swearing on the Bible. More substantially, Christian teachings and Bible instruction remained part of education at every level. Civil law often reflected some specifically religious concerns, such as regarding marriage and divorce, Sabbath observance, or laws against blasphemy. Polite society usually maintained an ethos of respect for broadly Christian beliefs.

How one evaluates such an informal religious establishment will differ according to one's own stance. But even from the point of view of traditional Protestants today, one would have to say that the benefits have to be weighed against the inequities toward those of other heritages. For instance, it might at least arguably be beneficial for a society that is overwhelmingly Protestant by heritage to maintain legislation limiting work and commerce on Sunday, making sure people are free to attend their churches. Yet such laws would look very different to Orthodox Jews who celebrated their Sabbath on Saturdays. Similarly, teaching Protestant Christianity in public schools and colleges would seem, from a Protestant perspective, to have obvious benefits for promoting that faith in the culture. Yet Americans who were Jewish, Muslim, Roman Catholic, or secularist had good reasons to resent the discrimination involved in such practices. Even so, it has also been said that certain aspects of the informal Protestant establishment benefited the whole society. Religious teachings in the schools, for instance, helped promote respect for the rule of law, something often needed, especially in frontier settings. Teaching religiously-sanctioned precepts like honesty, avoiding greed, honoring parents, or helping neighbors in need had undeniable social benefits. The American founders rightly believed that cultivating virtue would be an essential component in preserving the health of the republic. Even those, such as Franklin and Jefferson, who themselves were a long way from traditional Christian teaching, welcomed such teachings as a way to foster such virtue. Every society needs some sort of informal establishment to promote the dominant culture's shared precepts and moral values, and Protestantism played a large role in that respect in the early United States. The challenge, to which predominantly Protestant America rose only partially, was how to promote what one regards as right and at the same time respect the viewpoints of minorities who would follow some other standard.

So the answer to the question of whether America was founded as a Christian nation is "no, it was not; it was a mix of Christians and non-Christian elements."[8] Further, it was mixed in several different ways.

First, in the purely descriptive sense, the early United States, like just about everything in the Western world, was deeply shaped by the broad heritage of Christendom. And specifically Protestant influences were crucially important in shaping some dimensions of the culture and polity. Rights of conscience, rule with consent of the governed, regard for the law standing above rulers, trust in natural laws known by reason as products of a Creator, specifics of moral law, and much else were shaped in part by the nation's Christian and Protestant heritages. But these outlooks were inextricably mixed with many others, such as ideas from ancient Greek and Roman thought or from Enlightenment trust in modern practical and technological reasoning.

Second, in an official or formal sense, the early United States was a mix of intentional disestablishment of religion and an informal Protestant establishment that allowed for and often protected by law all sorts of Protestant privilege.

Third, in the normative sense, even from a traditionalist Christian perspective, the early United States was a mixture, so far as being a society with standards and practices that people should wish to imitate or go back to today. Many of its characteristic beliefs, practices, and emphases were truly laudable and worthy of imitation. But these many positive features were mixed with all the sorts of inequality, discrimination, violence, cruelty, vices, and injustices that are characteristic of any society. Some practices that seemed acceptable as a matter of course in much of eighteenth-century Protestant society seem outrageous today. Enslavement of Africans is the most conspicuous. One quick way to see what a mix of the admirable and the abominable early American society was is to ask whether the early United States was a Christian society from an African-American point of view.[9]

An intriguing turn in the story is that, even though by the end of the Revolutionary era, around 1800, the early United States may have seemed less religious than in colonial days, the trends proved to be not all in a more secularized direction. As the new republic expanded in the early nineteenth century, Americans would actually become more religious by most standards. Even so, their dominant ways of life would also remain a mix of the religious and the profane, as is characteristic of all human societies. And sometimes, as both religious zeal and secularizing material forces expanded, the paradoxes created by their mixture would become even more striking.

CHAPTER 3

The Age of Democratic Revivals

It was pretty ornery preaching—all about brotherly love, and such-like tiresomeness; but every-body said it was a good sermon, and they all talked it over going home, and had such a powerful lot to say about faith and good works and free grace and preforeordestination, and I don't know what all, that it did seem to me to be one of the roughest Sundays I had run across yet.

Mark Twain, *The Adventures of Huckleberry Finn* (1884)

Lyman Beecher (1775–1863), a leading Congregational evangelist and one of Connecticut's champions of antidisestablishmentarianism, later said that the ending, in 1818, of state tax support for Congregationalism was "the best thing that ever happened to the state of Connecticut." It threw the formerly Puritan churches "on their own resources and on God" and increased their influence "by voluntary efforts, societies, missions, and revivals."[1]

Most observers have agreed with Beecher that despite forces from the Enlightenment, Revolution, and denominational rivalries that might have undermined Christianity's cultural impact, churches actually gained influence during the succeeding era. Although church membership statistics for the era are somewhat unreliable, reported membership percentages doubled between 1800 and 1860. Far more people apparently attended churches than met the rigorous criteria of most Protestant churches for full membership. In 1860, church seating was available for an estimated three-fifths of the American population of thirty-one million.[2] These figures suggest that if you had visited the United States on a Sunday at that time, perhaps 30 to 40 percent of the people would have been in church.

Cultural impact, however, is more difficult to measure. Alexis de Tocqueville remarked in the 1830s regarding religion and its cultural influence that "I do not know whether all Americans have a sincere faith in their religion—for who can search the human heart?—but I am certain that they hold it to be indispensable to the maintenance of republican institutions." Other foreign visitors have said much the same.[3]

The great dynamo generating this remarkable American religious vigor was continuing revival. The period from about 1795 to 1865 was marked by recurrent outbursts of revival throughout the states. In 1801, spectacular new camp-meeting revivals occurred among both whites and blacks, especially on the Kentucky frontier. At the other end of the social spectrum, that same year, Timothy Dwight, president of Congregationalist Yale College, spurred a campus revival that helped inspire a whole generation of Connecticut Yankees in spreading the gospel into the new settlements of the West (now Midwest) and throughout the world. Meanwhile, the Methodist movement, which had become an independent denomination, was growing at a spectacular rate among the common people, surpassing even Baptists in numbers by 1820. At the same time, countless local revivalists sprang up, often with highly popularized and democratic versions of the gospel. Innovators formed several new denominations, each marked by grand expectations for ushering in a new age of the Spirit. By the 1840s and 1850s, impressive percentages of enslaved people had turned to Christianity, which became the overwhelmingly dominant religion of their culture. While women were usually the majority in these revivals, in 1857 and 1858 urban revivals among businessmen in the North drew them to noontime prayer meetings in numbers unlike anything anyone had seen. During the Civil War, notable revivals were reported in both the Union and Confederate army camps.

Just the overview of these remarkable developments lends plausibility to the estimate of renowned historian Perry Miller that "the dominant theme in America from 1800 to 1860 is the invincible persistence of the revival technique." The revival fire, said Miller, "sometimes smoldering, now blazing into flame, never quite extinguished (even in Boston) until the Civil War had been fought, was the central mode of this culture's search for cultural identity."[4] William McLoughlin goes even further to say, "The story of American Evangelicalism is the story of America itself in the years 1800–1900, for it was Evangelical religion which made Americans the most religious people in the world."[5] Though many other forces must be acknowledged, as well, for the dominance of religion, evangelical Christianity was unusually significant in shaping nineteenth-century American cultural values.

This way of characterizing American culture in the national era may seem odd, given the prevailing image of a dominant secular outlook introduced with the American Revolution. Indeed, the cultural impact of the Revolution has been aptly depicted as driving religion off center stage. As Edmund S. Morgan has written: "In 1740 America's leading intellectuals were clergymen and thought about theology; in 1790 they were statesmen and thought about politics."[6] As the new century opened, the American republic seemed to be set on a secular course. In 1801, Thomas Jefferson, an avowed Deist and a champion of the secular state, became president. His vice president was Aaron Burr (1756–1836), who was a grandson of Jonathan Edwards. Like many young men who came of age in the Revolutionary generation, Burr rejected the Christian faith. The violence, ambition, and intrigue that were parts of enlightened American culture were conspicuous when, in 1804, Vice President Burr killed the Federalists' most brilliant leader, Alexander Hamilton (1757–1804), in a duel.

The United States, however, contained a paradoxical society in which strong religious impulses survived side-by-side with the secularism of political life. The dual heritage can be illustrated by noting that another of Edwards's grandsons was Timothy Dwight, the president of Yale who helped spark the nineteenth-century revivals that began the same year that Jefferson and Burr were sworn into office.

If the era is viewed in a broader perspective that includes the ongoing revivals, one can see that the development of American culture involved a major religious dimension that paralleled and sometimes modified the better-known secular political, social, and economic developments. With this perspective, the era of the American Revolution can be seen, in a sense, as an interruption of a longer trend of awakening that started in the 1720s and continued long after the Civil War. The Second Great Awakening, as the nineteenth-century revivals have been called, was surely not the only thing shaping American culture in this era, but it was one major force.

Today, the cultural impact of these revivals is largely forgotten when we look at the dominant northern culture of the United States because other major developments have since changed the culture's character. Nonetheless, some dimensions of the nineteenth-century outlook have been preserved in other segments of American culture where religious expression is still prominent. The two major cultures in which the revival style has survived, although in differing ways, are the African-American culture and the white Protestant cultures of the South and the Midwest heartland. Although these cultures have changed in many ways since the mid-nineteenth century, they have also held onto much of their religious heritages. In the mid-nineteenth century, almost the whole nation, North and South, was a Bible belt. Even though American society had many nonbelievers, much violence and vice, and many secular forces, evangelical Protestantism had become the default religion. The Huck Finn quotation at the beginning of this chapter, which describes part of his visit with the feuding Shepherdsons and Granger- fords, suggests the pervasiveness of religious culture, as well as some of its paradoxes.

America's Revivalist: Charles G. Finney

One can get some idea of the cultural impact of these revivals by looking briefly at the career and character of Charles G. Finney (1792–1875), the most famous revivalist of his day. Finney was not quite to the Second Great Awakening what Whitefield had been to the first. By the nineteenth century, American religion had too many competing sects for one person to be cen- tral to the whole movement. Finney, nonetheless, was popular because he embodied so many typical traits of the American evangelical spirit.

Finney had been a schoolteacher and then a lawyer in New York State. In 1821, he experienced a dramatic religious conversion. He closed his law office and dedicated himself to evangelism. By the mid-1820s, his revival campaigns in western New York had made him a national sensation. West- ern New York, being rapidly settled largely by New Englanders with intense religious backgrounds, was perfect tinder for revival fires. Several of the era's more exotic religious movements, including Mormonism, Adventism, Shakerism, Spiritualism, and the Oneida community, had western New York bases. These grew in the context of almost constant evangelical reviv- als sweeping the new territories. Eventually, after decades of such intensity, generated especially by Finney and his followers, the area became known as the "burnt-over district."

Finney's revival tactics, or "new measures," that first brought him dra- matic success in the 1820s, raised sharp controversy. Frontier revivals at turn-of-the-century camp meetings already involved some controversial methods and results. The camp meetings were originally interdenomina- tional affairs at which large numbers of frontier people gathered for days or weeks of revival preaching. These meetings generated some spectacular physical responses as people experienced dramatic changes of heart. These spiritual "exercises" at the camp meetings included sometimes-involuntary responses such as jerking, dancing, falling, running, shouting, and barking. These ecstatic phenomena were at the time somewhat peripheral to most American religion and even died out in the camp meetings, which were taken over largely by the more disciplined Methodists. Finney now brought milder versions of the frontier revival methods to the more settled areas of the Northeast.

The biggest similarity between Finney's work and the camp meetings was that Finney systematically did what the meetings had happened upon— he built up and sustained spiritual intensity. His meetings were protracted, being held in one town or city for a week or more. While he did not look for or get ecstatic exercises, Finney did bring about many life-changing conversions. He used methods such as "the anxious bench," on which those actively seeking conversion could sit as special objects of preaching and prayer. He carefully prepared his campaigns and did not hesitate to name names and specific sins that could bring people to their knees. He urged people to testify to each other about their spiritual experiences, and in a revolutionary step, he specifically encouraged women to do so.

Evangelicalism and American Culture

By the mid-nineteenth century, evangelical religion was a major force shaping dominant American values. Rather than conflict with democratic and republican ideals inherited from the Revolutionary era, evangelicalism coalesced with, reflected, and reinforced such values. The United States was different from most of Europe in this respect. Revolution in Europe was associated with the strongly antichurch sentiments of the French Revolution. Christianity was, therefore, often associated with antiliberal political outlooks. In the United States, more than anywhere else, the most popular religion embraced and reinforced many of the political values and assumptions regarding human nature growing out of a liberal Revolution. At the same time, revivalist Christians modified these values by placing them in explicitly Christian contexts. Hence, it can be seen in the resulting amalgam that traits of evangelicalism were also traits of much of the greater American culture.

The Free Individual

One example of how evangelicalism reflected and reinforced broader American traits is the evangelical emphasis on the free individual. Conversion was becoming more and more a question of individual choice. This was revolutionary in that it took place in the context of a Protestant culture that had generally taught the opposite. Most of American Protestant evangelicalism through the eighteenth century had been Calvinist. Calvinists emphasized the sovereignty of God and the belief that humans in their sinful state could not simply choose salvation. Rather, first God had to provide a change of heart that would then enable the person to choose to put God first, rather than self. In practice, the distinction was subtle, since salvation still involved voluntary human choice. But Calvinists wanted to acknowledge that God controlled all things and humans were always dependent beings.

With new views of human nature developing in the eighteenth century, however, challenges to the Calvinist view grew. Especially important were the formulations of John Wesley and Methodism that placed more emphasis on individuals' abilities to freely choose than the Calvinists did. Wesley's teachings not only fit with revivalists' practice of urging people to make an immediate, decisive commitment, but they also matched the emerging American spirit of freedom and self-determination. Such teachings, combined with an efficient system of modern, centralized organization, developed under the leadership of Bishop Francis Asbury (1745–1816), led to spectacular growth. While most traditional Protestant churches relied on well-educated, settled clergy, Asbury organized hundreds of young circuit riders who could bring an intense revival message to almost every town and hamlet, including the expanding frontiers. At the outset of the American Revolution, there had been less than a thousand Methodists in the new nation. By 1820, the Methodist Episcopal Church was America's largest denomination and was continuing to grow.

Charles Finney's work can be understood in the context of Methodist success. In effect, he brought an essentially Methodist outlook into the old Calvinist denominations of the northeast. During his career, Finney was affiliated with either Presbyterian or Congregational churches, which at the time of the Revolution had been America's two largest denominations and were still disproportionately influential on middle-class culture. Like the Methodists, Finney talked about the ability of sinners to make a choice for Christ. Also, following Methodist examples, he emphasized a strict moral discipline and even taught that Christians could reach a state of moral "perfection," or freedom from voluntary sinning. Debates over such theological issues preoccupied many of the best minds of the day and dominated much of American intellectual and academic life.

At a more practical level, debates over revivalism and its characteristic theologies continued the challenge to the authority of the elite that had begun in the Great Awakening. In the early days of the American republic, it was predominantly assumed that in both politics and religion the educated elite would govern. Increasingly, however, such assumptions gave way to more democratic tendencies. The congregational self-rule of Baptists of all varieties reflected democratic polity, and the Baptist movement grew almost as fast as the Methodists among the less educated. Preachers increasingly claimed that formal training and formal worship were inhibitions to the gospel and that the common person with Bible in hand was a more reliable guide to authentic Christianity. These preachers succeeded in recruiting more people to their churches with an informal, popular, vernacular style of preaching accompanied by another nineteenth-century development, the rise of the gospel hymn.[7]

In these respects, as in his tempering of Calvinist theology, Charles Finney was a bridge between the older Calvinist elite culture and the newer democratic styles of the popular Methodists and Baptists. Finney himself was not anti-intellectual. He viewed his approach to sinners as primarily logical, like a lawyer pleading a case. After some spectacularly successful urban revivals in cities such as Rochester, New York, and New York City, Finney in 1835 accepted a position as professor of theology at the newly founded Oberlin College in Ohio. He continued to hold revival tours and also published some formidable books on theology and the theory of revival.

This was an age of oratory, and the spoken word was crucial to the revival. Nonetheless, the standards of oratory were still set by a culture dominated by print as a primary form of communication. Hence, despite the simplifications of much populist preaching, logical arguments were still highly admired as a way to authenticate one's viewpoint. So just as crowds would flock to hear Abraham Lincoln debate Senator Stephen A. Douglas before the Civil War, so also would they turn out to hear Methodists, Baptists, and the like debate their differing theologies. Popularized techniques that appealed more to emotions were gaining ground as the most prominent aspect of evangelical religion; but in many cases, these styles were taking place alongside a continuing respect for intellect.

Education

Many of the most popular evangelical movements started out disparaging formal education. Appealing to American democratic impulses, they challenged the authority of the educated elite and insisted that it was not necessary for clergy to have a higher education. Such emphases promoted rapid growth, especially among Baptists and Methodists. While more traditional denominations such as Anglicans, Congregationalists, and Presbyterians could not train nearly enough clergy to serve the numerous frontier communities, Baptists and Methodists could reach ordinary people with messages these people could understand.

Views of education were, however, closely related to social class, and built into evangelical religion was a tendency toward upward social mobility. Evangelicalism taught rigorous moral discipline, which included giving up vices such as drinking. It encouraged hard work and responsibilities toward families. Inevitably, many people who adopted such disciplines prospered economically. Once they prospered, they and their children began to take on more middle-class values, including respect for education that an earlier generation might have spurned. The Methodists, for instance, who had founded no colleges before 1820, were the most active denomination in founding colleges in the period from 1840 through 1860.

That churches should be leaders in education reflected a long tradition in Western culture. In the United States prior to the Civil War, that tradition was only beginning to change. In higher education, religious dominance was conspicuous. By far the majority of college presidents were clergymen. This was true even in state schools. State colleges typically required Protestant chapel attendance, taught the Bible and Protestant doctrine, and sometimes required church attendance of their students. "A state university in this country should be religious," declared the president of the University of Michigan in 1863 in a typical statement of the era. "It should be Christian without being sectarian."[8]

Most American colleges were founded and operated by denominations. In towns and villages throughout the nation, people from various denominations would band together to provide colleges. Most of these colleges were also evangelical. New Englanders, who had a long heritage of higher education, were especially prominent in spreading Christian principles through their colleges.

Evangelical—and often New England—dominance was commonplace at lower levels of education, as well. Most people took it for granted that religious training would be part of a good education, and both private and public schools routinely taught Protestant doctrine (often to the chagrin of Catholics and others). The standard American elementary textbook until around 1830 was *The New England Primer*. This work exalted Protestant martyrs and taught Calvinist theology, most famously by "In Adam's fall, we sinned all," a sentence used to illustrate the letter A. Similarly, when the most widely used grade-school texts of the era, *McGuffey's Eclectic Readers*, were first published in 1836–37, they also taught a strongly theistic, Calvinistic, and biblically oriented worldview that emphasized that life is only a preparation for the more important life after death.

Science and Technique

Educated evangelicals in the early republic did not see the learning of the day, especially science, as conflicting with Christianity. Rather, as products of the peculiar American alliance of enlightened and dissenting Protestant-ism, they regarded science as the best of their allies. They thought, in fact, that natural science should be the foundation on which to build irrefutable proofs of the truth of Christianity. Just as, if one found a watch on a de-serted beach, one would have to infer a skilled watchmaker, so in the face of scientific discoveries of the laws of nature, one should infer a wise Creator. *McGuffey's Eclectic Readers* contained a story in which George Washing-ton discovered cabbage plants growing in a pattern that spelled his name. When little George correctly guesses that his father planted them that way, his father teaches him the lesson that everywhere in the "beautiful, orderly, purposeful world," we see evidence that "there must have been a designer."[9]

Evangelical intellectual leaders typically went one step further in arguing that "*the theology of natural science is* in perfect harmony with *the theology of the Bible.*"[10] This affinity of nature and the Bible, they believed, was par-ticularly strong in the moral order. The self-evident principles of morality of Enlightenment common sense conformed to Scripture. "So complete is the coincidence," argued Francis Wayland, the Baptist author of the most popular college texts of the day, "as to afford irrefragable [irrefutable] proof that the Bible contains the moral laws of the universe; and hence, that the Author of the universe—that is of natural religion—is also the Author of the Scriptures."[11]

Typical of evangelical educators, Charles Finney combined concern for eternal souls with respect for science. Finney was especially interested in the practical applications of science to revivals. Whereas earlier Calvinists insisted that revivals were simply the work of God, Finney introduced planning techniques to make revivals succeed. Producing a revival, said Finney, was just as scientific as producing a crop of grain: God did it, but he used means that we can predict and control.

Charles Finney was, in fact, one of the progenitors of modern advertising technique. Rather than concentrate on just the message, he analyzed the audience and the conditions under which people were likely to respond. His pioneering work paved the way for later radio and television evangelists and megachurch leaders to master mass communication techniques. Ironically, in the hands of religious hucksters, scientific technique came to be widely combined with simplistic anti-intellectual messages and sensational claims, which marketing science proved was what sold the best. And already in Finney's day, free enterprise combined with ever-expanding settlements made the huckster, whether in commerce or religion, a common phenomenon.

Primitivism

American respect for science often went hand in hand with a trait among revivalists that might at first seem wholly unrelated: the desire to go back to the practices of the New Testament churches. This principle, called primitivism, paralleled the scientific method. In both, one starts by freeing oneself of traditions and prejudices, thus getting back to the facts—either the facts of nature or the facts of the Bible.

An excellent example of primitivism was the Disciples of Christ, one of the most successful new denominations, founded by Alexander Campbell (1788–1866). Campbell appealed to popular audiences in the western regions of the country, but his writings were filled with appeals to logic, natural law, and the "common sense" principles of a Christian version of Enlightenment philosophy. One of the early colleges of the Disciples, Bacon College in Kentucky, was in fact named for Francis Bacon, the seventeenth-century progenitor of the scientific method. Bacon was such a popular figure among evangelicals in general that one historian has described their typical stance as the "beatification of Bacon."[12]

Campbell's appeals to Baconian science fit not only with the spirit of the times but also with the revolutionary approach to Christianity for which he became famous. The church would rely on the facts of New Testament Christianity alone and so follow only primitive Christian practices. For instance, it would include the New Testament ceremony of foot washing but not allow musical instruments, which are not mentioned as part of New Testament worship. This extended the Puritan principle of "the Bible alone" as the authority for the church. This principle, however, was now reinforced by the popular Enlightenment conception of true scientific reason. Just as Enlightenment scientists believed that if the proper methods were followed, all rational persons would agree with the laws thus discovered, so Campbell believed that a new fellowship, built on the Bible and scientific reason, would eventually draw all true Christians to it and, hence, end the divisions of Christendom.

Back to the Bible and the New Order for the Ages

This "back to the Bible" theme, which became one of the most pervasively popular slogans throughout much of American Protestantism, fit perfectly with the Enlightenment scientific method of starting over. The nation itself was perceived as an experiment in establishing a *novus ordo seclorum* (new order for the ages), as the motto on the one-dollar bill puts it. Many popular churches and sects, likewise, saw themselves as a new Christian order for the ages. They believed their renewed group would then become the basis for the renewal of civilization.

Such appeals were democratic, since they challenged existing authorities based on traditions. The Bible was crucial in such challenges, since the reformer could always appeal to the accepted Protestant principle that the Bible was the only supreme authority, standing above all traditions. The common person who stood by the plain, common-sense meaning of the Bible could confidently disregard the authority of educated clergy or prestigious churches.

Such popular appeals were effective because almost all American Protestants agreed in principle that the true church and the true civilization would have to be based on the Bible. People in all walks of life spoke of the Bible as an authority on all sorts of subjects, including history and the sciences, as well as theology and ethics. Throughout the nineteenth century, American school children read lessons from *McGuffey's Eclectic Readers* with titles such as "The Bible the Best of Classics" and "My Mother's Bible."[13]

Americans often defined themselves in biblical terms and imagery. They followed New England Puritan precedents in this regard, still speaking of themselves as a New Israel and a covenanted people. The covenantal concept—that the success and prosperity of the nation were the results of blessings from God and hence dependent on national morality—was an important practical belief, influential in every political movement for moral reform. Moreover, biblical cadences influenced rhetorical usage; the speeches of Abraham Lincoln are a prominent example. The Bible provided much of Americans' literature, and their knowledge of history was confined largely to biblical history.

The idea of a new order for the ages based on the Bible had dramatic implications for the future. The Bible, regarded as equally reliable for prophecy and history, spoke of a millennial age, or a thousand-year reign of Christ, as the culmination of human history on earth. Many Christians through the ages, and some American Protestants in the nineteenth century, took the millennium to mean a literal one-thousand-year reign following Jesus's return to earth. Among nineteenth-century American Protestants, the most common view was postmillennial, or a belief that Jesus would not return until *after* the millennium.[14] According to this view, the meaning of the predicted millennium was that the last great era in world history would be a golden age marked by the reign of the *spirit* of Christ, or the Holy Spirit. It would be brought in by increasing great awakenings, the evangelization of the world through missions, and the turning of the nations to Christ. The final era of human history would be marked by moral and material improvement. Such views fit with nineteenth-century optimism about social progress.

Missions

Many nineteenth-century American Protestants thought a new age was beginning and that they, together with their British brothers and sisters, were its vanguard. Forgetting by then most of their anti-British prejudices of the Revolutionary era, American Protestants typically identified themselves with the worldwide advances of the essentially Protestant Victorian empire. They saw their cause as part of a transatlantic effort in which English-speaking people would lead the advance of Protestantism throughout the world.

Concretely, that meant the organization of concerted foreign missionary efforts, a practice that was not well developed among most Protestant churches prior to the nineteenth century. The spread of evangelical doctrine, with its emphasis on conversions to save souls, inspired efforts in preaching the gospel in non-Christian lands. The American Board of Commissioners for Foreign Missions (ABCFM), an interdenominational agency dominated by New England Congregationalists, was founded in 1810 and became the leading foreign mission agency of the era. The ABCFM was particularly successful in its mission to the islands of Hawaii. Altogether, about two thousand Americans served abroad in missionary efforts from 1810 through 1870, laying the base for a vast expansion of missionary efforts by the early twentieth century.[15] Altogether, the proportion of the world's population identified as Christian rose from about 23 percent in 1800 to nearly 35 percent by 1914. The church had not grown so fast, proportionately, since its early centuries. The proportion of non-white adherents grew from about one-eighth of the Christian total in 1800 to almost one-fourth in 1914.[16]

Evaluations of expanding Christian missions vary greatly according to one's perspective. For some they are viewed simply as a dimension of Anglo imperialism. Others might view missions as a way of tempering the economic and military aspects of imperialism with genuine spiritual and moral concerns. From a Christian missionary perspective, such activity can be viewed as making the nineteenth century a "great century" of missions, bringing the gospel message to all sorts of people and far exceeding the total foreign missionary efforts of any earlier era.[17]

Reform

Millennial imagery, which often helped inspire missionary efforts, had important implications for Americans at home, as well. Many Americans regarded their nation as "a city on the hill," a beacon for the advancement of civilization. Evangelicals often combined classic republicanism, Protestant dominance, and religious freedom into a belief that American civilization would be in the forefront of an outpouring of the Holy Spirit that would usher in the last millennial, golden age of world civilization.

Such an age would combine spiritual, social, and political advances. Not only would individual hearts be changed in revivals, but as a result, the whole nation would improve as biblical principles were voluntarily applied to all aspects of life. Vices would be suppressed; wars and oppressions would cease. Evangelicals, especially in the North, accordingly formed a host of societies to combat what they saw as the leading vices of their era, such as dueling, prostitution, use of alcohol, Sabbath-breaking, and (most controversially) slavery. These, together with home and foreign missionary societies, Bible societies, Sunday school societies, tract societies, and education societies, formed what has been called an "evangelical united front." Most of these societies had British counterparts and fostered a transatlantic dimension in the movement. In the United States, the combined budgets of this evangelical empire rivaled that of the federal government. Evangelical institutions were thus providing some of the nation's leading forces for cultural change.

Charles Finney can, again, be used as an illustration. Not only was he the best known revivalist of his day, but he was also in the forefront of American social reform. He and other evangelists with whom he worked closely were leaders in the often unpopular causes of the abolition of slavery and greater equality for women. Oberlin College in Ohio, Finney's base after 1835, was the Americas' first coeducational college. Moreover, it was notorious as a hotbed of abolitionist sentiment and a center for the Underground Railroad, the network that helped enslaved Africans escape to free states and Canada.

Divisions within the Evangelical Camp

The existence of slavery suggests that the transformation of the United States into a Bible-based nation that would usher in the millennial age was much easier to preach than to put into practice. For one thing, even though evangelical Protestantism was the most common religious outlook in America, most Americans were not active evangelicals. For another, evangelicals themselves were divided into competing denominations. By the mid-nineteenth century, Methodists and Baptists were the largest religious groups, followed by Presbyterians and Congregationalists. These groups accounted for 83 percent of American Protestants and claimed populations (including many not active as church members) that accounted for over half of Americans.[18] Underneath their doctrinal rivalries, these groups also had a tradition of some cooperation and, in principle, considerable unity of purpose.

In practice, however, they were divided more sharply by social realities. Class differences and expectations of higher education for their clergy separated staid traditionalists from popular folk-oriented groups. Even deeper divisions were ethnic. America was a land of immigrants, and religious affiliations were usually the strongest elements in providing an immigrant group with a distinct identity. Many Lutherans, for instance, tended to remain aloof from other Protestants and American-style revivalism, not simply because of a slightly different theological heritage, but also because of German versus Anglo traditions.

By the mid-nineteenth century, however, the deepest religious divisions among the dominant evangelicals had become regional. In 1844, the largest national denomination, the Methodist Episcopal Church, divided between the North and South over the slavery issue. The next year, they were followed by the largest Baptist denomination. Presbyterians had already divided more-or-less regionally over a complicated set of issues, including abolitionism. These schisms in the nation's most influential denominations appeared to foreshadow an inevitable division in the nation itself. Abolitionists in the North argued vehemently that, based on the Bible, the spirit of Christianity forbids the enslavement of one race by another. Slavery's defenders in the South argued just as vehemently that the Bible itself did not condemn slavery but took it for granted. Each side hurled charges of heresy and hypocrisy at the other. Religious beliefs did not create the conflict, but they intensified it. When people in each camp are sure they have the Bible, and hence God, on their side, there is no room for argument. Common evangelical convictions, rather than bringing people together, thus helped heat up the regional rivalries and increased the likelihood of secession and war.[19]

The American Paradox

The institution of African enslavement itself illustrates poignantly a central paradox in the character of American culture. At a time when the United States was known for both its Christianity and its concerns for human rights, not only was slavery practiced, but in some respects, it was more unjust and inhumane than the slavery of less modern epochs. For one thing, modern American slavery differed from most earlier slavery in that it involved the enslavement of one race by another. It was built on the premise that, simply because of race, it was permissible to do to black Africans what would have been considered a violation of sacred human rights if done to white Americans. Moreover, enslaved Africans in America were treated in some respects as though they were not humans. This was particularly conspicuous in the legal definitions of slavery. American slave codes treated enslaved persons as though they were simply property. Before the law, they were treated like farm animals or furniture. Not only could they be bought and sold, but their servitude was permanent and transmitted from generation to generation. Being defined as property, they had no rights of family, and so children could be separated from parents, husbands from wives, and "sold down the river."

These laws might not have been so astonishing if they were typical of slavery in all times and places. The fact was, however, that the American system was unusual. Throughout history, the status of slaves was often a temporary condition. Moreover, even in Latin America, slaves typically had a better legal status. For instance, the Roman Catholic Church recognized them as persons who had rights of marriage and family. In practice, however, Latin-American slavery conditions were often more severe than those of their North American counterparts. Moreover, the harshness of North American slavery was tempered sometimes by kindness and charity at the personal level. Legally, however, the slave codes in Protestant America were strikingly more harsh. They were all the more astonishing in that Protestants professed to have a high view of the sanctity of marriage and the family.

A number of factors contributed to such harsh codes. Racism, reinforced by wide cultural differences between transplanted Europeans and imported Africans, was certainly a major force. The firm conviction of owners of enslaved people that Africans were inferior was essential to rationalizing such a massively discriminatory system. Just as important, however, was the economic factor. In many places, especially on large plantations in the South, African slavery seemed essential to sustaining the whole economic system and way of life. In such circumstances, people are inclined to find rationalizations for what otherwise might seem inexplicable behavior.

The economic factor in US definitions of slavery has been aptly depicted as reflecting "the dynamics of unopposed capitalism." Latin-American slavery, which was defined earlier than in the United States, was based more on a medieval model, with some affinities to serfdom. Enslaved people were recognized as persons by the church, even if they were bound in servitude. In America, however, settled at the beginning of the modern capitalist era, no other strong institutions or traditions opposed the capitalist motives. Therefore, as has been true in important segments of American life, the question was resolved purely on the basis of utility, rather than on religious or moral concerns. Ultimately, the economic dimension of life, combined with the rationalization supplied by racism, defined the status of the enslaved Africans.[20]

The irony of this arrangement reveals a deeper irony in Western civilization. Modern economic and technological superiority has depended on the ability to differentiate and isolate areas of life that can be treated on a purely rational basis. In contrast to medieval and most other periods, in which spiritual considerations can pervade everything, modern Europeans and Americans have almost entirely rationalized some major activities, such as economic life. The Reformation inadvertently contributed to this by despiritualizing the medieval world of saints, sacred places, and miraculous powers. In general, the more rationalized outlook helped Protestant nations economically. The price, however, was that Westerners were removing spiritual considerations from certain aspects of their lives, and the price was vast.

The Western world, especially those parts with a Protestant heritage, however, was also producing revolutionary views of humanity and human rights that would eventually provide counterforces to some of the depersonalizing tendencies of modern, rationalized civilization.

Some of the earliest critiques of slavery had religious origins. As early as 1657, George Fox, the founder of the Society of Friends, was condemning slavery and arguing that all humans should be treated equally regardless of race. Such ideas spread slowly. In the mid-eighteenth century, John Woolman (1720–72), a Quaker who saw the desire for wealth and security as the source of most human oppression, took the lead in trying to arouse moral outrage at the enslavement of one race by another.

It was not until the era of the American Revolution, however, that antislavery views began to spread widely. Enlightenment views concerning the equal rights of individuals, combined with Christian moral concerns, led a vocal minority to question the anomaly of slavery in a nation that proclaimed "all men are created equal." In the era after the Revolution, some churches in both the North and the South took stands condemning slavery and slaveowning. However, such stands prevailed only in areas where the economic and social reasons for perpetuating slavery were not strong. Hence, slavery was gradually eliminated in the North. In the upper South, however, where antislavery sentiment was considerable for a time, both churches and politicians soon found they would lose their constituencies if they took a strong stance. In the Deep South, more economically dependent on the slavery system, abolitionism never had a chance. After Nat Turner's slave insurrection in Virginia in 1831 and the rise of militant abolitionism in the North, most white southerners retreated to defenses of slavery as a God-ordained social system. By the 1840s, the differing moral perceptions in the two regions were strong enough to lead to schisms in the major denominations.

No one depicted better than did Frederick Douglass (1818–95) the cultural paradox that the worst practices of slavery flourished in some of the places where churches were the strongest. Douglass was formerly enslaved himself and became a leading advocate of social reforms, including for abolishing slavery. In his autobiographical *Narrative of the Life of Frederick Douglass* (1845), Douglass, a licensed preacher, wrote this classic depiction of the American paradox:

The slave auctioneer's bell and the church-gong bell chime in with each other, and the bitter cries of the heart-broken slave are drowned in the religious shouts of his pious master. Revivals of religion and revivals in the slave-trade go hand in hand together. The slave prison and the church stand near each other. The clanking of fetters and the rattling of chains in the prison, and the pious psalms and solemn prayer in the church, may be heard at the same time. Dealers in the bodies and souls of men erect their stand in the presence of the pulpit, and they mutually help each other. The dealer gives his blood-stained gold to support the pulpit, and the pulpit, in return, covers his infernal business with the garb of Christianity.[21]

Religion of Enslaved People

Despite their harsh treatment in Christendom, many enslaved Africans themselves eventually came to see evangelical Christianity as transcending the white culture from which they had learned it. While most immigrant groups found their particular religious traditions important for preserving their distinct identities, the Africans who were brought involuntarily to North America were removed as far as possible from their African religious heritage. Members of tribes were scattered so that formal religious practices varied for Africans on any given plantation and were difficult to retain. What they preserved longest were African worship styles and practices that various local African religions had in common. Eventually, many of these were incorporated into their Christianity. African Americans, like many white Americans, also retained interest in occult magical practices such as voodoo. However, unlike some communities of enslaved Africans in Latin America and the Caribbean, where African religions survived intact, by the time of the emancipation in the United States, virtually the only organized religion among black people was Christianity. Not all African Americans were religious, of course, and black culture contained as many paradoxes between Christian practices and their opposites as white culture. Nonetheless, by the time of the Civil War, Christianity was overwhelmingly the religion of black Americans.

This remarkable cultural development, like so much else in American history, dates back to the Great Awakening. The openness and expressiveness of the Baptist and later the Methodist services had some affinities to African religious styles and allowed for the introduction of more demonstrative and ecstatic practices. Moreover, while more traditional Protestantism tended to emphasize hierarchical order and deference to authority, evangelicalism, while not being socially revolutionary, presented Christianity as a religion of the poor in which values would be reordered. According to evangelicalism, the lifestyles of the aristocracy were evidence of moral degeneracy. The simple Christian, no matter how poor materially, could be morally and spiritually superior in a higher realm of reality.[22]

The first substantial numbers of Africans were converted to Christianity during the eighteenth-century awakenings, especially in the South during the 1750s and 1760s. Though blacks usually attended churches with whites, a number of independent black preachers emerged, in both the North and the South, by the end of the eighteenth century.

The most famous of these was Richard Allen (1760–1831). Born enslaved in Pennsylvania, Allen was converted to Methodism, earned his freedom, and in 1794 founded an independent black congregation. In 1816, he and other black preachers in Philadelphia took the further revolutionary step of establishing a black denomination, the African Methodist Episcopal Church. Allen thus helped set an American pattern in which the church would be the most important agency for establishing black leadership and independence.

Although in the South there were sometimes a few independent black churches, most black churchgoers sat in separate sections of white churches. On plantations, where the majority of enslaved blacks lived, formal church activity was usually under white supervision. Nevertheless, increasingly during the nineteenth century and especially in the two decades preceding the Civil War, blacks were adopting evangelical Christianity.

The major impetus for this transformation of black culture came from within their own communities. Once they adopted Christianity on a wide scale, that religion became extraordinarily important for binding the black community together, introducing a new sense of communal identity. The most meaningful worship for plantation blacks often took place in secret meetings in cabins or "hush harbors," to which they would "steal away." Spirituals, which were composed and sung communally, became a leading cultural expression. During the Civil War, a white Union officer observed of black regiments that, with a few exceptions, the only songs they would sing were spirituals.[23]

In the spirituals and throughout their religious expressions, African Americans typically saw themselves as a biblical people. This belief, found in the popular religion of many other Americans, was accentuated and shaped in unique ways by the black experience. For one thing, black culture was of necessity oral. The biblical narrative, eloquently repeated and sung, became accordingly a primary means of building self-identity. Typically, the blacks saw themselves as new Israelites, enslaved in a new Egypt. They celebrated their own version of a millennial hope when they preached or sang of the coming day of God's deliverance, when a new Moses would rise up to lead them out of Egypt, or a new Joshua would lead them to the promised land. They could rejoice in the hope of the "day of jubilee" when Jesus would deliver them or they would be released to heaven.

Such understandings had double meanings. Their primary meaning was clearly spiritual and otherworldly. For an oppressed person, the hope of heaven where one could "lay my burden down" is not to be treated lightly.[24] The overwhelming testimony of the enslaved people themselves was that the heavenly hope had a literal meaning. Nonetheless, such hope was fully compatible with another hope: the hope for deliverance in this life also, just as God had rescued the Israelites from slavery in Egypt.

Only occasionally in North America did this hope take revolutionary form. When it did, as most famously in Nat Turner's brief insurrection in 1831, biblical imagery was central. Turner saw himself as literally a new prophet of God.

Totally denied access to political power, black culture in North America developed around the churches and leadership among the clergy. On the plantations, black preachers often became the respected leaders of the community, and among free blacks both North and South, black leadership emerged in churches. Deprived of so much else, Bible religion for blacks— even more than for most of their white contemporaries—provided crucial resources in shaping their views.

Nonevangelical America

For better or for worse, evangelical Protestantism, because of its dominant role at a formative stage, played a crucial role in shaping mainstream American culture. At the same time, just as crucial is the counterpoint of the uniquely pluralistic American culture. A pivotal theme in American religious and cultural history is the interplay between these two motifs, Protestantism and pluralism. Neither makes sense in the American experience without the other.

Native Americans as Outsiders

Even though evangelical Protestantism—while sometimes an ally of oppression—transformed much of black culture in North America, among Native Americans, both evangelicals and other Christians had a more peripheral, though equally ironic, impact.

During the colonial era, the most extensive Catholic missions to the Indians took place in areas that eventually became parts of the United States. French Catholic missionaries made heroic efforts, sometimes with modest success, in evangelizing tribes in the vast territories of the upper Midwest. The most tangible artifacts of Catholic missionary endeavors are the chains of Franciscan missions in California, begun in the late eighteenth century by Junipero Serra (1713–84). These missions were built as part of an effort to establish a Spanish presence in California, but they also won substantial numbers of converts.

Protestant missions to the Indians increased with the Great Awakening of the eighteenth century and enjoyed occasional success. Nonetheless, most Native Americans resisted Christian incursions and continued their traditional religious practices.

Indian religions varied greatly by tribe, although most involved beliefs in various spiritual powers that controlled different dimensions of nature and beliefs that life should be lived in harmony with these powers. Resistance to European conquests sometimes had important religious dimensions. Pontiac's Rebellion, which in 1763 united tribes of the upper Midwest in formidable resistance to the British, was inspired in part by Neolin, the Delaware prophet who called for a return to Indian ways. Similarly, Tecumseh's uprising, which ended with his death in battle in 1813, was supported by the religious teachings of his brother, Tenskwatawa, "the Prophet."[25]

Native Americans generally perceived that when Christian missionaries appeared, invasion could not be far behind. In fact, individual missionaries, although trying to change Indian culture by the introduction of Christianity, were also attempting to provide an alternative to the more violent imperialism of white people. White culture, as we have seen, was never simply Christian or simply aggressive-acquisitive but always a paradoxical mix. Time and again, the story of Christian missions in North America was the story of some missionary successes, the establishment of relatively stable communities of Christian Indians, and then the destruction of those communities by other white settlers. Whites and Indians were frequently at war, ever renewed by the whites' insatiable quest for new settlements. War barbarizes the outlook of everyone involved so that large numbers of white Americans, including a good many who went to church, came to believe that "the only good Indian is a dead Indian."

A striking example of the injustices arising even from the most controlled of such encounters is the nineteenth-century mission to the Cherokees. During the early decades of the century, missionaries successfully evangelized large numbers of Cherokees living in eastern Tennessee, western North Carolina, and northern Georgia. These missions became models for Christian civilization-building. The Cherokees patterned their government on the United States Constitution, built schools and churches, and were developing an educated native leadership. Nonetheless, other whites not interested in the missions wanted the Cherokee territories and insisted that the Cherokees be displaced to the West. The president of the United States was Andrew Jackson, a Presbyterian who made a name for himself partly by fighting Indians; Jackson shared the dominant views of white Westerners that they were always in a virtual state of war with all Indians. Jackson, accordingly, ignored the Indians' rights. In the face of an adverse ruling from Chief Justice Marshall's Supreme Court, Jackson reportedly quipped: "John Marshall has made his decision; now let him enforce it." Despite the bitter protests of both missionaries and Indians, most Cherokees were removed to what is now Oklahoma amid much suffering along a "Trail of Tears."

Such treatment of Indians meant that, even when the missionaries were most successful, most Indians would remain outside the dominant culture. For most Native Americans, their traditional religions would increasingly become important in attempting to preserve tribal identity.

The Catholic Church: Outsiders with an Insider Heritage

Much of American history and politics has revolved around ethnoreligious conflicts, although the mythology of the dominant Protestant groups, who emphasize assimilation and consensus, has played this down in the retelling of the nation's history. Nonetheless, the United States is overwhelmingly a nation of immigrants, and much of the nation's political history can be understood as efforts of the earliest dominant groups to keep control. Race, ethnicity, economics, and religion are all major forces in these struggles, but their interrelationships follow no simple pattern. The elimination of substantial religious differences between the dominant white community and the black community did little to alter blacks' social and economic subordination. On the other hand, in the case of Roman Catholics, religious prejudices were more important than race and often more important than nationality. For example, German Protestants could assimilate more quickly into the mainstream Anglo-Protestant culture than could German Catholics. Moreover, the long-standing Protestant-versus-Catholic cold war had helped create some deep national antagonisms that carried over to America.

Catholics themselves were divided ethnically; a good bit of Catholic history in America is a combination of external struggles against dominant Protestant culture and internal friction among competing Catholic national traditions.

The Roman Catholic Church in America through the early national era was small and dominated by English gentry from Maryland. Despite the anti-Catholicism implicit in the American republican tradition, many of these English Catholics supported the American Revolution. The promise of religious freedom in the United States was preferable to legal restrictions for Catholics under British law. Because of the lack of adequate numbers of priests, this early American Catholic church developed its own style, including lay trustees, which provided some congregational governance over their own affairs, and a plain style of worship.

Such early trends in American Catholicism were, however, soon overwhelmed by massive immigration. Between 1790 and 1830, the Catholic population grew almost ten times to about three hundred thousand and then between 1830 and 1860 grew ten more times to over three million, almost a hundred-fold increase in seventy years. By the end of this period, the Roman Catholic Church in the United States was larger than any single Protestant denomination, although Catholics represented only about one-tenth of the total American population.

Because the overwhelming numbers of Catholics in this era were foreign-born, the position of Catholics in American life was largely that of insecure outsiders. Nonetheless, Catholics brought with them a tradition of being insiders, since Catholicism was the official state religion in most of the nations from which Catholics emigrated. The political dimensions of international Catholicism helped keep long-standing Protestant religious prejudices alive. The recently arrived Catholic immigrants in America had to face not only these prejudices but also ethnic resentments and biases against the poor.

Poverty was especially an issue with regard to Irish immigrants who began to flood northeastern cities in increasingly large numbers beginning in the 1820s. Most of the Irish were fleeing their native country because of a famine that became especially severe in the 1840s. Their poverty compounded resentments, both within and outside the Catholic Church, regarding their ethnic ways. Within the churches, they brought an authoritarian style and an emphasis on ritual, devotion, and elaborate decoration with artifacts dedicated to saints. Irish Catholics also brought with them a tradition of political authoritarianism, often supported by the church, and thus, despite their deep loyalty to their new land, were soon perceived by established Protestants as a threat to American ways. Prejudices against Irish Catholics were sometimes almost as severe as prejudices against African Americans.

The other major immigrant group swelling the Catholic population at this time was the Germans. The massive German Catholic immigration tended to be farmers who moved to the Midwest in the "German triangle," an area from Cincinnati to St. Louis to Milwaukee. Although typically not so poor as the Irish, they were separated from mainstream America not only by their religion and ethnicity, but also by their language. For many in the German communities, this was an important source of pride and identity. In general, they were not eagerly awaiting the day when they would become like Protestant Americans but were proud of what they regarded as cultural and religious superiority. Preserving their language was hence an important ingredient in preserving the faith. "Language saves faith" was a typical slogan. Consistent with this outlook, Germans were leaders among American Catholics in insisting on building parochial school systems as alternatives to the essentially Protestant public schools. Such policies helped maintain closely knit ethnoreligious communities that preserved solid German and Catholic identity for generations.[26]

Sociologically, people in immigrant communities were very dependent on each other, and churches in such communities were important social centers, often more important than the churches in their native countries. Such communities and churches also tended to be conservative, placing a strong emphasis on preserving ethnic and religious traditions as a means of maintaining identity and communal cohesiveness.

Protestant Outsiders

Such characteristics of immigrant communities were not unique to Catholic enclaves. For instance, many German immigrants were Protestant, mostly Lutheran, but many were German Reformed church members (Calvinists). Although for Protestants it was somewhat easier, especially in the second

78

generation, to leave the immigrant community and to blend with the larger American society, many German settlers, especially in the Midwest, retained their ethnoreligious communities and identities in much the same way as German Catholics. This was especially true of groups with a strong Lutheran heritage, which did not have an exact British counterpart. The Missouri Synod Lutherans, founded in 1847, preserved use of the German language, separate school systems at all levels, and a strongly conservative theological tradition. Many other Lutheran groups, such as the Scandinavians who later settled Minnesota, did much the same. So did most other ethnoreligious communities, including various ethnic Reformed, Methodists, and Baptists. As Garrison Keillor exemplified in his long-running radio show, *A Prairie Home Companion*, which often portrayed Lutheran traits in the mythical Minnesota town of Lake Wobegon, even in recent times, the best way to understand many American communities, especially in the Midwest, is to find out their ethnoreligious identities.

Common Values

Despite these ethnic and religious diversities, most of the population sub-scribed to many common values. Almost all had inherited largely the same Judeo-Christian heritage and believed in a moral system built upon the Ten Commandments. God was to be reverenced and worshipped; parents and those in authority were to be respected. Most Americans believed people should control their passions and desires, not commit murder or adultery, steal, lie, or succumb to envy and greed. In general, these precepts were interpreted in a typically early-modern republican fashion, emphasizing in moderate ways the rights and responsibilities of individuals. Individual character was seen as the chief force in history, and virtue of the individual was seen as the key to a healthy society.

The conventionally shared outlooks of the day were in many ways con-servative, more conservative than might be expected from reading the liter-ary leaders of the era. A study of the letters and diaries of ordinary Ameri-cans reveals a considerable commonality in religious outlook, regardless of denomination or religion. Religion, which was prominent in these ordinary private expressions, was largely a matter of accepting God's providence. One should not expect to control one's destiny, but rather, one should learn to accept what God willed. Nineteenth-century Americans, for whom life was dramatically precarious, were not so far from Puritan attitudes of preparing how to die by cultivating a submissive spirit in the meantime. Most were a long way from later American emphases on personal fulfillment and control. These earlier attitudes were strikingly different from later times in that the self, rather than to be celebrated, was seen as a willful entity that needed to be controlled and subordinated to God's will. The individual was important in the sense that one had no one to blame but oneself for one's actions. Religious people often judged personal success in terms of overcoming overly ambitious aspirations, rather than, as in more recent times, in terms of being able to surmount any obstacle.[27]

Diversity: A Changing America

While such commonalties crossed many traditional religious lines, tradition itself was beginning to be challenged in pre–Civil War America. New, alternative views seemed present everywhere. This was especially true of religion, which was the principal channel for ideological innovation. Nineteenth-century America was in the forefront of nations by allowing religious freedom. The ideologies of the new republic encouraged new beginnings, and vast tracts of land offered space for religious and practical experimentation.

The result was that the United States was remarkable in providing not only a haven to preserve many imported traditions but also remarkably fertile soil for the growth of new religious movements.

Most of the variations developed within the older Anglo-Protestant communities. These communities were dominated religiously by an evangelicalism that generated a constant religious intensity. Part of this intensity focused on renewals of, and attempted improvements on, more-or-less traditional evangelicalism itself; another part sparked new religious emphases or movements.

Among these innovations were some liberal or progressive movements. As a rule, such views usually develop among well-established elites, whose social position is secure enough to seek change without fearing ostracism. In general, groups in firm control can afford to be liberal or tolerant, while religious movements among less mainstream groups will be more likely to enforce strict doctrinal or behavioral codes as a means of encouraging personal self-discipline or of preserving their distinct identities. Because of their elite statuses, liberal groups in America, despite relatively small sizes, have had disproportional influence on the public culture.

The Literary Renaissance

Such disproportional influence is particularly true of a small group, mostly New Englanders, who were associated with the American literary renaissance in the mid-nineteenth century. This group included Ralph Waldo Emerson, Henry David Thoreau, Nathaniel Hawthorne, Herman Melville, Margaret Fuller, and Walt Whitman.

Most of these writers were so progressive that they were outsiders intellectually, even if insiders socially, although it is true that Emerson became very popular on the polite lecture circuit and Whitman's poetry was sometimes patriotic or sentimental enough to gain a following. Most of American intellectual life, however, was considerably more conservative. The talents of Thoreau or Melville, for instance, were not appreciated much in their day. American academic life was still dominated by the churches. Nevertheless, the literary elite, because of their talents and an openness that made them forerunners of future trends, have been far better remembered than those, mostly theologians, who were considered the intellectual powers of their day.

Romanticism and Transcendentalism

The American literary renaissance in the decades following 1830 was shaped especially by European romanticism. Romanticism took many forms, but for the purposes of this discussion, its most important emphasis was the primacy of the spiritual over the material dimension of ordinary reality. American culture was intensely practical, built primarily on technical mastery of the material world. Most Americans, therefore, valued the scientific ways of looking at things emphasized during the Enlightenment. They looked for fixed laws of nature that could be objectively discovered, which could be supplemented by various traditional Christian beliefs and experiences that brought one in touch with another higher supernatural or spiritual realm. The usual outlook, therefore, was that of a two-layered reality: the natural and the supernatural. Romanticism, a broad mood with many varieties, typically stressed that the superior spiritual dimension of reality could be discovered in ordinary experience only if individuals remained open to the subjective, intuitive, imaginative, and emotive dimensions of their experience. One could intuitively see through the natural to the transcendent. Thus, special revelations became relatively less important, while the creative dimensions of each unique individual became relatively more important.

The archetypical American romantic of the most progressive or transcendentalist variety was Ralph Waldo Emerson (1803–82). Emerson was reared in the progressive part of New England around Boston, where, by the early 1800s, many people had already turned from Puritan Calvinism to Unitarianism. Developing their beliefs about the same time as the American Revolution, Unitarians combined an Enlightenment optimism concerning human abilities with more-or-less traditional Protestant teachings. Such moderate liberals exercised influence in the cultural center around Boston and controlled Harvard College. Emerson became a Unitarian minister, but in the 1830s, he resigned. His turn from rational Enlightenment optimism to more radical transcendentalism, in fact, shocked his moderate Unitarian friends. When at the Harvard Divinity School commencement in 1838 Emerson declared that each individual could be a "newborn bard of the Holy Ghost," Harvard professor Andrews Norton felt it necessary to publish a scathing disclaimer. Nonetheless, Emerson preached his radical doctrine of the ability of each individual to know the divine directly. This was an exciting doctrine in the emerging democratic culture in which deference to spiritual authority remained strong. In contrast to the self-deprecating conventional piety of the day, self-reliance was the watchword of Emerson's gospel.

Somewhat like the earlier outbursts of spiritual egalitarianism during the English Civil War and the later countercultural movement of the 1960s, radical American romanticism came at a time of unusual upheaval and openness. The 1840s, especially, were a decade of unrest and experimentation. Spiritually motivated groups formed experimental communities, such as the transcendentalists' Brook Farm, established near Boston in the 1840s. People wanted to go back to nature, as Henry David Thoreau did at Walden Pond. Others from the well-to-do classes were looking for spiritual realities in more exotic movements. Many middle-class people were experimenting with mesmerism, or hypnotism, which was believed to provide access to spiritual reality. Other sorts of spiritualism that were widely popular, especially among middle-class New England women, involved mediums who claimed they could make contact with spirits from the past and control other psychic phenomena. Often related to this innovative religious spirit were health regimens, including bloomers or other looser clothes for women, water cures, and vegetarian diets.

Sectarian Innovations

Though such religious and quasi-religious experimentation was found primarily in the older Anglo-Protestant communities, it was not confined to the leisure classes. Less-educated and less-prosperous people provided the primary constituencies for alternative sets of religious innovations, departing from the evangelical mainstream by moving in a sectarian direction. A sect is a religious group that has very sharp boundaries of belief and behavior separating its members from the larger society. In general, such movements appeal to poorer and less-educated people who are more likely to feel alienated from the prevailing order and hence are more open to a radically new value system.

The general rule one can glean from American history is that the more sectarian and economically poorer groups tend to preach doctrines that heighten emphasis on spectacular and miraculous divine interventions in their lives and in history. Typically, they claim special exclusive revelations, identify a group of spiritually separated believers who adopt distinctive behaviors, and promise a dramatic end to the present age leading to the inauguration of a millennial kingdom. Innovations among the more well-to-do classes tend, on the other hand, to be inclusive, emphasizing the availability of spiritual forces to all people, as in transcendentalism or spiritualism.

A classic example of American sectarian innovation is the Seventh-Day Adventist movement. This movement developed among followers of William Miller (1782–1849), who predicted that the end of the world and the return of Christ would take place between March 21, 1843, and March 21, 1844. Miller's teachings were accentuations of many typical American evangelical traits. His millennial calculations were based on quasi-scientific mathematical calculations and literal interpretations of biblical prophecies. As the days for the predicted end approached, Miller's teachings created sensation in evangelical America. He gained perhaps one hundred thousand followers, some of whom sold their goods and ascended mountains for the final hours of the wait. When Jesus failed to materialize by March 21, 1844, Miller recalculated and discovered that October 22, 1844, was the correct deadline. With the world still intact after that date, many followers dispersed. Some, however, remained true believers. The most significant group of Seventh-Day Adventists eventually followed the leadership of Ellen White (1827–1915), a prophetess who incorporated many of the popular health regimens of the day into church teachings. Sylvester Graham of graham cracker fame and

John Harvey Kellogg of cereal fame became the most successful advocates of the Adventist meatless-diet health programs.

Politically, the most significant sectarian innovators were the Mormons, organized by Joseph Smith (1805–44) in New York State in 1830. Whereas Adventists accentuated evangelical Protestant themes, Mormonism, or the Church of Jesus Christ of Latter-day Saints, was a new religion combining Christian elements with unique teachings. Smith taught, for instance, that there was more than one god and that the principal deity who ruled the universe had a body. Through direct revelations, Smith found resolutions to the competing religious claims of the day. He said that an angel led him to a set of inscribed golden tablets deposited in the fourth century AD by American Indian descendants of the lost tribes of Israel. Smith translated these tablets, which became the Book of Mormon, one of the bases for unique Mormon teachings. Smith and his followers soon established a community in Kirtland, Ohio. Another group moved to Independence, Missouri, which Smith said was revealed to him to be the site of the original Garden of Eden and the center for a coming millennial age. There, on the frontier, Mormons were severely persecuted by other settlers.

The Mormons then consolidated their efforts in Nauvoo, Illinois. Voting as a block, they became a significant political force in the state. In 1844 (the same year the Adventists were ascending to mountaintops), Smith announced his candidacy for the presidency of the United States. He continued to have revelations and secretly taught that he and some other Mormon leaders were allowed to have several wives. Threatened with exposure, Smith closed a dissident press in Nauvoo. This violation of the freedom of the press led neighboring citizens of Illinois to abandon whatever commitment they had to freedom of religion. Smith and his brother were arrested, but an irate mob dragged them from jail and murdered them.

The main body of Mormons then made a trek to Utah under the leadership of Brigham Young (1801–77). There they found for themselves a promised land that they turned into an ordered and stable new Zion. While many other American religious groups talked of a return to biblical models, Mormons acted it out. They lived in what amounted to a continuing biblical time, with ongoing prophets, priesthood, miracles, and promises of a millennial age when they would rule the earth.

Even at a distance, American tolerance of Mormonism was strained. In 1857, President James Buchanan sent a military expedition to bring the territory under more than nominal federal control. One motive was pressure to eliminate the Mormon practice of polygamy. The Mormons resisted, and the

United States backed away from full-fledged war. Not until after dealing with slavery and reconstruction in the South did the government return to the Mormon problem. During the 1880s, the government enforced antipolygamy legislation and threw some Mormon leaders in jail. In 1890, the Mormon Church president announced a divinely sanctioned end to polygamy. By the twentieth century, Mormons became some of the most patriotic of Americans and champions of traditional values.

In the mid-nineteenth century, however, not only the Mormons but a number of other American religious groups attempted to radically redefine what many regarded as the most sacred institution of Victorian society—the monogamous family. One group that had already been doing so for close to a century was the Shakers. Founded around the time of the American Revolution by Mother Ann Lee (1736–84), Shaker communities did away with the traditional family entirely, insisting on celibacy for communal members.

At the other end of the spectrum was John Humphrey Noyes's Oneida community in upstate New York. Noyes (1811–86), a radical Christian perfectionist, taught that perfect love should allow "complex marriage" and sexual relations between all the men and women in the community. Noyes formulated his radical notions on sexuality in the 1840s, about the same time that those of the Mormons were also made public. Like the Mormons, Noyes's community was constantly harassed by outraged Victorians, and by 1879 Noyes had to give up teaching complex marriage.

The Age of the Spirit and Woman's Place

All three of the communal groups described in the preceding section were millennialists, announcing dramatic versions of the prevalent evangelical doctrine that a new age of the Spirit was at hand. In the millennial age, traditional relationships would be restructured or done away with as humanity discovered a whole new value system. Quakers had already announced such teaching in the 1600s. Radical sects of the nineteenth century suggested variations of the theme.

Such trends had particular significance for revaluing the roles of women. Some of the sects, notably the Shakers and the Seventh-day Adventists, had women leaders. Others, such as the Mormons, taught a rigid doctrine of the subordination of women. More important in a broad cultural sense than these particulars, however, was the mainstream evangelical belief that civilization was on the verge of a new spiritual or millennial age, encouraging some pioneering rethinking about social relationships, especially of women's roles. Such trends, supported by democratic rhetoric of human equality, also fit well with and augmented the more open romantic spirit in many segments of America from the 1830s to the 1850s.

The prevailing view of women, however, was conservative, and this view was reinforced by both Christianity and a romantic spirit. Western civilization was built around ordered, hierarchical relationships. In such hierarchies, women were almost always subordinated to men. Families, not individuals, were the basic unit of society, and men were the legal heads of families. Christianity, although in principle limiting the harshness of the subordination, generally was used to support these social arrangements. Moreover, because of explicit New Testament statements and tradition, the governance of the church was almost always confined to men, and in most Christian groups, women were not ordained into the ministry or allowed to preach. Such traditions were particularly strong in the nineteenth century among Catholics and other non-Anglo immigrants, and also among southerners. In the influential Anglo community of the North, patriarchy, or the dominance by males, was overwhelmingly the prevailing view as well. The difference, however, was that in these communities some alternatives were being suggested.

Though women were subordinated, their importance to society was celebrated in what has been called the cult of domesticity. Middle-class Victorians lauded women's calling to be wives, mothers, and homemakers. By making the family strong, women were considered the backbone of society. This ideal had a strong spiritual component. In an expansion of their roles, women were expected to be the spiritual leaders in the home. They were the guardians of traditional Christian virtues such as service and self-sacrifice. Men, on the other hand, were regarded in the popular literature of the day as prone to violence and lust. As mothers, women were to train their sons in more Christian virtues, and as wives, they were to save their husbands from their selfish passions and vices.

This mythology had some basis in reality. One of the social realities was that, for the middle class, economic activities were increasingly moving away from the home and family, becoming exclusively male domains. These areas of life were also becoming increasingly rationalized; that is, they were being conducted more on a scientific-technological assumption that tended to lessen the importance of personal relationships and increase emphases on the impersonal considerations of efficiency and maximizing profits. Increasingly, larger areas of male activity were being depersonalized and hence exempted from traditional factors of moral review.

In addition, warfare was always an exclusively male domain that, to say the least, often undermined Christian virtues. Nineteenth-century society with its large frontier was a society in which ordinary men were often armed and dangerous. After the 1828 election of General Andrew Jackson (who had earlier killed a man in a duel) as president, the typical profile for presidential candidates turned from the educated intellectual to the fighting man. American male pastimes typically included drinking, gambling, and violence. Churches strongly opposed most forms of violence, drinking, gambling, sexual promiscuity, and other perceived vices. Women, who were often victimized by these activities, were the strongest allies of clergy in opposing them.

In this society, women were carving out a spiritual domain in church and developing power domestically. This provided them with meaning, vocation, and a sense of moral superiority to those who held formal power in society. By the moral standards of the day, the destiny and even the survival of Christian civilization depended largely on the work of women, who constituted the majority of Protestant church members and who often took over spiritual and moral leadership in the home.

New Public Roles for Women

The openness to spiritual innovation in mid-nineteenth-century America also began to provide some more public roles for women. As in the Quaker movement two centuries earlier, openness to an age of the Spirit suggested that old barriers would be removed. This was true of radical movements that departed from traditional Christianity, such as Transcendentalism, Spiritualism, and Christian Science, in which women's leadership was prominent; it was also true of the spiritually radical evangelical right. The dominance of Ellen White among the strict Seventh-day Adventists is the most striking example.

Closer to the Anglo-evangelical mainstream, the holiness movement developed in mid-century, particularly among American Methodists. Phoebe Palmer (1807–74), for instance, led influential Tuesday prayer meetings in New York City for over thirty-five years. Teaching a rigorous holiness doctrine that every believer should experience a "second blessing" leading to a holy life, she became the chief spokesperson for a major movement within the denomination. Palmer also kept a strenuous schedule as a traveling evangelist, although she did not call her sermons preaching and never sought ordination.

Between the first and the second Great Awakenings, over a hundred women are known to have been preachers, mostly in small, breakaway evangelical groups.[28] Meanwhile, a few traditional Protestant denominations were also moving toward ordination of women clergy. The first ordained female minister in a fully traditional group was Antoinette Brown (1825–1921), ordained by New England Congregationalists in 1853. Baptists and Methodists, who allowed lay exhorters, occasionally had lay women preachers. Jarena Lee (b. 1783), for example, was a noted early black preacher in the African Methodist Episcopal Church. In the mid- to late-nineteenth century, ordination of women became common in some new separatist holiness denominations. The Salvation Army, an English import, is the best-known example of such a theologically strict group with room for women's leadership in the post–Civil War era. Ordination of women, however, remained rare among the great majority of mainstream middle-class evangelicals.

The most broadly based advances in public roles for women in pre–Civil War America were in the many reform and missionary societies of the time. Since most of these societies were interdenominational rather than under direct church control, women could find in them substantial outlets for expressing their expanding roles as allies of the clergy and as the spiritual and moral guardians of society.

Promoting the public roles of women was among many reforms proposed. While most women subscribed to the cult of domesticity, some visionaries campaigned for seemingly radical proposals such as legal equality and the right to vote. As with other reform movements, religious motives provided some substantial impetus to these campaigns.

While most of the dramatic changes in public roles for women came from within the reform societies themselves and in a few churches, another foundation was being laid in new educational ventures, one of the components of the voluntary reform movements. Although it was rare and radical to attempt coeducation—as at Charles Finney's Oberlin College—other schools for women, though usually more domestically oriented than men's colleges, played important roles in providing the beginnings for women's higher education. Typically women's colleges included a strong religious component.[29]

Literature was becoming another important avenue for women's expression. While women were not formally trained in theology and usually had only limited opportunities for public speaking, in writing popular educational literature they were finding an acceptable means of expressing some religious leadership.

Religion and American Politics

We can see from the foregoing discussion that religion was a strong influence in shaping American culture, its values, its institutions, its reforms, and the ways that people thought about reality. It is not surprising, then, that we should see its impact on politics, which rightly or mostly wrongly is often taken to be the center of American life, or at least of American history. In US politics, the impact of religion is usually indirect and difficult to measure. The separation of church and state meant the institutional distancing of religion and politics. The two, however, were always connected both in the rhetoric of civil religion and more substantially by the fact that they both dealt with the same questions of morality. "Religion in America," Tocqueville observed, "takes no direct part in the government of society, but [nevertheless] it must be regarded as the first of their political institutions."[30]

Religion's importance in politics is indicated by the religious divisions in pluralistic America that have often been the best predictors of voting behavior.[31] This striking correlation should not be so surprising, since religious affiliation and political behavior both tend to reflect a number of the same variables: ethnicity, class, and region. Even though social forces and interests are major determinants in political behavior, religion has often influenced or reinforced the values that determine larger political goals.

In general, we can view the religious dimensions of pre–Civil War American political behavior as a contest between those who can be considered as broadly in the Puritan-evangelical tradition and those who are not. In the nineteenth century, the Puritan-evangelicals were usually of older British stock, strongest in the East and especially in New England, and affiliated with mainstream denominations, such as Congregationalist, Presbyterian, and some types of Baptist and Methodist. They were Puritan primarily in the sense of applying religious principles to shaping the social order. Usually they were evangelical or conversionist, emphasizing that changed individuals are the key to a changed society. They also emphasized that individuals must cultivate the virtues of self-discipline, such as industry, thrift, and sexual purity. Converted individuals, they believed, should band together in their denominations, in voluntary societies, and in political parties to promote such values in all levels of society through educational institutions and social reforms.

From the founding of the nation, other Americans resisted this broadly Puritan agenda. Jeffersonians, for instance, did not share New Englanders' zeal for making the government the regulator of morality. Such differing moral agendas help account for the early split between Jefferson and New Englander John Adams.

That being said, it also needs to be recognized that often religion is not the primary variable in determining such lineups. By the mid-nineteenth century, white southerners, many of whom shared the evangelical heritage, were forced by their defense of slavery to reject the Puritan belief in federal regulation of society's morality. Though many southerners offered religious justifications for their views, their political behavior was more deeply shaped by economic considerations, regional loyalties, and race prejudice.

In general, however, religion was one of the significant factors in determining where Americans would line up politically, especially when combined with class, region, and ethnicity.

By about the 1840s, the classic patterns of American politics were taking shape. The massive numbers of Catholic immigrants were not likely to affiliate with political parties that included a strongly reformist Protestant agenda. They, accordingly, soon became the backbone of the Democratic Party. Protestant religious groups who were also outsiders in the sense of not identifying themselves with the Puritan heritage tended in the same direction. Some strictly confessional Lutherans, such as the Missouri Synod in the Midwest, did not think America was likely to become a Christian nation and so tended to vote Democratic. Similarly, even among a seemingly insider group such as the Presbyterians, the more strictly confessional Calvinist group ("the Old School") tended to vote Democratic. This was related to their strong Scotch-Irish ethnic identity, since the Scotch-Irish did not always get along well with New Englanders. The other main group of Presbyterians ("the New School"), by contrast, was closely allied to New England Congregationalists and usually voted for the Whig Party, which promoted the Puritan-evangelical ideals of virtue and hard work.[32]

Some other, smaller sects were evangelical but did not share the Puritan vision of Christianizing America. Rather, these groups, such as some Baptists and primitivists, stood closer to the tradition of Roger Williams, seeing the American civilization more like Babylon than the new Israel. They, too, tended to vote Democratic. At the other end of the ecclesiastical spectrum, Episcopalians had a long history of antagonism to Puritanism and often did not share the Puritan-evangelical political agenda.[33]

These lineups help explain what otherwise might seem a total aberration in American political history: the Anti-Masonic Party of the 1820s and 1830s. Anti-Masons consolidated around the indignation—especially in New York State—toward the influential Masons, or Freemasons, for the apparent murder in 1826 of William Morgan, a former Mason who threatened to reveal secrets of the order. In 1828, the Anti-Masons delivered nearly half of New York's electoral votes to John Quincy Adams. In 1831, they held the first American political convention, patterned after a convention of a religious voluntary society. They soon merged with the new Whig Party, of which they became an important "conscience wing," and included strong proponents for antislavery such as Thaddeus Stevens (1792–1868) and William H. Seward (1801–72).

This crusading impulse was largely an expression of culturally reformist Protestantism. The secret order of the Masons, which had elaborate rituals and covenants within its brotherhood, appeared to the Anti-Masons to be a competing religion appealing to freethinkers. Radical nineteenth-century evangelicals thus attacked Masonry as a false religion, much as later twentieth-century fundamentalists attacked "secular humanism." Such attacks fit with antislavery since the goal for evangelicals was to build a culture in which reforming evangelical morality would prevail. A telling example of the connection is Charles G. Finney, a long-standing evangelical proponent of abolitionism. Once the emancipation of the slaves was accomplished in the 1860s, he turned his political energies back to the now outdated agenda of the 1820s—Anti-Masonry.

The evangelical connections to shaping American political patterns were more than a curiosity, however. They were a major concern for the Whig Party from the 1830s to 1850s. The Whigs had a strong moral agenda and a strong Anglo-Protestant and Yankee constituency (although they had a southern wing as well). Whigs cultivated the ideal that the "virtuous" middle class should take responsibility for building a society based on individual morality, self-help, and education. Though the party was also shaped by the business concerns of this class, its elitist evangelical-Puritan connections were so strong that it has been aptly characterized as "in many ways the evangelical united front at the polling place."[34]

The next major political party on the scene in the turbulent years of the mid-nineteenth century was more purely of this kind but without the dignity of the Whigs. The American, or Know-Nothing, Party was a resurgent political expression of nativism and anti-Catholicism. The huge Catholic immigration at that time brought such long-standing antagonisms once again to a head. Protestant leaders had been warning for decades that Catholic immigration could lead to a political takeover. One reason for building Protestant colleges throughout the nation was to counter Catholic expansion. Public schools also taught broadly Protestant doctrine and included

Protestant religious exercises. When Catholics asked for equal tax support for their schools, they were denied.

By the early 1830s, a number of prominent Protestants, such as Samuel F. B. Morse (1791–1872), inventor of the telegraph, and Lyman Beecher (1755–1863), the New England evangelical and father of a family of reformers (including Harriet Beecher Stowe), were issuing dire warnings concerning a growing Catholic power in America. The more popular counterparts were sensational anti-Catholic books that anticipated the standards of more recent "fake" news. Marie Monk's *Awful Disclosures of the Hôtel Dieu Nunnery of Montreal*, a Protestant best-seller in 1836, for instance, told of a girl from a Protestant family being converted to Catholicism and then becoming enslaved in prostitution in a convent. A secret tunnel connected the nunnery to the priests' residences, and unwanted babies were buried in the cellar.[35]

In the 1840s, violence replaced sex as the most conspicuous motif in anti-Catholicism. In a number of eastern cities, rioting broke out between Protestant laborers and the newer Catholic immigrants. The most serious was in Philadelphia, where St. Michael's and St. Augustine's churches in the industrial suburb of Kensington were burned to the ground.

Such sentiments spawned nativist anti-Catholic protection societies and local political parties. In the early 1850s, these consolidated into the Know-Nothing Party. In the off-year election of 1854, this nativist group seemed on the verge of becoming a new national party replacing the collapsing Whigs. It included southerners as well as northerners, swept the elections in Massachusetts, and gained other local congressional victories. In 1856, the Know-Nothings, renamed the American Party, nominated as their presidential candidate Millard Fillmore and carried 21 percent of the popular vote.

The slavery issue, however, overwhelmed anti-Catholicism, and the American Party quickly disappeared. Its northern antislavery members merged into the new Republican Party.

The Republican Party, which emerged from indignation over the Kansas-Nebraska Act of 1854 and the threatened expansion of slavery, brought together many of the reforming sentiments, although on a regional basis. Though antislavery overshadowed all other issues, Protestant reformers saw in this party a new hope of building their version of a Christian America. Former Anti-Masons, anti-Catholics, Prohibition campaigners, and other champions of a national morality helped shape the new Republican ethos, an outlook that would dominate American politics from 1860 to 1912. Though Republicanism involves a philosophy of support for big business (also dominated in the nineteenth century by Protestants), its moral stance was integral to its platform.

A famous political blunder of the next era illustrates the point. In the presidential election of 1884, a supporter of the Republican candidate, James G. Blaine, remarked that the Democratic Party was the party of "Rum, Romanism, and Rebellion." The remark overstepped the bounds of explicitness with which religious issue could be mentioned in public. Nonetheless, the Blaine supporter was celebrating the fact that the coalition that formed the early Republican Party had brought together opponents of rum, Romanism (in other words, Catholicism), and rebellion.

The irony of the fusion of antislavery and anti-Catholicism in the Republican Party is a poignant one. It aptly illustrates that the issues surrounding the relationship of religion and public life are not simple. Religion is one, albeit not the only, force that attempts to impose moral standards for national life. Yet moral codes that are appropriately defined within a religious system may not be appropriate standards to apply publicly in a pluralistic society. Anti-Catholicism or anti-Protestantism are attitudes that most people would deplore today. Prohibition of alcoholic beverages, although it was popular enough by the early twentieth century to become national policy, is also today considered to have been a failure. On the other hand, most people today think that their nineteenth-century forebears should have taken a more aggressive stance toward outlawing slavery.

White southerners, by way of contrast, viewed antislavery much the way that Catholics viewed Protestant nativism. They saw themselves as every bit as Christian as their abolitionist northern counterparts—in fact, more so. Our own moral indignation at their tragic disregard for the rights of an entire people should not obscure our understanding of how most southerners viewed the matter. To them, defense of the white southern way of life was the defense of Christian civilization, a civilization in which Christianity and the republican virtue of limited central government were ideally combined. Every civilization, they said, had a poor laboring class. Seldom did the poorest workers have so much security as did enslaved people. They could also see more clearly than the northerners themselves that the supposed "free" society of the North was oppressive in many ways, economically and socially, and far from truly Christian. Besides, they argued, slavery had been practiced throughout history and was not condemned in the Bible. Hence, they saw the abolitionist reformers as self-righteous and hypocritical imperialists.[36]

To the enslaved African Americans, however, the abolitionists appeared to be nothing less than prophets of the Lord, and the northern armies seemed sent from Jehovah to rescue his people. The black version of evangelical millennialism included the literal expectation that his faithful people would be freed from bondage. The seeming fulfillment of this biblical promise increased their commitment to their faith.

Whites in the North were, in the meantime, much more ambivalent. Radical abolitionism had the support of only a small minority. John Brown (1800–59), a militant Calvinist who believed he had a call from God to raise an army and personally free the enslaved Africans, was executed after he failed in an attempt to mount an insurrection in 1859. Although for antislavery advocates Brown became an important symbol of selfless sacrifice to high principle, most northern whites were far more conservative. Many were overtly racist. Abolitionists, while influential, were also controversial. In 1837, an angry mob murdered Elijah Lovejoy (1802–37), an abolitionist editor and a protégé of Charles Finney. Other abolitionists often were attacked by irate northern mobs as well.

Nonetheless, by 1860, the North strongly supported Abraham Lincoln's moderate policy of containing slavery within its present territories without abolishing it. Even such a restrained stance, however, presented by a president elected by a purely sectional vote, was sufficient to convince southern leadership of the necessity of secession to preserve their way of life.

Civil War: Two Rival Versions of Christian America

Once the Civil War broke out, the dominant view in the North took on a strong crusading tone. Even though slavery was not abolished until 1863, many saw the war as a sacred cause with explicit millennial overtones. In the dominant rhetoric, the Union itself was a sacred object essential to the advance of Christ's kingdom. Julia Ward Howe's "The Battle Hymn of the Republic," published in 1862, captured the mix of militant nationalism and biblical millennial themes. Drawing on imagery from the book of Revelation, Howe spoke of the Lord as "trampling out the vintage where the grapes of wrath are stored" and as having "loosed the fateful lightning of his terrible swift sword." These images were not only familiar to most Americans, but seemed appropriate to apply to the "sword" of their own armies. The millennial promise of "the coming of the glory of the Lord" was virtually equated with the success of the Union. Protestant-Republicans had high hopes to build a virtuous civilization. The popular post-millennial views of the day promised moral advance, such as the ending of slavery and other oppression as steps toward a culminating golden age of human history that would manifest the reign of Christ.

The realities of life in the North of the Civil War era were a long way from these millennial ideals. Even in the towns and countryside only a minority of the population were active in their churches. The urban areas of early industrial growth were marked by poverty, squalor, and vast inequalities of wealth. Prejudice and discrimination based on race, ethnicity, and religion were widespread. There were powerful economic interests involved in preserving the Union. And raising armies and fighting an incredibly bloody war against a determined enemy was often anything but glorious. Nonetheless, even aside from millennial or biblical themes, the Union itself had become a sacred entity. This was the era of the rise of the nation-state. In the United States that came with a creed that celebrated liberty and justice. For many people the nation had become a more important source of identity than the church. Baptists did not often worry that they might be killing other Baptists. The state had become a religion. In the rhetoric and enthusiasm for the Union, it was often impossible to disentangle Christian and biblical motifs from unqualified patriotism.

In the South, the rhetoric was typically less grandiose, lacking the millennial themes and celebrations of national and moral progress. Yet southerners had no less sense that they were fighting for a Christian civilization than did their Yankee counterparts. They differed though in what it meant to be a Christian nation. Through the revolutionary era, white southerners' social and political ideals had been similar to those found in the North. The presence of slavery, however, and then defensiveness toward abolitionists, especially after 1830, had chilled most white southern enthusiasm for a mutual heritage celebrating progress and change.

Most mid-nineteenth-century white southerners emphasized instead the traditional belief that the deity ordained humans to live in a socially ordered world. This had long been the dominant social view throughout the Western, or European, world. Just as God created hierarchies in nature, with some creatures clearly more skilled and powerful than others, so God created orders in society. In every society, some classes had wealth and power and others were less wealthy and called to do the menial tasks. Social health, southerners argued, depended on not disrupting such God-ordained orders. The Bible, they claimed, said as much.

At the same time, however, the southerners were themselves enough the products of Thomas Jefferson's revolutionary America to preserve a firm attachment to a form of American individualism. God had ordained individual liberties, guaranteeing equality before the law, personal and economic liberties, and freedom from undue governmental regulation. As most Americans did, southerners believed such liberties applied fully only to males; but unlike northerners, they applied none of these principles to people of African descent. So, compared with northern leaders, they spoke less of universal liberties and emphasized more that the orders of society, whether patriarchal family or paternalistic slavery, were ordained by God.

The Civil War, then, can be understood at one important level as a conflict between two moral and religious visions of society. These competing moral visions, though having multiple roots in various traditions of political thought (such as classical, Enlightenment, or British), as well as in distinctly Christian teachings, were widely regarded on each side as having evident divine sanction. People are more willing to die for a cause if they believe that God is on their side. One result of this was the bitter irony that Lincoln commented on in his second inaugural speech: "Both read the same Bible, and pray to the same God; and each invokes his aid against the other."

CHAPTER 4

Protestant and Progressive America: 1860–1917

The grandfather, who was in college sixty years ago, asked in dread and fear, "Is my soul saved?" . . . The father, who was in college thirty years ago, . . . asked, "Is your soul saved?" The son does not ask either question. He is content to live the life of the Christian. Salvation is taken for granted in a world of, by, and full of goodness.

C. F. Thwing, president of Western Reserve University,
The American College: What It Is and What It May Become (1914)

If one had visited the United States on the eve of the Civil War, then returned a half century later at the height of the Progressive era, one would have seen many continuities in the dominant culture. Political power was still held firmly by white Protestants who had every intention of keeping it that way. Their crusading spirit was as strong as ever. Sentiment was growing in the Protestant-Republican North for national legislation prohibiting the sale of alcoholic beverages. Protestant southerners were willing to forget deep regional antagonisms long enough to join in this crusade, which was directed in part against perceived threats arising from new immigrant populations, especially Catholics, but also Jews and perhaps even German Lutherans. A parallel effort at Anglo-Protestant dominance was the "blue laws," which forbade commerce in many localities on Sundays. This practice was important to moralistic Anglo-Protestants but not to most Lutherans or Catholics, and it was directly discriminatory against Jews because they observed a different Sabbath. The United States was already an amazingly diverse culture, but the cultural insiders with whom every immigrant group had to cope were still predominantly Anglo-Protestant.

During this era from the 1860s until the 1910s, insider Protestants—despite the faults that seem always to accompany wealth and power—had some reason to be proud of the civilization they dominated. The United States was viewed by much of the world as a model society where people from many nations could live together in relative peace and as a place with unusual opportunities for economic success. Whatever injustices, discriminations, and poverty were in the United States, one could find far worse in other quarters of the globe. Among the essential premises of the dominant American thought of the era were (1) the superiority of Western civilization, (2) that Anglo-American democratic principles were the highest political expression of that civilization, and (3) that these principles were almost bound to triumph throughout the earth.[1] Without necessarily saying so explicitly, Protestants saw these ideals as an outgrowth of their heritage.

Moreover, Protestant moral reformers, which included women as much as men, could claim leadership in the major efforts to make the United States a more just society. Most of the Progressive reforms of the day were brought in by prodding the conscience of the dominant middle class. One estimate suggests that 85 percent of all social reformers of the era had some connection with evangelical Protestantism.[2] Catholics and Jews might also have been ardent champions of reform, but Protestants held the leadership and the power.

Prohibition and Sabbath legislation could even be seen as social reforms aimed at drug and labor problems. Progressive reformers, however, had a much larger moral agenda for cleaning up government, regulating big business, protecting consumers, fighting poverty and the vast inequities in wealth, and building a more participatory democracy. All these reforms had strong middle-class Protestant support and reflected an ongoing Puritan spirit of civic responsibility. Their impetus came not primarily from class or religious conflict but from appeals to conscience that people from most traditions might share. Given the upbeat and often successful reforming ethos of the day, it did not seem incongruous that the theme song of Teddy Roosevelt's Bull Moose (Progressive) Party convention in 1912 was "Onward, Christian Soldiers."

Despite such continuities with themes from 1860, the sharp-eyed visitor to the United States at the end of this era would also be struck by some vast differences. The dominant Protestant culture, its increasing enthusiasm notwithstanding, was struggling to keep control. Though it was not obvious to most participants that they were at the end of an era, realities were threatening to make the rhetoric hollow and obsolete.

The changes of this period were vast. The most obvious of these changes were urbanization, industrialization, and immigration, all of which threatened to undermine the dominant ethos which was implicitly built around the assumption that the world was made up of communities similar to a New England town. Growing sentiments also favored drastic limitation of immigration to keep ethnic ratios stable.

Threats to the Protestant cultural establishment were not simply external. Within the establishment, the forces of change were taking their toll. Intellectual changes were especially important for many individuals because they led to practical changes in belief and value systems. Increasing numbers of educated people abandoned traditional Protestant teaching and trust in the authority of the Bible. Others modified traditional doctrine to accommodate modern thought. Debates over these issues were threatening to split the Protestant community from within.

While the dominant American culture around 1910 in many ways resembled that of the culture of 1860, it was being pushed near the breaking point by both external and internal pressures of momentous proportions. This chapter and the following chapter will examine the tensions this culture faced, looking first at the successes and changes within the dominant Anglo culture, and then at how this world looked to other Americans who were still kept away from most centers of cultural power.

The Gilded Age

Northern evangelical clergy typically described the Civil War in both covenantal and millennial terms. In speaking of a covenant, the clergy looked back to their Puritan heritage, which had been thoroughly blended with the American principles of government. "While the Union is all in all, the very ark of the covenant to us and our children," declared a leading New York Presbyterian in a typical statement in 1862, "it is everything to the race. It is freighted with better hopes for freedom and humanity than any other nation in existence."

With victory, the nation could look forward to "millennial days" when peace, justice, and the principles of Christ would reign.[3] Once the nation abolished one of history's most glaring injustices, many ardent Protestants proclaimed, the future of moral reform should then be unlimited. Even "government," said the well-known theologian Horace Bushnell at the end of the Civil War, "is now become Providential—no more a mere creature of our human will, but a grandly moral affair."[4]

The golden age of the reign of morality somehow went missing, however. Instead, the nation experienced what Mark Twain (1835–1910) and Charles Dudley Warner (1829–1900) aptly characterized as "the Gilded Age." The rhetoric of a Christian civilization, Twain and Warner were suggesting, was a thin veneer painted over secular and immoral realities. In their novel, *The Gilded Age* (1873), the leading character, Senator Dilworthy, is involved in endless circles of corruption. Yet when he runs for reelection, he waxes eloquent as a Christian statesman, addresses Sunday schools and ladies' missionary societies, "and even took a needle now and then and made a stitch or two upon a calico shirt for some Bible-less pagan of the South Seas, and this act enchanted the ladies, who regard the garments thus honored as in a manner sanctified."[5]

The period that began with the assassination of Lincoln and included the trumped-up impeachment of President Andrew Johnson; the Black Friday Scandal of 1869, the Credit Mobilier Scandal, the Whiskey Ring, and other corruption in the Grant administration; the corruption of Reconstruction and the reneging on the promise of equality for blacks; the possible stealing of the election of 1876; and the 1881 assassination of President Garfield (to mention only highlights) invited such a characterization. Henry Adams, the grandson of John Quincy Adams, scion of the best of the heritage of New England civic responsibility, anonymously published the novel *Democracy* in 1880. In it the heroine, seeking the virtue that should be at the heart of a republic, finds instead that her principal suitor, a Republican leader, is like a "moral lunatic," who "talked about virtue and vice as a man who is colour-blind talks about red and green."[6]

Mark Twain and Henry Adams were, of course, not typical figures of the era. Yet each was reared in the prevailing Anglo-Protestant culture, although at opposite ends of it. Adams was from the New England aristocracy; Twain from the new West. Twain's character Aunt Polly, from the novel *Tom Sawyer*, seemed a universal personage in Protestant America. Almost everyone, it seems, had encountered in their upbringing such strict, evangelical Puritan piety. Writers such as Twain and Adams, who rejected their religious heritage and felt alienated from it, were perhaps in the best position to see its contradictions from within.

Adams (1838–1918), a historian by profession, provided the most profound overall analysis of this era. In his autobiography, *The Education of Henry Adams* (1907), a particularly telling passage is entitled "The Dynamo and the Virgin." In it Adams reflects on his experience while visiting the Paris Exposition of 1900. At the center of this world's fair was a great dynamo, which Adams saw as representing the technological power that lay at the heart of modern civilization. Modern culture, and nowhere more than in the United States, was based on harnessing physical energy. From Paris, Adams traveled to Chartres, where he saw the spectacular medieval cathedral that dominates the landscape. What sort of force, asked Adams, did it take for such an economically and technologically limited civilization to produce such a magnificent work of art? That civilization, he said, was run by a spiritual power, the power of dedication to the Virgin. "All the steam in the world," he remarked, "could not, like the Virgin, build Chartres." American civilization, by contrast, had a superficial spirituality in Adams's view. Its real power was in brute force. The idea of great art in America, Adams observed, was a statue of General Sherman on a horse.

It was not that traditional Christianity was declining in America by any usual standard of measure. Churches of all sorts were growing, and Protestant churches were keeping up with population increases, even though much of the new immigration was not Protestant. Major Protestant groups, such as the Methodists, Baptists, Presbyterians, Disciples, and Congregationalists, tripled their combined memberships in the period from 1860 to 1900. In 1880, Robert Ingersoll, the most famous skeptic of the post–Civil War era, who traveled the country attacking the Bible and Christian teaching, announced that "the churches are dying out all over the land." Charles McCabe, head of the Methodist Church Extension Society, wired to Ingersoll the following message:

All hail the power of Jesus' name—we are building more than one Methodist church for every day in the year, and propose to make it two a day!

McCabe had reason to be optimistic, as indeed most Protestant leaders were in his day. The statistical strength of the churches could be matched with their continuing moral impact. James Bryce, a British visitor in the late 1800s, observed that the clergy were America's "first citizens" and that they exerted "an influence often wider and more powerful than that of any layman." They seemed to be, as much as anyone, the definers of the values that made up the culture. It was an era of Christian crusades. Theodore Roosevelt remarked that he "would rather address a Methodist audience than any other audience in America" for "the Methodists represent the great middle class and in consequence are the most representative church in America." As historian Winthrop Hudson observed, "In 1900 few would have disputed the contention that the United States was a Protestant nation."[7]

How are these strikingly conflicting estimates to be resolved? What was Henry Adams seeing that most of his contemporaries in 1900 were ignoring?

In essence, the differing estimates reflect the two sides of what has been and will be observed throughout this book as an essential paradox in American civilization: it is both intensely spiritual and intensely materialistic. In part, this combination is an inevitable one that can be found in all so-called Christian civilizations throughout the ages. The spiritual dimensions never cut nearly as deep as some of the public expressions of the leaders would suggest. This is true even of medieval Western civilization, of which Henry Adams held a somewhat romanticized view. The paradox in Western civilizations reflects a paradox deep in human nature.

Nonetheless, Adams was pointing to a real difference between modern civilization and those that had gone before. Modern technology has greatly enhanced many people's access to material pleasures. So, among modern people who remain religious, the paradoxes between the spiritual and material sides have been greatly intensified.

Understanding Secularization

To understand this intensification of the paradox, one should consider the way secularization has taken place in America. *Secularization*, as it is used here, simply means the removal of some area of human activity from the domain, or significant influence, of organized or traditional religion. In the modern Western world, this has happened for two primary reasons. First, secularization has been promoted by those who have been hostile to traditional religion, especially Christianity. This hostility might take the form of resistance to the practical, ethical restraints of Christian teaching from, for instance, the business person, the politician, the free spirit, or the no-good person who wants to carve out an area of life governed by principles other than those of Judeo-Christian morality. The hostility may also arise primarily from ideological commitments to an alternative secular belief system. As shall be illustrated, especially after 1865 in America, increasing numbers of ideological secularists appeared who insisted that traditional Christian (or other theistic) teachings were untenable and should be replaced by higher principles that, frankly, were based on human inquiry alone.

At the same time, traditional Christians, practicing Jews, and other ardent theists may also promote secularization. In fact, one of the most important characteristics of the modern world since about 1700 is the promotion of such secularization by religious people. The reasons for this are closely related to the characteristics of the eighteenth-century Enlightenment, which was discussed earlier. Enlightenment thinkers of the eighteenth century began applying the inductive scientific model, so successful in the areas of physical science and technology, as the basis for understanding other domains of human activity. Christians as well as non-Christians saw the advantages of this approach. If areas of reality could be analyzed and organized rationally and free from prejudice, it was widely held, these areas could be vastly improved. Most modern people accept this principle with respect to technology. Even though people may have deep religious commitments, they want to keep certain technical areas free from religious influences. To offer a contemporary example, most strongly religious people would not be happy if the pilot of their airplane announced that passengers should not worry about landing in the storm since he or she would just be trusting in the leading of the Lord.

In modern America, therefore, Christians and other religious traditionalists have often adopted a stance that can be called "methodological secularity" for an increasing number of their activities. Scientists and technicians of all sorts, no matter how religious, are expected to check their religious beliefs at the door when they enter the laboratory. Of course, they may pray about their work, engage in it with a purpose to serve, and perhaps ponder how nature reflects God's design; but the activity itself will be, for methodological purposes, essentially secular.

One of the best examples of this technological principle being applied beyond the simply physical world is the design of the US government. The Constitution is, in a sense, a technical mechanism to regulate potentially conflicting forces. Many Christian groups, notably the Baptists, were fervent proponents of such secularization, which involves simply separating out areas of religious and nonreligious activity. Religion would inevitably influence legislation, but the moral principles involved could be argued on the basis of natural law in public forums. Government could also sponsor formal ceremonial religious activities, although (like the technician who prays before entering the lab) these were expected not to have substantive bearing on the business of governing.

Crucial to the development of America was, as in the case of the US Constitution, that such applications of technological principles did not involve any essential hostility toward traditional Christianity. This contrasts importantly with the experience of the French Revolution, which became the chief symbol of modern politics and the model for much later sociological thinking on the subject of secularization. In France and in much of Europe, liberal politics came to be associated with direct opposition to the clergy and Christianity. The secularization of the government, or the removal of direct religious influences on it, had definite anti-Christian implications.

The American development was far different. Secularization of many areas of American life accelerated during the nineteenth century, but most often it followed the model of a methodological secularization, as exemplified by the US Constitution, which was essentially friendly to traditional Christianity. Dominant Protestantism, in turn, was essentially friendly to such secularization and could even bless and celebrate much of it.

Gradually, a largely peaceful differentiation of religious and secular domains took place. One important factor that eased this transition and even made it difficult to perceive was that as areas of life were removed from substantive religious influences, these areas might well at the same time continue to be baptized in more superficial ways in harmony with the general principles of Christian civilization. One could not, therefore, plot a neat contraction of religious influence in America. Rather, in many ways, religion could be seen spreading its influence even if, as in the singing of "Onward, Christian Soldiers" at the Progressive Convention in 1912, that influence might be increasingly thin.[8]

Religion and Politics: The Link Continues

One area in which the phenomena and paradoxes of the simultaneously religious and secular occur in American life is politics. Religion continued to be one of the best indicators of political behavior, especially when religion was combined with ethnicity, as it almost always was. In general, the Republican Party remained predominantly the party of northerners affiliated with mainstream evangelical denominations, such as Methodists, Baptists, Presbyterians, and Congregationalists. These groups had evangelical traditions, emphasizing the conversion of individuals who are then expected to live pious lives. These concerns were still connected with something broadly like the Puritan ideal of building a Christian society. Hence, these groups encouraged government regulation of personal behavior according to evangelical standards, as the proposed prohibition of alcoholic beverages best symbolized. In general, this evangelical political program was opposed by more liturgically minded religious groups, such as Catholics, Episcopalians, and some Lutherans. While there were many exceptions, this pattern was the general rule.[9]

Religion could at times have a lot to do with politics since it helped shape and reinforce competing moral visions that infused political debates. Often, however, other political concerns overrode religious differences; the firmest political alliance of the era was that within the Democratic Party, between Catholics and white southerners. The latter generally belonged to evangelical denominations and disliked Catholics, but the two groups were politically allied due to their common disdain for the Yankee Republican establishment.

The role that religion played did not have to be explicit. In fact, it generally had to be subtle since both parties wanted to recruit supporters from the other's constituency. For instance, the notorious remark in the 1884 presidential campaign that the Democrats were the party of "Rum, Romanism, and Rebellion" was widely criticized. Republicans needed to court Catholic support and occasionally got it. Archbishop John Ireland of St. Paul, Minnesota, one of the leading Catholic "Americanizers" of the era, for instance, was an active Republican.

Democrats were also trying to broaden their constituency by cutting into the Republican evangelical base. In 1896, they fostered an important party realignment by nominating dark-horse agrarian William Jennings Bryan, an ardent evangelical, to be president. He was also a prohibitionist, thus taking from the Republicans one of their traditional distinctions.[10] With the fervor of an evangelist, Bryan preached the moral urgency for social reform. By the Progressive Era, both parties were preaching moral reform and each presented a vision of America as the land where God's will should be done.

What we can see, then, is a pattern where both parties reached for a consensus built on moral claims that could bring people of all religions into what was regarded as essentially a melting-pot ideal. Despite the public toning-down of religious factors and the emphasis on moral commonalities, the basic patterns of the differing religious (and regional) platforms of the two parties persisted until new ideological and moral issues began to displace them in the 1960s.

The Republican Party and the Incorporation of America

While the religious factor promoting various moral visions in politics is undeniable, we can see the basically paradoxical character of religion and culture by looking more closely at the development of the Republican Party, which was usually dominant from the Civil War to World War I.

In addition to emerging from the Civil War as the party of the northern pietist moral reform, the Republicans also championed the rise of big business. Business is a realm that tends to have a logic of its own, built upon the principle of maximizing profits. Individual and social moral demands may restrain business to a degree, but these demands weaken, especially as businesses become larger and more depersonalized and in boom times when huge financial rewards come to those who can most efficiently organize and mobilize. Such forces were strong in America after the Civil War, and for some people, these forces were irresistible, hence giving the Gilded Age its notorious reputation for political and economic corruption.

In addition to mere greed, however, more fundamental changes appeared in the fabric of American economic life. Most importantly, the mammoth industrialization of the nation was accompanied by the social revolution of urbanization and the economic revolution of incorporation.

Both of these forces created vast new areas of life that were less susceptible to religious and moral control. The teeming cities, despite the presence of ethnic enclaves, fostered large populations that were detached from their original religious communities. Anonymity, which had not been a choice in small towns and rural America, was now possible. Organizations such as the Young Men's Christian Association (YMCA) and Young Women's Christian Association (YWCA), which were evangelical agencies, and urban revivals tried to counter these trends. Evangelical churches also grew most among people who had recently moved to the cities. In terms of membership, urban churches often thrived. Yet the sheer size of cities also made them centers for secularity.

At the same time, the incorporation of American business, much of which took place in the decades between 1865 and 1900, created another largely secular domain. In incorporation, the state grants a business the status of a person so that it has an ongoing life of its own, is owned by stockholders, and is run by an essentially self-perpetuating board of directors. Owners (stockholders) are not personally liable for the debts of the corporation—only for their investments. As the new captains of industry mobilized resources during this volatile period of growth, the corporation was the preferred method of organization. Though individuals such as John D. Rockefeller, Andrew Carnegie, and John Pierpont Morgan were prominent in this process, it eventually made the corporate person—the business—a less personalized entity; that is, corporations were identified less with any individual. This distancing of businesses from their owners also made the owners less susceptible to moral standards that would normally be expected of individuals.

Most of the mainline Protestant churches (that is, the older and respected northern denominations such as Presbyterian, Congregationalist, Methodist, and Baptist) that had solid, middle-class constituencies supported such trends. Churches tend to follow the mood of their constituents. When, after the Civil War, many of the same constituencies that had agitated for abolition and other causes became disillusioned with reform, their churches followed suit, in general supporting the social status quo and whatever seemed to favor business.

As industry, urbanization, and immigration expanded, the most pressing social problems of the day had to do with the relationship of capital to labor. Laborers were organizing, striking, and agitating for better working conditions. Occasionally, there were riots, as in the 1886 Haymarket affair, in which the Chicago police tried to break up a labor rally, someone tossed a bomb at them, and the police fired back, killing some protesters. Subsequently, a number of anarchists, some of whom were not present at the incident, were convicted and given death sentences for agitation that was believed to have led to the bombing.

Many mainline church people reacted to such violence with alarm. The *Congregationalist*, one of the most respected New England religious papers, commented: "When anarchy gathers its deluded disciples into a mob, as at Chicago, a Gatling gun or two, swiftly brought into position and well served, offers on the whole, the most merciful as well as effectual remedy."[11] One senses in such remarks that the quality of Protestant mercy had become strained.

Nevertheless, such overreactions can be better understood if they are seen in terms of the broader ideal for civilization that they reflected. Fear concerning anarchists was built on the deep commitment of the Anglo-Protestant establishment (and of Catholic leaders, for that matter) to law and order as the basis for a free society. New socialist and anarchist ideas were usually promoted by recent immigrants, so that Protestants saw in them a foreign threat to their civilization. Such fears often outweighed the fact that evangelical Protestant laborers were often active in the unions and in demands for greater equity.[12]

Beneath such issues were economic views that led many Protestant Republicans (and many others, of course) to oppose labor strikes of any sort and also to oppose government regulation of industry. The self-interest of their class, and particularly the self-interested demands of business leaders were, of course, primary incentive for promoting such views. On the other hand, it should not be supposed, as is sometimes remarked, that they lacked genuine social concern. They had very strong concerns for the welfare of society, but they had become convinced that free enterprise plus individual initiative were the best ways for that welfare to be accomplished.

Hard Work as a Social Program

Essentially, the outlook of such Protestants reflected a self-help ideal that, as with most American beliefs, combined Enlightenment ideals with some Christian principles. This outlook was based on the belief, widespread in the eighteenth and nineteenth centuries, that human agency was central to historical change. This same outlook produced the popular theory of the time that history is determined by "great men" and that the great issues in history therefore concern morality. The American revolutionaries had held such views. In the nineteenth century, most Americans still believed that what applied to the great applied as much to ordinary people: individual choices were crucial to success or failure.

The standard view, which was still taught in both college economics texts and popular literature after the Civil War, was built upon the premise that God created the world with a system of rewards and punishments. People who worked were rewarded, while lazy or profligate people suffered from poverty. The right to own private property was considered a sacred right, since it was essential to the operation of the reward system. It was also important not to interfere with the natural mechanism, as in the form of strikes or government interference. Charity was an important duty toward the truly needy, such as the disabled, widows, and orphans, who could not help themselves. To artificially aid the able-bodied, however, was simply to destroy individual initiative. The logic of the system made it seem God-ordained.[13]

The question in the late nineteenth century was whether this outlook, which had some obviously beneficial applications in small-town settings that were economically rather simple, would work in the emerging mass societies of the cities. Protestant leaders insisted that it would. Henry Ward Beecher (1813–87), the best-known preacher of the post–Civil War era, for instance, was confident that "even in the most compact and closely-populated portions of the East, he that will be frugal, and save continuously, living every day within the bounds of his means, can scarcely help accumulating."[14]

The key to success and social welfare was, in this view, for individuals to work hard and help themselves. Conversion to Christianity could be an important first step toward such discipline. In any case, the ethic was a gospel of work.

McGuffey's Eclectic Readers, still the standard reading texts in thirty-seven states in 1890, helped transmit these values to the next generation and to new Americans. Honesty, kindness, thrift, industry, and patriotism were recurrent themes. The lessons included stories like "The Little Idle Boy," "The Idle Boy Reformed," and "The Advantages of Industry." The latter concludes with the idle boy, named George Jones, seen years later "a poor wanderer, without money and without friends." The narrator admonishes: "The story of George Jones, which is a true one, shows how sinful and ruinous it is to be idle. Every child who would be a Christian, and have a home in heaven, must guard against this sin."[15]

The emphases on hard work and self-reliance could be valuable in a society where most people started poor, but many older-stock white people had unparalleled opportunities for economic advance. It is important to note also that the worldview also included lessons on the dangers of riches, emphasizing that the virtuous poor were happier than the greedy rich. It likewise focused on the importance of charity.

"Acres of Diamonds"

Opportunity in America often was interpreted as a gift from God. The most famous clerical promoter of this view was Russell H. Conwell (1843–1925). Conwell, a Baptist preacher in Philadelphia, was a self-made man who amassed a fortune, as well as establishing an "institutional church" that served the local community not only by religious services but as a community center. Among Conwell's projects was the founding of Temple University. His fame, however, rested on the speech "Acres of Diamonds," which he delivered an astounding six thousand times. Everyone had acres of diamonds of opportunity in their own backyards, he proclaimed. When asked why he did not preach the gospel instead of preaching how people could get rich, Conwell replied, "Because to make money honestly is to preach the gospel."[16]

An essential tension was emerging as Conwell and others in the self-help school emphasized honesty, charity, civic responsibility, and other such virtues. Another side of the individualistic ethic encouraged business leaders to do whatever it took to maximize profits, and as huge industries burgeoned, that profit motive tended to overwhelm many moral concerns. In practice, that meant that expanding areas in American life were free from the religious and moral restraints that might be expected in more personal relationships.

A classic illustration of the tensions involved in America is seen in the career of John D. Rockefeller Sr. (1839–1937). The Standard Oil magnate was a devout Baptist who prided himself on his personal integrity. Yet in the fierce competition for control of the oil industry, Standard Oil used ruthless tactics to drive its competitors out of business. Muckraking journalists, who by the 1890s were exposing business corruption, saw Rockefeller as chief among the "robber barons." American monopolies were developing techniques that would outrage moral sensibilities in personal relationships, such as exploiting a weakness to drive a struggling neighbor out of business. Yet given the internal logic of the emerging competition, Rockefeller himself was convinced that "the Lord gave me my money." Like other captains of industry, Rockefeller followed the logic of the individualistic ethic to share some of the excess of his profits with the community. Notably, he endowed the University of Chicago, founded in 1890, to be a great Baptist center for learning.

An Age of Reform

Another side to the picture, however, tempered the trend of letting freewheeling capitalism shape American society regardless of ethical consequences. Many Americans from the dominant classes were intensely moralistic, with a strong sense of civic responsibility. Civic responsibility and charity, lessons that were always taught alongside the work ethic, tempered individualism. Such sensitivities can be traced back to the Puritan heritage of a covenanted nation. Reform in America often has a middle-class base, appealing to the Judeo-Christian principles that each person has responsibilities for the welfare of all his or her neighbors.

Beginning with the middle decades of the nineteenth century, when business expansion became a major political issue, the mood of America began to oscillate between eras of reform, when moral restraints were prominent, and eras when the quest for material advance more often overrode such restraints. The pre–Civil War age of reform was followed by the conservative Gilded Age, which was followed by the Progressive Era of reform—lasting from about the 1890s until it was displaced by the conservative 1920s. That, as we will see in upcoming chapters, was followed by the New Deal, then the conservatism of the 1950s, and then the reform mood of the 1960s. Since then the patterns have not been as clear, although the tensions between business interests and reform interest still persist.

Women and Reform

As in the pre–Civil War reforms, middle-class women played a prominent, though still not controlling, role in the demands for moral reform during the Progressive Era. While most women accepted their assigned primary role as guardians of the home and, secondarily, as subordinate partners in the churches, their situation was changing. Increasingly, women were developing their own networks of organizations. By far the largest number of these organizations were local church organizations, such as women's societies for charity and especially for missions. Nondenominational voluntary reform societies, which supplemented local church organizations, continued to provide women with their most important public role—as moral guardians of society, an extension of the widespread nineteenth-century expectation that women would be the moral guardians of the home.

The idea that women had a significant social role to guard the moral sector, although part of a package that usually limited full-time career opportunities for women, was based on more than mythology. Since men held exclusive sway in industry, which was increasingly dominated by rationalized principles of seeking efficiency, male roles operating under rules of ruthless competition and survival of the fittest were accentuated. Most women, on the other hand, continued to operate largely in the home and in the neighborhood, where traditional standards of personal ethics were appropriate.

As in the society at large, religious options for women were broadening. After the Civil War, many middle-class women turned to spiritualism and the occult, sometimes as ways of communicating with the dead, especially those lost in the war. Though such views led to exotic new sects—such as Theosophy, founded by Madame Helena P. Blavatsky (1831–91) and Henry Olcott (1832–1907) in 1872 in New York, or Mary Baker Eddy's (1821–1910) Christian Science—most of the new spiritualistic experimentation probably supplemented more-or-less traditional Christian beliefs. The reign of dogmatic systematic theologies, controlled by male theologians, was beginning to wane in many of the Northern Protestant denominations; the women's counterpart was often a more romanticized version of Christianity open to innovation.

The Christian dimensions of the women's reform efforts remained conspicuous. The most striking example was Frances E. Willard (1839–98), leader of the most influential women's movement of the era. Willard was reared in a pious family of evangelical New Englanders, transplanted to Wisconsin. Part of her early inspiration came from hearing Charles G. Finney preach. In her own work, Willard, a devout Methodist, likewise combined traditional evangelical theology, an emphasis on holiness, and ardent social reform. She worked principally with the Women's Christian Temperance Union (WCTU), the largest women's organization of the time. Assuming its presidency in 1879, Willard pushed the WCTU toward supplementing its preeminent temperance concerns with other reform interests, such as support of labor unions and especially women's right to vote. Willard was one of those who effectively turned the arguments for women's domesticity around by accepting the stereotypical image of women as naturally more virtuous than men. Rather than see this as a reason for women to stay home, Willard and others used it as an argument for women to save society. "What the world most needs is mothering," said Willard.[17]

Willard and other activist women also pushed for women's equality in the churches. Here they met stiff opposition from the established Protestant denominations. The Methodist General Conference denied Willard the privilege of addressing them in 1880, and in 1888 it refused to seat Willard and other elected women delegates. Nonetheless, the effective organization of women was helping pave the way for new policies in the mainline churches, as elsewhere in American society. Just as within a generation, by 1920, women were granted the vote at the national level, so mainline Protestant churches began opening up at least some offices to women.

Missions

The period from the Civil War to World War I was the great age for American Protestant missions, an enterprise in which women played a major role, both in the field and in supporting societies. In 1869, American world missions were about the same size as the total for continental European countries and half the size of British missions. By 1910, American missionaries outnumbered continentals by over two to one and had surpassed even the British.[18] Counting those who were married, women made up about 60 percent of the missionaries. Meanwhile, women's supporting agencies at home had a membership of some two million.[19]

Enthusiasm for missions reflected a combination of motives. The primary motive arose from the traditional Protestant and revivalist belief that without faith in Christ, the heathen would spend eternity suffering in hell. People who do not hold such a worldview may dismiss this motive; but if one took this view absolutely literally, as many Americans did, it was easily a sufficient motive for high-minded people to give up their earthly comforts and risk their lives in bringing the gospel to a distant land. Added to this motive was the further conviction that Christianity was not simply an otherworldly religion but a civilizing benefit to all people. Even some who, by the end of this era, may have doubted the exclusiveness of Christianity as a means of eternal salvation could continue to support a worldwide social gospel dedicated to transforming humanity through the principles of Jesus.

Moody and the Shaping of the Missionary Ideal

One can get some sense of the missionary fervor by looking at the most prominent promoter of American missions of the time. Dwight L. Moody (1837–99) was to the generation from the 1870s through the 1890s what Charles Finney had been to the pre–Civil War era—America's chief evangelist. Moody was a homey, self-educated and self-made man, the epitome of the American Horatio Alger figure, the boy who, through luck and pluck, rose from modest beginnings to fame and fortune. Converted through the work of the YMCA (then a leading evangelistic agency), Moody eventually gave up a lucrative career as a shoe salesman in Chicago and turned to evangelistic work. After effective local ministries in Chicago during the 1860s, Moody and his song leader, Ira Sankey, toured the British Isles from 1873 to 1875. Success abroad catapulted them to immense fame and popularity at home. During the next quarter century, Moody held revivals in American cities. Preaching a simple, old-time gospel of salvation through rebirth in Christ, Moody charmed audiences with sentimental stories and the conventional moralism of middle-class Victorian Protestantism.

In 1886, Moody made a tour of college campuses that led to a dramatic summer gathering of students at Moody's campground in Northfield, Massachusetts. There a hundred top collegians pledged their lives to missions. Their enthusiasm spread quickly to their campuses, and in two years, when they formed the Student Volunteer Movement (SVM), the number who pledged had grown to thousands. Out of the SVM arose most of the Protestant missionary leadership of the next generation. The watchword of the SVM—"The Evangelization of the World in This Generation"—matched the crusading and ebullient spirit of the day.

"Our Country"

Though Moody's message of the salvation of souls was a primary inspiration for young men and women to give their lives to missions, those who supported missions stressed its civilizing benefits, as well. Most prominent of these was Josiah Strong (1847–1916), who in 1885 published the best-selling volume *Our Country*. Strong, a proponent both of missions and of social reform, firmly proclaimed that the world's destiny lay with the Anglo-Saxon race. Anglo-Saxons had two great contributions to offer the world: love of liberty and a "pure spiritual Christianity."[20] Missionary efforts promoted both of these.

Strong, like many of his contemporaries, held views that now seem outdated and racist. In part, he and others based such views on what they saw as the proven moral superiority of civilizations and in part on the social science of the day that included social-Darwinist views on race. According to such views, races or national groupings were always locked in struggles for superiority and dominance. Some races were past their prime and had reached a sort of racial senility. According to the Anglo-Protestants, the Latin race, including southern European Catholics, was of this sort. In Roman times, this race produced a great civilization. Now, they were being surpassed by more vigorous Anglo-Protestantism. On the other hand, other races, such as the African, were seen as being in their infancy. To lift up and help such peoples was, as Rudyard Kipling put it, "the white man's burden."

Such views fit American foreign policy at the time of the Spanish-American War in 1898. Americans saw themselves dealing with "savage and senile races."[21] Spain represented a decadent Catholic civilization. The Filipinos, freed from Spanish rule by the Americans, needed American guidance. As President McKinley explained to a Methodist audience, he reached his decision to acquire the Philippines after spending many evenings on his knees praying for divine guidance: "And one night late it came to me this way. . . . There was nothing left for us to do but to take them all and to educate the Filipinos and uplift and civilize and Christianize them, and by God's grace do the very best we could by them, as our fellow men for whom Christ also died."[22]

Americans as a nation were beginning to encounter the rest of the world but usually with the confident sense of their cultural superiority. In 1893, progressive religious leaders sponsored, in conjunction with the World's Columbian Exposition in Chicago, a World's Parliament of Religion to promote understanding among the various religions of the world. To the consternation of some conservatives, representatives of many of the world's faiths gathered and even bowed their heads together as the Roman Catholic prelate, James Cardinal Gibbons (1834–1921), recited the Lord's Prayer. Despite the new respect for other faiths that such a gathering inevitably engendered, even the most progressive Americans did not abandon their sense of cultural superiority. As John Henry Barrows, one of the principal organizers of the parliament, put it, "Civilization is the secular name for Christianity."[23]

From such sentiments, which so thoroughly blended the dominant American secular and religious goals, it was not a far step to Woodrow Wilson's motto that the purpose of World War I was "to make the world safe for democracy."

The Social Gospel

In the meantime, middle-class Protestant sentiments for reforming American civilization were growing. The Progressive impulse, however, was too broad to be attributed to any one social group or tradition. Like much else, it reflected a mix of secular motives and religious concerns. Some sentiments had grass-roots origins in the Populist movement, but Progressivism reflected a change of mood in America in the two decades before World War I. Most simply, this change of mood seems to have involved a collective awakening of national conscience. As historian Richard Hofstadter pointed out, key words in the national vocabulary of the Progressives included *law, character, conscience, soul, morals, service, duty, shame, disgrace, sin,* and *selfishness.*[24] Progressives typically attributed the evil in society to violations of moral law.

Since much of American society was professedly Christian, these moral appeals often had strong Christian overtones. Jacob Riis, whose photographs and narrative in *How the Other Half Lives* (1890) helped arouse the nation to the urgency of its urban problems, was an active churchman. Henry Demarest Lloyd's *Wealth against Commonwealth* (1894), an effective exposé of the ruthlessness of modern monopolies such as Rockefeller's crushing of his competition (mentioned previously), had an explicitly Christian message. Lincoln Steffens, in *The Shame of the Cities* (1897), advocated the golden rule as the key to social progress. One of the most popular novels of the whole era, and one of the most revealing of the moral sensibilities that could be aroused among middle-class Americans, was *In His Steps* (1896), authored by Charles M. Sheldon, a Kansas Congregationalist pastor. Sheldon envisioned what it would be like if the people of a small city consistently asked, "What would Jesus do?" Just by following this simple rule, Sheldon suggested, business and personal relationships could be revolutionized, and American civilization would move into a golden age.

The emerging social gospel movement, of which Sheldon's book was an early popular expression, can best be understood if you consider that it appeared only thirty years after American Protestants in the North were making the most extravagant predictions about the onset of a millennial age. The social gospel, which in many ways was "the Progressive movement at prayer," revived this millennial vision, though in a more moderate form. Whereas the earlier social millennialism grew out of revivalism (as in Charles Finney's era), the millennialism of the new social gospel earned its name as *social* gospel because it focused more strictly on saving the social order than on saving individual souls. "The kingdom of God" that Jesus had preached about was central to the social gospel. Social gospelers often played down the otherworldly aspects of understanding the kingdom and emphasized its relevance to the social problems of the day.

The two most important spokespersons for the social gospel were Washington Gladden (1836–1918) and Walter Rauschenbusch (1861–1918). Gladden, the pastor of a Congregational church in Columbus, Ohio, pointed out that the mainline Protestant churches were failing to reach the working classes. The reason, he thought, was that the laissez-faire economic theories of the day perpetrated injustice and hence alienated laborers. The ethics of Jesus, he insisted, would lead to economic theories that were more just to all classes of society.

Rauschenbusch, the other major spokesman, was a middle-class Baptist whose social conscience was quickened by work in a New York City church near the infamous Hell's Kitchen neighborhood. In 1897, he joined the faculty of Rochester Theological Seminary, where he produced major theoretical justifications for the social gospel. Rauschenbusch explicitly rejected traditional theologies that he believed distracted Christians from their social obligations. Even more strongly than Gladden, he rejected laissez-faire ethics as un-Christian and advocated moderate socialistic reforms. Concepts of God, he argued, had to be adjusted to the modern age. In the democratic age, the true meaning of the "Kingdom of God" must be understood as a social system working for the equality of all people. Such reforms, Rauschenbusch proclaimed, in broadly millennial terms still shared by many Americans, would lead to a "Christianizing of the social order."

Pragmatic Progressivism

While the moral impulse was central to Progressivism, and Christianity was explicitly or implicitly behind much of its moral fervor, another dimension of the Progressive outlook had almost nothing to do with religion. This was a scientific or social scientific attitude that, while subordinate before World War I, signaled the direction in which American public life would soon move.

Probably the clearest illustration of this outlook and its practical implications is in the work of Oliver Wendell Holmes Jr. (1841–1935), a justice on the United States Supreme Court from 1902 to 1932 and considered to be the most influential legal theorist of his day. Holmes argued that it was a misconception to think of civil law as either a question of morality or some natural law principles built into the scheme of the universe. Thus rejecting the characteristic eighteenth-century viewpoint with its implicitly religious assumptions, Holmes pointed the way to a typical twentieth-century outlook. The law, like everything else, was simply the product of social forces. Understanding it was a purely pragmatic exercise. "The object of our study," said Holmes, "is prediction, the prediction of the incidence of the public force through the instrumentality of the courts."[25] In other words, the lawyer was like a social scientist, who predicted what the courts would do and obtained the best for the client under the circumstances. The courts in turn could view the law as an evolving social experiment and use the best of modern social theory to improve its function. Moral absolutes were irrelevant.

A number of Progressives took a similar, purely pragmatic approach to reform. Among historians, for instance, one of the most famous was Charles A. Beard (1874–1948). In 1913, Beard published *An Economic Interpretation of the Constitution of the United States* in which he argued that the Constitution, far from being a quasi-sacred embodiment of natural law, was largely the product of its originators' economic interests. By challenging the myth of the Constitution's sacred origins, Beard helped clear the way for reinterpretations of the Constitution based on modern, pragmatic understanding of social needs. Though still in the minority, influential writers in many fields were questioning traditional absolutes.

A Revolution in Education

Views such as Holmes's and Beard's reflected a massive revolution in American education that had been taking place since just after the Civil War. Since schools are major transmitters of the society's values and train its most influential spokespersons, this revolution was of far more than academic interest.

This revolution had especially profound implications for mainline Protestants since, at the beginning of this era, they controlled most of American education. In public education, as we have seen, this control was substantial earlier in the nineteenth century. When the common school system spread during the first half of that century, most public schools were virtually Protestant.

Beginning in the middle decades of the nineteenth century, Catholic protests forced some secularization of the public schools. Protestants found this solution preferable to providing Catholics and other religious groups with tax support for their own schools. Protestants usually were satisfied with the more vaguely Christian ethos of the public schools. Although *McGuffey's Eclectic Readers* continued as the most popular texts throughout the nineteenth century, the later editions contained little of explicit Protestantism. In order to serve the larger public, the editors had replaced any identifiably theological concerns with broad lessons in middle-class morality, values, and patriotism. Protestants generally were not alarmed by that degree of secularization. As historian Robert Lynn put it, they simply had a firm belief in "the inherent and inevitable harmony of public education and the Protestant cause."[26]

During this same period, a similar process happened in American higher education, but with more momentous implications for a continuing Protestant dominance. At the end of the Civil War, most American colleges were explicitly Protestant. The vast majority had clergymen as presidents, required students to attend chapel, possessed strict moral codes, and taught Protestant theology and Christian ethics in courses. In 1865, the book most highly regarded by the majority of American academics was the Bible.

By 1917, the situation changed drastically. Although many of the most respected schools still had some church control, the sectarian features of their programs had disappeared or become optional. As the quotation at the beginning of this chapter suggests, evangelical Christianity had given way to religion defined as moral concern. Most professors would have been embarrassed to claim the Bible as an authority, except perhaps as a moral inspiration.

Revolution in Beliefs

At the heart of this transformation in collegiate education was a profound revolution in the fundamental beliefs that educated Americans took for granted. It would be difficult to overestimate the impact of this transformation, especially for religion. Traditional beliefs that were accepted as the height of educated respectability in 1865 seemed by 1917 badly out of step with intellectual fashion.

The specific changes in belief were almost all part of a greater pattern. Intellectual inquiry was shifting from concern with discovering fixed, absolute truths toward looking for natural explanations of how changes take place. At a time when Western civilization was rapidly changing and diversifying, understanding the processes that caused change seemed especially intriguing. Such analysis was attractive because it employed the newly revered scientific methodologies.

This transformation was a major turning point in Western thought. Ever since the Greeks, intellectual inquiry had been directed at discovering fixed truths that were assumed to be built into the scheme of things. Now the modern intellectuals were proclaiming that truth is culturally bound and always changing and that the natural and cultural forces that produce various beliefs are the only forces to be looked at.

The new social sciences were an important manifestation of this transition. Through them, traditional norms could be relativized. Rather than inquire how civil law might reflect natural law, as America's founders had, the new social sciences could view social norms and laws as customs, explained by the social forces shaping a society. Auguste Comte (1798–1857), an early European prophet of social science, had proclaimed that human society went through three ascending stages: theological, metaphysical, and positive stages. The theological stage was when the society claimed divine sanction for social laws. The metaphysical stage was when truth was sought in a philosophy of natural law. Finally, the highest, or "positive," stage was when social law would be based on scientific inquiry. Science thus promised a secular millennium.

William Graham Sumner (1840–1910) of Yale, an early proponent of social science in America, held a similar view. Trained for the ministry, Sumner found a new faith in scientific analysis of natural forces. Later in his career, he remarked that one day he had put his religious beliefs in a drawer; twenty years later he opened the drawer and the beliefs were gone. The conclusions of Sumner's social science reflected the rugged individualism of the Gilded

Age. A champion of what had become known as social Darwinism, he considered religious and moral factors "sentimental." In a striking depiction of humans as products solely of nature, he proclaimed that "man" had "no more right to life than a rattlesnake; he has no more right to liberty than any wild beast; his right to the pursuit of happiness is nothing but license to maintain the struggle for existence. . . ."[27]

As the Progressive Era approached, America's new social scientists turned from dog-eat-dog individualism toward a view that the government, informed by social science, should employ the human mind to control social developments for the good. Such reformist views took for granted moral values worth fighting for. Moreover, not all the early social scientists had abandoned explicit Christianity as thoroughly as Sumner. Richard T. Ely (1854–1943), for instance, the prime mover in the founding of the American Economics Association in 1886, was a champion of the social gospel. Modern economics, he held, could be used for Christianizing society.

Ely, however, represented a transitional stage. John Dewey (1859–1952) was more representative of the way American academia was moving. Dewey was a significant exponent of pragmatism and a promoter of influential modern educational theories. Until the 1890s, Dewey held definite Christian views; gradually, however, he adopted a social outlook that was essentially an updating of Auguste Comte. He believed that human society had long been enslaved by restrictive religious restraints. True progress was possible only if we recognized that we live in "an open world" where "change rather than fixity is the measure" and science is used to reach limited human goals.[28]

The Symbol of Darwinism

Darwinism was part of this larger thought pattern and became its chief symbol. Charles Darwin's (1809–82) views on biology, announced in *On the Origin of Species* in 1859, made the same explanatory move that was being made in many other fields at the time. Just as Karl Marx was explaining social change through the laws of "scientific socialism" and Sigmund Freud later explained psychological difficulties through attempts to understand the unconscious mind, Darwin explained the development of biological species by a hypothesis based on the premise that changing natural forces were the only relevant considerations.

Darwinism was immensely important for Western thought, since prior to that time no one proposed a plausible explanation for human origins that did not involve some sort of designer and creator. Although many intellectuals had doubted the truth of Christianity, few were atheists, since the design in the universe seemed to entail a designer. This was especially true in America, where there had been few professed atheists.[29]

While Darwin left many questions unanswered, his explanation made it intellectually plausible to believe that human life was the product of a chance universe.

Darwin offered his explanation at a time when many intellectuals were eager to break away from the constrictions of traditional Christianity. This was especially true in England, where the Anglican Church still had a firm control on university education and where anticlerical feeling was strong among some intellectuals. Such intellectuals enthusiastically adopted Darwin's biology, in part because it supported their larger naturalistic worldview, that is, a view in which only natural explanations of things were allowed. England's T. H. Huxley, nicknamed "Darwin's Bulldog," coined the word "agnostic" in 1869 to describe the new outlook. In contrast to atheists, who denied God's existence, agnostics said they simply did not know if God existed since science could not answer such questions.

In the United States, the advent of Darwinism and similar outlooks limiting explanations to scientific analyses of natural changes coincided with the transitions from colleges to universities. The old-time colleges were like advanced preparatory schools with strict discipline and a combination of classical and Christian learning. Professors, many of whom were clergy, were often generalists. In order to transform these institutions into universities, it was necessary to professionalize and to specialize. Similar developments were taking place in many areas of late-nineteenth-century American life, including business, law, and medicine. For the developing universities, the new scientific learning was especially useful. The standards of natural science provided a model for establishing specialized expertise in other disciplines. The new science's bias against introducing explicitly religious concerns into learning offered a rationale for breaking with the older, sometimes amateurish, Christian learning.

Darwinism could be especially useful for such campaigns. Andrew Dickson White (1832–1918), for instance, was the first president of Cornell University, founded in 1868 as a center to train people in technical expertise. The university avoided religious connections and was accused by some local clergy of being too secular. In 1869, White lectured to a New York audience on "The Battle-fields of Science." Eventually, he published a two-volume *History of the Warfare of Science with Theology in Christendom*, one of a number of books promoting the warfare metaphor as a way to understand the relationship between Christianity and science. Ignoring that Christians had been the leading proponents of modern science and that earlier battles were largely *among* Christians, White and others argued that science was on the side of modernity and progress and that traditional Christianity represented the superstition and prejudices of the Dark Ages.[30]

While Darwinism itself did not immediately create the sort of consternation among the clergy that is sometimes supposed, the ambivalence of the churches toward the new science lent some credibility to the warfare idea. Protestants typically cited the scientific evidence of design in the universe as a chief argument for a designer. Darwinism threatened this argument, putting the prestige of science on the opposing side. Moreover, in American folk Christianity, the Bible was often taken very literally. Especially in the South after the Civil War, Darwinism was cited as evidence of growing apostasy in modern Yankee civilization and a turning from the Bible. In the latter decades of the nineteenth century, a number of southern professors lost their jobs for teaching that biblical creation and evolution could be harmonized.

Despite such opposition, the broader reaction of the Northern Protestant establishment to Darwinism was toward harmonizing the new science with Christianity. So long as one did not accept Darwin's premise that natural forces were *all* there were, evolution could be seen as God's method of creating, much as photosynthesis could be viewed as God's way of providing crops. Conservative biblicists in the North often added that God could have intervened in the evolutionary process to create the human soul, as described in Genesis.[31] Such issues could seemingly be resolved. The more ominous issue for the Protestant establishment was not so much Darwinism itself as the rise of an exclusively naturalistic worldview, of which Darwinism was an important part. If a purely naturalistic science became the civilization's highest authority, what room would be left for Christianity?

Higher Criticism of the Bible

The focal point for the encounter between the two worldviews was at first not so much biology as the Bible itself. At the same time that Darwinism and other new scientific outlooks were being debated, the educated American Protestant community was being hit with shock waves of new biblical criticism. Modern biblical criticism, which went back to the Enlightenment, had already developed in the prestigious German universities during the first half of the nineteenth century. When it was imported to America during the second half of the century, it arrived in mature and formidable forms.

The new "higher criticism" was based on the same premises as the other nineteenth-century sciences. Modern scholarship, it proclaimed, should consider only natural causes that explained change or development. This approach involved an entirely new way of looking at the Bible, which up to that time most American scholars regarded as supernatural in origin. If viewed, on the other hand, as a purely natural product, the Bible appeared quite different. It was simply the product of the evolving religious experience of the Hebrew people and the early Christians. The miracles, which were always taken as evidence of the Bible's authenticity, now became problems.

The premises of the new scholarship also challenged the uniqueness of Christianity. In thoroughly nonsupernaturalistic explanations, Christianity would be viewed exactly like other world religions—as the product of historical and cultural causes.

In the late nineteenth century, the most serious social and intellectual challenge faced by the American Protestant establishment was what to do with the claims of this new scholarship. Although most of its conclusions were simply restatements of its radical naturalistic premises, it had on its side the prestige of the best historical science of the day. Moreover, some of the specific issues it raised about traditional understandings of the Bible, such as who authored some of the books, were difficult to answer on any premises.

The Modernist Impulse

This crisis over the Bible and the uniqueness of Christianity triggered a major shift in theology among some of the leadership in mainline Protestantism, especially at theological seminaries where clergy were trained.

Although there were various solutions to the problems, the broad outline can be described as typically fitting the rise of the modernist principle. Although the term *modernism* did not arise until the early twentieth century, by the late nineteenth century, American Protestant leaders were endorsing the idea. To save Christianity from higher criticism of the Bible, these Protestant leaders asserted that Christianity was not as exclusively dependent on the authority and accuracy of the ancient book as had been previously supposed. Rather, the Bible was the seed from which a higher Christianity evolved in modern civilization. When we have the oaks of civilization, said Henry Ward Beecher, America's most famous preacher of the post–Civil War era, why should we "go back and talk about the acorns?"[32] The modernist principle, then, reflected the optimistic and progressive principles of the era: a higher Christianity had evolved from the Bible and could be found in the best of modern civilization.

New Theologies

Such emphases coincided with a growing reaction against traditional theologies. Since the days of the Puritans, American theology had been dominated by Calvinist groups. Calvinism emphasized the sovereignty of God and the absolute dependence of humans on God's grace: all humans deserved damnation because of their rebellion against God, but God had chosen to save some through the atoning work of Christ. In the eighteenth and nineteenth centuries, popular Methodist theology slightly tempered Calvinist teachings by providing people with a more cooperative role in salvation, but the hard teachings that, except for God's saving grace in Christ, people would deservedly be damned were still standard teaching.

The new views of the Bible triggered a reaction against such traditional theologies. For one thing, they suggested that the Bible need not be taken as literally as it traditionally was. Rather, the more positive essence of the Christian message could be emphasized. This essence would be more in harmony with the increasingly optimistic view of human nature that had been building in America since the Enlightenment and was reinforced during the romantic era. In these more modern views, humans were not regarded as naturally depraved or sinful. Rather, they were seen as potentially good, though often misguided. In the new liberal or modernist theologies, Christian teaching blended with such emphases.

Such new theology gradually developed on the American Protestant scene in the decades leading up to World War I. Because the process was gradual, and because it was generally an era of optimism and church growth, these new theologies did not precipitate a severe crisis. Proponents of the new views often continued to use traditional biblical language, only giving it new meanings that nonetheless retained some continuity with the traditional spirit of American Protestantism.

Two such emphases particularly helped theologians and preachers meet the challenge of the new science and biblical criticism. One was that Christianity was basically a matter of the heart. Hence, Christians who knew Jesus in their hearts did not need to fear modern scientific challenges. Religion dealt with a higher level of truth than science. Secondly, and just as important, the new theologies emphasized that the essence of Christianity was morality. Like the emphasis on the heart, morality had always been strong in the American revivalist heritage. Popular Protestantism, moreover, was often antitheological, stressing that your actions were more important than the details of what you believed. Modern theology was thus a theology of action. The social gospel was one manifestation of its spirit. Cooperative action could unite Christians and transform the world.

Filled with such assurance, establishment Protestants, despite the deep challenges they faced, moved with confidence toward what to them looked like an unlimited future. The twentieth century would be "The Christian Century," as the title of one of their church magazines labeled it. Working together, the major denominations formed the Federal Council of Churches in 1908. The new federation immediately produced a progressive social creed and set up commissions for cooperative missions and evangelism. The era of ecumenical Christianity seemed well under way, and optimists talked of a full union of Protestant churches as older theological issues faded.

By dropping some of the offensive and exclusive features of the evangelical heritage but retaining the moral fervor and some substantial symbols of piety, liberal Protestants were successfully drawing people from many of the diverse American tribes into their melting pot. Liberal Protestants still dominated American politics, education, and public life. In a pluralistic society, such dominance would have been difficult to maintain if they had continued to preach the exclusivist dogmas of their evangelical forebears. Now, however, they could hope to control a broadly Christian civilization that emphasized common moral ideals that could be widely shared.

CHAPTER 5

Pluralistic America: 1860–1917

If there were one religion in England, its despotism would be terrible; if there were only two, they would destroy each other; but there are thirty, and therefore they live in peace and harmony.

Voltaire

If one way to understand the formative years of the emerging modern United States is to look at the dominant culture that attempted to shape and control a national consensus, an equally important theme is that of America as a diverse pluralistic society. Much of American history reflects the ongoing tensions between these centripetal and centrifugal forces shaping the culture. Moreover, for each new subgroup that was not Anglo-Protestant, a major question would arise concerning what its central identity would be. To what extent would it conform to the Anglo-Protestant model, and to what extent would the subgroup retain another distinct identity? For answering such questions, religion often played a crucial role.

The Varieties of Catholic Experience

These themes were played out on the largest scale in the American Catholic communities, especially in the era from the Civil War to the early twentieth century. During this time, the Catholic population continued its amazing growth. In 1860, Catholic Americans numbered over three million; by 1930, the number had grown to almost twenty million, or about one-sixth of the American population and one-third of church memberships. In numbers, the United States was not nearly as Protestant a country as it was in tradition. By 1928, a Catholic, Al Smith, was the Democratic nominee and made a serious run for the presidency.

Throughout this era, American Catholicism was continually being shaped by ethnic communities made up largely of new immigrants. In such communities, religion often played a larger role than it had in the immigrants' native lands, since religion became one of the most tangible ways of retaining a distinct identity. Moreover, the church provided the principal social organizations for ethnic groups in cities. For instance, in a typical working-class Chicago Irish parish in 1896, the church sponsored twenty-five societies that provided everything from charitable organizations to baseball teams and enlisted well over ten thousand members.[1] Such networks were especially important for ethnic communities where English was a second language. Moreover, each of life's major turning points, from birth to death, was marked by a solemn church sacrament and was an occasion for the most important gatherings of family, friends, and neighbors.

Catholicism, embracing people from many nations and traditions, was far from monolithic; hence, it had its own internal versions of the perennial American problem of unity and diversity and of relating the many subtraditions to the one church. Ethnic loyalties continued to be the principal source of tension among Catholics, and inevitably, these tensions grew as new ethnic groups swelled American cities. In the mid-nineteenth century, the principal rivalries were between Germans and Irish. By the later nineteenth century, the Irish emerged as the dominant group in church hierarchy, a situation that was deeply resented by almost everyone else. In the late nineteenth and early twentieth centuries, millions of Italians and Poles emigrated to America, each creating major communities with distinctive religious styles and strong ethnic loyalties. Groups of French, French Canadian, Portuguese, Belgian, Slovak, Croatian, Hungarian, and Spanish-speaking Catholics each built smaller communities as well.

Immigrant communities were often divided within themselves, not only over questions of how much to Americanize but also by regional attitudes imported from their native countries. Italian Americans, for instance, were deeply divided between northern Italians, who came from more urban, industrial areas, and southern Italians and Sicilians, who had preserved a peasant culture. Northerners were especially critical of the southerners' festivals and folk religion, which they considered superstitious and feared gave all Italians an unfavorable, "backward" image. Italians were also divided politically. Italy had just been united in the 1860s under a democratic and nationalist regime. This regime was bitterly opposed by the papacy, which lost most of its lands and political power to the unification movement. The papacy accordingly discouraged Catholics from participating in Italian politics. Such tensions between modern democratic secularism and the church were imported to America, dividing the immigrant community and complicating the processes of Americanization. Though the particular patterns were different in each case, every immigrant community embodied such serious internal divisions.

Despite this bewildering diversity both among and within ethnic groups, it is still possible to perceive an overall Catholic style, as well. Most Catholic immigrants to America came from peasant backgrounds, sharing some common European heritages. Catholic historian Jay Dolan, while noting variations between older and newer American Catholics and among the many imported traditions, still characterizes a "Catholic ethos."

While eighteenth-century American Catholics were influenced by the republican heritage, by the late nineteenth century, Catholic communities were conspicuous, first of all, in their emphasis on authority. The overriding authority of the church was one of the things that had always distinguished Catholicism from Protestantism. In the nineteenth century, Catholic authoritarianism was reinforced by the inherently conservative nature of immigrant communities. The church in America was technically a missionary church until 1908 and was directly under the authority of the Vatican. The Vatican, in the meantime, had its own problems, making it more authoritarian than ever. When the Vatican lost its political power to Italian nationalism, the church responded at the first Vatican Council in 1870 by strengthening its spiritual authority. The council declared, among other things, the infallibility of the pope when officially speaking on spiritual matters. American Catholics were in general receptive to such declarations. *Roma locuta est; causa finita est* ("Rome has spoken; the case is closed") became a popular motto in America.[2]

The second feature of the Catholic ethos, an emphasis on sin, was one that was shared by many nineteenth-century American Protestants as well. Christian Americans of all sorts would hear similar messages instructing them to avoid worldliness and sins such as drunkenness, violence (except in warfare), and personal impurity. Catholics, like Protestants, had periodic revivals, called parish missions, in which visiting priests would warn the Catholics of the dangers of hell if their sins were not forgiven. The principal difference in the message was that while Protestant preaching tended to emphasize individual experience of commitment and personal resolve to live a pure life, Catholic preaching stressed reliance on formal church practices, especially the regular confessions of sin to one's priest and acts of penance and devotion. Salvation was believed to come from the grace of God in either case, and the life of faith for either Protestant or Catholic was largely a matter of self-discipline. For Catholics, however, the institutional church was the reservoir of grace, so that grace was channeled through its sacraments, and the life of faith was guided by following prescribed church practice.[3]

These theological understandings led to other distinctions of the Catholic-ethos emphasis on ritual and openness to the supernatural. Not only did typical Catholic spirituality involve faithful observance of the church's rituals and ceremonies, but it also usually involved personal devotional exercises, such as praying the Rosary or other prayers to an array of saints who had special functions in helping the faithful in everyday life. Although Protestants as well as Catholics would expect answers to prayer, in general the Catholic emphases on numerous saints and tangible rituals kept them more open to the supernatural dimensions of reality than their Protestant counterparts. In either case, and especially among almost any people with agrarian ties, such beliefs were often mixed with considerable folk religion that went beyond specific church teachings.[4]

The central theme for Catholicism in America remained that of establishing their own identity in relation to the host culture.

One of the most practical areas where this theme emerged concerned schools. Initially, almost all schools in America were Protestant. A "public" school was simply a school that performed a public function; religious agencies, private organizations, or communities could all sponsor public schools and expect tax support. When Catholics became a sizable religious group, they soon found they were not welcome to participate as equal partners in this arrangement. When they suggested that their own Catholic schools receive tax support, they were rejected.

The key battles over this issue were fought in New York City in the 1830s and 1840s. The Public School Society, which operated the public schools, was a private agency run by Protestants. The Catholic bishop, John Hughes, insisted that Catholic schools receive equal support. He pointed out that the public schools taught Protestant doctrine and included Protestant religious exercises, such as reading from the King James Version of the Bible. A political campaign to obtain justice for Catholic schools failed. Protestants were forced to make their schools somewhat less sectarian and more secular, but they preferred to have more secular schools for everyone than allow any tax support for Catholic schools.[5]

Bishop Hughes and other Catholics had little choice but to build their own parochial school systems. This was a matter of some dispute in the Catholic community, since some Catholics saw the alternative schools as hindering the process of Americanization. Nonetheless, by the late nineteenth century, Catholic parochial education became one of the most important institutions perpetuating the identity of Catholic communities. The schools were especially important in non-English-speaking communities since they helped preserve ethnic and religious identity as well. Some Protestant ethnic groups, especially the Missouri Synod Lutheran and the Dutch-American Christian Reformed, who had a strong confessional heritage that separated them from American evangelicalism, built their own school systems for similar reasons.

The Americanist Controversy

For Catholics, as for every immigrant community, the debate over how far to Americanize was an ongoing one. The Catholic situation was complicated by the politically conservative stance of the Vatican in reaction to nationalism and political liberalism. Some Catholics, by contrast, shared the more progressive American outlook of the day and thought that Catholicism should adjust to that spirit. One of the early leaders of this Americanist movement was Isaac Hecker (1819–88), a mid-century convert to Catholicism who founded the Paulist Fathers, an order of priests. Throughout the rest of the nineteenth century, a small but very influential group of Irish Catholic leaders, including most prominently James Cardinal Gibbons (1834–1921), archbishop of Baltimore, worked for modest changes in emphasis, such as less stress on devotional supernaturalism and more openness to political liberalism, that they thought would keep the church up-to-date with its American setting. Unlike the Protestant liberals of the day, they generally did not suggest departures from traditional doctrine—only changes in style and tone. One item, for instance, that brought opposition from German-American Catholics was that the Americanists joined the Protestants in advocating prohibition of alcoholic beverages, one of the leading progressive reforms.

The more basic stance of the Americanists, however, precipitated a serious crisis. Pope Leo XIII (1878–1903) had seemed a friend to progressive causes, particularly in his encyclical *Rerum Novarum* of 1891, which, while condemning socialism, called strongly for justice for organized labor. The pope, however, soon put the brakes on any incipient progressive American

Catholicism, issuing another encyclical in 1895 that declared the American separation of church and state was not the ideal condition for the Catholic Church. Rather, said the pope frankly, the church would be better off if "in addition to liberty, [the church] enjoyed the favor of the laws and the patronage of public authority." Much to the chagrin of the Americanists, the pope was saying that the Catholic Church ought to be established by the state.

The next incident increased the papal pressure against the Americanists, though in part it was based on a misunderstanding. In 1897, a translation of a biography of American Catholic reformer Isaac Hecker was published in France. The translator suggested that Hecker's less authoritarian American style should be the model for modern Catholicism. This provided fuel for some Catholic liberals in France who were unhappy with papal authority. The Spanish-American War in 1898 did not enhance the pope's view of America. In 1899, he issued another encyclical, addressed directly to Cardinal Gibbons, condemning Americanism. The pope's definition of Americanism fit the views of French theological liberals better than it did American progressives, whose theology remained quite orthodox. Cardinal Gibbons replied that he knew of no American Catholic "who has ever uttered such enormities" as the pope condemned. Despite the fact that the pope was condemning what the American leaders called a "phantom heresy," their campaigns for an American church in tune with the spirit of the age were effectively intimidated.

The Triumph of Catholic Conservatism

The sequel to the incident described above almost entirely shut down progressive Catholicism. The more basic issue when the popes talked about "Americanism" was theological liberalism, which they saw as the inevitable outgrowth of any general policy of adjusting religion to the spirit of the times. One manifestation of this concern was that in 1898, at the height of the Americanist furor, the Vatican condemned Father John C. Zahm, a professor of physics and chemistry at the University of Notre Dame, for teaching theistic evolution—God could use evolutionary means as a method of creation. A broader step was the papal condemnation of theological "modernism," issued by Pius X in 1907. "Modernism" covered all the efforts in adjusting Catholic doctrine to the spirit of the modern age, especially to modern science and biblical criticism. While many American Protestant churches were moving rapidly to new theologies, the early growth of Progressivism in American Catholicism was effectively nipped in the bud.

The outcome was, thus, a triumph for the conservative forces that had always been strong in the American churches in any case. In the battle for self-identity, a more distinctly Catholic definition triumphed over a more typically American one. During the next generation, while many mainline Protestant institutions lost much of their distinctiveness, Catholics built a solid framework of their own institutions. The intellectual life of their universities was conservative, dominated by the classic, medieval Catholic outlook of Thomas Aquinas. While during this time Catholic schools provided little intellectual leadership outside their immediate circles, nonetheless, unlike their mainline Protestant counterparts, they retained schools at all levels with a distinctly Catholic outlook. This was just one manifestation of the wider American Catholic experience during the first half of the twentieth century. Ethnic neighborhoods in American cities retained their coherence, and the church remained an important defining feature. Catholics were in many ways becoming the most typical of Americans, yet they knew they were Catholics. Through preservations of neighborhoods and of distinct practices, such as eating fish instead of meat on Fridays, they retained a Catholic identity.

Support of conservatism varied by class. The church-going Americans most likely to adopt progressive or modernist theological views were middle-class, white northerners of older ethnic stock who belonged to the most prestigious mainline Protestant denominations. Churchgoers who did not fit that profile, Protestant as well as Catholic, were more likely to support more traditional emphases on the supernatural dimensions of Christianity. Hence, the social location of most Catholics, as ethnic working-class outsiders, fostered strong popular support for the conservatism of the international church and its American hierarchy.

Non-Anglo Protestants

The vast immigrations of the era from the Civil War to World War I included many Protestants as well as Catholics. Most of these Protestants were from non-English-speaking regions such as Germany, Scandinavia, and the Netherlands. High percentages of these immigrants settled in the rich farmlands of the Midwest, though substantial numbers also crowded in ethnic ghettos in the cities, following the dominant Catholic pattern.

In each of these groups, the tensions over Americanization were as strong as among Catholics. Retaining one's native language and an ethnic community was crucial to retaining identity, especially for first-generation immigrants. A strong, homogeneous religious heritage could reinforce this impulse, since holding onto such a spiritual heritage was framed as a matter of loyalty to God himself.

The largest group of such non-Anglo Protestants was Lutheran, primarily from Germany and Scandinavia. Substantial numbers of Germans had settled in the New World since the eighteenth century. Germany, however, before 1871 was a collection of separate states divided among Protestants and Catholics. Beginning around the 1840s, German immigration to the United States vastly increased, and as among the Catholics, by the early twentieth century, the numbers of new Lutheran immigrants overwhelmed the older Lutheran groups in America.

The result was that Lutheranism, while vigorous in America, was divided in a bewildering number of ways. Already, before the mass immigration at mid-century, Lutheran churches were divided between American Lutherans, who emphasized affinities with the dominant evangelicals, and traditionalists, who stressed the uniqueness of the Lutheran confessions, a staid and non-revivalist style, and services often in the German language. The new immigrant groups were already divided by additional language and ethnic differences. Moreover, in each of these communities, the struggles over Americanization were recapitulated, often continuing well into the twentieth century. America's crusade against Germany in World War I provided incentives for German Americans to abandon the German language and to Americanize. Most other national groups were moving toward English worship services at about that same time. Some successful unity efforts merged many of the smaller local Lutheran synods into national denominations, a process that continued throughout the twentieth century. Nonetheless, some sizable Lutheran groups retained their independence, and others, especially those in rural areas with fairly stable populations such as Minnesota, retained strong identities that were both ethnic and Lutheran.

Dutch immigration, while much smaller in numbers, provides a similar variation on the Americanization story. Most Dutch Protestants were Reformed, or Calvinist. The early Dutch Reformed Church from the colonial era had by the nineteenth century come to look much like other American evangelical churches. When numbers of Dutch immigrants swelled after the Civil War, some of the Reformed immigrants joined the existing Dutch Reformed church, the Reformed Church in America. Others, usually coming from groups that had already broken away from the state Reformed Church in the Netherlands, deemed the Reformed Church in America as too American and lax. They formed their own Christian Reformed Church, which fostered a strong separate identity by building its own complete educational system and carefully preserving its confessional and ethnic heritage.

Eastern Orthodox Churches

Some ethno-religious groups had fewer opportunities for blending into the American scene. This was especially true for later immigrants whose traditions were new to the United States. Asian immigrants, for instance, had little choice but to remain in separate enclaves where they were usually content to preserve their own religious heritage. Much less distinct, because there was no racial factor involved and their religion was Christian, was the experience of Eastern European immigrants who belonged to the Eastern Orthodox Church. Nonetheless, their distinctive heritage made them seem outsiders much more than non-Anglo Protestants or even Catholics.

The Eastern Orthodox Church had roots as far back as the ancient churches of the Eastern Roman Empire. In medieval times, after the Eastern Empire was separated from the West, these Eastern churches and the Roman Catholic Church separated. In the modern era, Eastern Orthodox churches remained the official state churches of Greece, much of Eastern Europe, and of Russia.

Eastern Orthodox churches seemed strange in the American setting, largely because immigrants from these countries were relatively rare before 1900. After that time, immigrants from nations with Orthodox churches numbered well in the millions, including Russians, Greeks, Ukrainians, Albanians, Bulgarians, Serbians, and Rumanians. As a result of this diversity, Orthodox churches in America have been divided into many ethnic subgroups, with the largest being the Greek, followed by the Russian. Survival of the Orthodox churches, accordingly, has depended largely on survival of ethnic identity. In the twenty-first century, far more Americans self-identify as Orthodox than are active in Orthodox churches. Due largely to their degree of isolation based on ethnic identities, Orthodox Christians as such have had little impact on the wider American life. Being transplants from old-world state churches, and not being nearly as large or as united as Catholics, they have preserved distinct identities. Their highly distinctive worship and liturgies represent one of the oldest traditions of Christendom, and these, together with their continuities with the theologies of the ancient church, have attracted converts from among other Americans looking for alternatives to the popular styles of much of contemporary Christianity.

Judaism in America

The role of Jews and Judaism in shaping mainstream American culture makes a startling contrast to that of Eastern Orthodoxy. Although the total numbers of the ethnic constituencies of the two groups have been comparable (maybe five to seven million in the twenty-first century, depending on how one counts), and although there are parallels in times of immigration and areas of origin, the Jewish impact has been vastly disproportional relative to numbers. More than any non-Protestant immigrant group, Jews have become an integral part of the cultural activities of the nation, but at the same time, they have retained their ethnic identity.

One reason for the contrast is that religion has played a different role in the Jewish community than it has for the other ethnic groups that have already been discussed. Most ethnic groups came from nations where their religion was dominant, usually established by law. In the new land, traditional forms of that religion played a crucial role within the immigrant community but provided little help in relating to the larger culture. Those from the ethnic group who wished to retain a clear ethnic identity were likely to be traditionally religious. The options were traditional religious practice, drifting away to occasional traditional practice, or a total Americanization that would involve leaving both the religion and the ethnic community.

Jews, on the other hand, had long lived as a minority group in lands dominated by another group's religion and politics. Jews already had generations of the ghetto experience that other immigrants found new. Likewise, their ethnic identity was not dependent on their religious practices. While for the traditional observant Jew, the religious practices of keeping the law and observing the proper ceremonies were central to one's membership in the community, one retained an identity with the community even if one were not observant. Jewishness was simultaneously an ethnic and religious status.

The unusually influential role of Jews in the United States also reflected an economic difference from most other non-Protestant immigrants. Jewish immigrants, although typically in poverty when they arrived in America, generally did not come from peasant backgrounds as most Catholic or Orthodox immigrants did. Rather, Jews, who were exempted from laws against usury (lending money with an interest charge) in Europe, had long traditions as a commercial class. The early Jews who came to America, mostly from Spain and Portugal, were few, hardly numbering more than a thousand by the end of the colonial era, but many of them prospered. During the early nineteenth century, most Jewish immigration, which did not bring the total population of Jews to over one hundred thousand until the 1850s, was from Germany, often peddlers and merchants. Some of these immigrants became part of a commercial elite. In the late nineteenth century, this group of prosperous Jews was overwhelmed in numbers by Jews from Eastern Europe, especially Poland and Russia. Economic and cultural differences separated the two groups and created rivalries. Nonetheless, the Eastern European Jewish men were predominantly skilled craftsmen who, after initial years of poverty, soon moved toward economic success.[6]

Another factor contributing to the remarkable integration of Jews into American life was their affinity to the dominant Protestant culture. Ever since the days of the Puritans, many of the dominant Anglo-Protestants in America thought they were establishing a biblical civilization. Both the Puritans and some of their influential successors in the national era spoke of America as a "new Israel." Calvinist culture, which shaped much of the early American religious heritage, was especially shaped by the Old Testament, or the Hebrew Scriptures. Calvinists, more than most Protestant groups, saw their religious task as building a Christian civilization. To do so, they looked especially to the Old Testament model. Hence, American culture, perhaps more than that of any other modern nation, was shaped by ideals drawn from the Hebrew Scriptures. Until the twentieth century (when Americans forgot most of both), most Americans knew the history of the Jewish patriarchs as well or better than they knew their own history.

These traditions meant not only that Jewish values and outlooks fit well with the dominant Americanism, but that they also helped mitigate some of the ever-present prejudice against Jews. Early Puritans, for instance, treated occasional Jewish visitors better than they treated other outsiders. Although there was real discrimination against Jews and Jewish political and religious practice in colonial America, it was relatively mild compared with European counterparts. In Europe, the Jewish experience had been to be grudgingly tolerated in various nations for a time but then to be sometimes subjected to severe waves of persecution and popular anti-Semitism. In the United States, although there was anti-Semitism and exclusion of Jews from most prestigious organizations and schools, the discrimination was at least tempered by enough exceptions to provide attractive contrasts to the European alternatives.

In addition to a common biblical heritage, American Jews shared with Anglo-Protestants influences from the Enlightenment. Like the Calvinists, who also had disproportionate influence in shaping America, Jews valued education and the written word. By the eighteenth century, therefore, their religious heritage was supplemented by high respect for the reason of the day. As an oppressed people, they had a passionate commitment to American Enlightenment doctrines concerning equal rights for all.

The initially dominant thinking in the relatively small Jewish communities during the first half of the nineteenth century was to draw on these commonalities in order to blend in with the mainstream culture. Beginning as early as the 1820s, enlightened American Jews made efforts to reform ancient rites, such as dietary laws, and rituals of synagogue worship that they found unsuited for modern times. Out of such sentiments, which had their origins among Jews in Germany, grew a major Reform movement, engineered primarily by Rabbi Isaac Mayer Wise (1819–1900). Though opposed by traditionalists, Wise helped build a Reform movement that made this type of Judaism strikingly like a Protestant denomination. Probably the closest parallel was the Unitarian movement that grew out of Calvinism at the same time and also flourished among the well-to-do in urban centers. For Judaism, practice is more central than doctrine, so the principal reforms came in vastly simplified requirements for Jewish observance. Reform services were held in English, they were shorter, worshippers sang hymns, choirs and organs were introduced, and in some cases services were even held on Sunday rather than Saturday, which is the traditional Jewish Sabbath.

The growing tensions between the leaders of Reform and traditionalist movements were brought to a head by a dramatic incident. In 1883, at a banquet honoring the first graduating class of Hebrew Union College in Cincinnati, the center for Reform, the menu announced an opening course of shellfish, an item forbidden by strict Jewish dietary laws. Traditionalists and moderates stormed out. The eventual result was a three-way division of American Judaism into Reform, Conservative, and Orthodox. The Orthodox were those who strictly continued traditional practice. Conservative Judaism was a moderate movement between the other two. This group was conservative in the classic nineteenth-century sense of affirming the value of distinctly Jewish traditions, but it also allowed these traditions to evolve over time. Hence, Conservatives preserved more traditional practices than did members of the Reform movement, but they allowed some updating in the forms of such observance.

One can see, for instance, the degrees of concession to modernity in the treatment of women during worship services of the three groups. Orthodox practice required strict separation of women from men in worship, which was conducted totally by males. Conservatives condoned family seating in worship and allowed women to participate alongside men in communal worship. Reform Jews, like liberal Protestants, allowed women to read from the Torah and eventually took the lead in encouraging women to be rabbis.[7]

This three-way division came just as the Jewish situation was beginning to change dramatically through immigration. The latter decades of the nineteenth century were a time of increased racism and ethnic nationalism throughout the Western world. One reason for this was a reverence for the social science of the day, which was used to provide a Darwinist explanation for the supposed superiority of certain races in the struggle for survival. Such factors only provided a rationale for unleashing ancient hostilities and modern rivalries. Jews were among the chief victims of such renewed hostility, and in Eastern Europe and Russia, they were often driven from their homes by popular pogroms and persecutions. Between 1880 and 1900, over five hundred thousand Jews emigrated to America, and by 1920, nearly two million more had made the journey. New York City became easily the largest center of Jewish population in the world.

The new immigrants were almost all Eastern European, speaking a Yiddish or Polish dialect, and were initially very poor, bringing with them all the problems that poverty entails. The older Jewish population of well-to-do German Jews was often appalled and embarrassed by the conditions of their coreligionists and feared these conditions would breed anti-Semitism. Sharp "uptown" versus "downtown" differences emerged, as the New York version of the issue was described. The well-to-do uptowners had ambivalent feelings toward the newcomers who crowded the lower east side. The uptowners organized charities for the newcomers, but they mostly seemed to want these newcomers to get rid of their "foreign" ways as quickly as possible. As the title of Israel Zangwill's 1909 play, immensely popular among the uptowners, put it, they should merge into *The Melting Pot*. Said Zangwill, "[Here] all the races of Europe are melting and reforming. . . . God is making the American."[8]

The situation did not prove to be so simple. The Eastern European immigrants brought with them two principal tendencies. Many in the first generation reacted to their uprooting in the fashion typical of most immigrant groups, holding on tightly to their traditional religious practice. Another substantial group had already, in their homelands, become explicitly secular or antireligious. This group typically championed socialist solutions to the world's problems. Even though most of the Jewish community tended not to be highly organized politically, partially in reaction to Irish Catholic power, these ideological socialists provided the immigrant community with an important secular alternative to the explicitly religious heritage.

This secularizing tendency was soon accentuated, consistent with a principle known as "Hansen's law" (named for an early historian of immigration, Marcus Hansen): "What the son wishes to forget, the grandson wishes to remember."[9] While many of the first generation of Yiddish-speaking immigrants attempted to preserve their old-world heritage and religious practice, many in the second generation attempted to get away from their traditions. During the early decades of the twentieth century, this law operated more conspicuously in the Jewish communities than any other. By the 1930s, fewer than one third of Jewish families were members of any congregation, and three fourths of Jewish young people between the ages of fifteen and twenty had not attended any services for at least a year.[10]

Nevertheless, this strong secular alternative did little to weaken Jewish identity, which had been established over millennia. Cultural identity could be sustained, at least for a time, even without religious practice. Widespread anti-Semitism reinforced a strong sense of distinctiveness. Excluded from many mainstream institutions, the Jewish community built flourishing networks of organizations to care for almost every dimension of social life. At the same time, the secularization of the communities, as well as their growing affluence and high educational attainments, made it easier for some Jews to participate in the mainstream of American life, particularly in the media and in entertainment, without the encumbrance of distinctive religious practices. Rather than blend into a melting pot, however, they established a model for twentieth-century American pluralism in which a group maintained a strong continuing identity while at the same time participated with civility in the mainstream of public life.

The Christianity of African Americans

The experience for African Americans since the Civil War contrasts dramatically with that of Catholics and Jews. For Catholics and Jews, religious differences reinforced ethnic rivalries with the Anglo-Protestant establishment. African Americans, on the other hand, were kept outside the power structures more decisively than other groups, *despite* their religious stance. Blacks were overwhelmingly Protestant, almost all Baptist or Methodist, and their churches flourished and grew. Yet their theological affinities to white Protestantism provided them with little social advantage. There is probably no clearer illustration of the point that, while religion has been immensely important in shaping American life, it often is not the decisive force. Just as warfare often has brought coreligionists to the point of killing each other, so also have racial antagonisms outweighed religious affinities. To pick just one striking example, perhaps no two groups have been more deeply separated from each other socially than white Baptists and black Baptists in the South.

One way to understand the experience of the freed people (former enslaved people) is to consider the analogy to that of immigrant groups in America. Once slavery ended, the position of African Americans was, in principle, similar to that of some new immigrants. Slavery, of course, had not been their only social problem. They still faced the deep poverty and economic dependence of unskilled laborers. Such problems were compounded by lack of education and the almost total illiteracy imposed by slavery. Although these obstacles were massive, they were not vastly different from those faced by many immigrants. These obstacles became almost insurmountable, however, when combined with a third factor—racial prejudice. Just as anti-Semitism intensified throughout the world in the late nineteenth and early twentieth centuries, so racism intensified against African Americans. In the United States, racial prejudice was the central motif in whites' attitudes toward blacks and, even after the end of slavery, it kept blacks on the bottom economic and educational rungs of society.

During Reconstruction, so long as northern moral and religious idealism remained strong, hopes were raised of giving blacks a place in political life and in building educational institutions so that blacks might eventually take their place as equals in American life. The majority of northerners, however, soon reneged on any promise of equality. When Reconstruction ended, control of southern society and politics soon reverted to southern whites only. Having lost the war, most southern whites were deeply determined that they would not give up the principles for which they fought. One of those principles was that the South would be "a white man's country." Blacks were soon effectively eliminated from political influence, and Jim Crow segregation laws soon gave legal sanction to white supremacy. The South, which had always been a society in which evangelical religion and violence were dual motifs, continued in the same vein. During the 1890s, there were on average, three lynchings of blacks per week![11]

As was also true for immigrant groups, churches became for African Americans their principal institutions both for coping with the hard realities of life and for building up a sense of community. In fact, because of always-limited economic resources for building other institutions and because the churches were the one black institution over which whites allowed blacks full control, the church usually functioned as the central and only black institution in a community. Fine church buildings often were major sources of community pride. The churches also provided almost the only opportunity for black leadership. In fact, black churches typically had strong pastors who personally controlled the network of church organizations that served the black communities. W. E. B. DuBois (1868–1963), the famous African American sociologist, at the turn of the century observed that the black pastors of his day were "among the most powerful Negro rulers in the world." He observed also that "in the South, at least, practically every American Negro is a church member. Some to be sure are not regularly enrolled, and a few do not habitually attend services; but, practically, a proscribed people must have a social center, and that center for this people is the Negro church."[12]

After the Civil War, the organizational separation of blacks and whites into their own churches was welcomed by both groups. In the South, until the war, the groups had worshipped together in the same churches, with blacks segregated to the balconies. Blacks now generally forsook the white denominations, preferring their own organizations to servile roles in white organizations in which they were unwelcome. Many joined Northern Methodist denominations, including the African Methodist Episcopal Church and the African Methodist Episcopal Zion Church. By 1870, the blacks remaining in the Southern Methodist Church had organized into the separate Colored Methodist Episcopal Church (now Christian Methodist Episcopal Church).

Even more African Americans formed their own Baptist churches. Baptist churches are controlled by local congregations and therefore are very easy for groups of believers to establish. This strength could also be a weakness. It was much more difficult for Baptists to organize nationally. For several decades after the Civil War, black Baptists struggled to unite as a national denomination. In the meantime they organized many of their churches into state conventions and formed national Baptist agencies to promote foreign missions, especially to Africa. However, not until 1895 was the National Baptist Convention established as the largest organization of black Baptists. Tensions continued, however, and in 1916, the convention split in two, the larger group calling itself the National Baptist Convention, Inc., and the slightly smaller group keeping the name National Baptist Convention. Localism plus a perennial lack of surplus funds made it difficult for black churches to maintain effective national organization.[13]

Black churches nevertheless provided immensely important centers for self-help and self-development. African American women especially found opportunity in church auxiliary organizations for the mutual support, community service, and leadership denied them in the larger society. During the Progressive Era of the early 1900s, large, national black-church women's organizations played major roles in promoting ideals of respectability that were regarded as essential if blacks were ever to be accepted in the larger society.[14]

A number of issues were strongly debated within the black communities. The most persistent was what blacks' relationship should be to white society and to the support of friendly northern churchgoers. Initially, during Reconstruction, newly freed blacks were largely dependent on support from northern whites. Especially in the field of education, many former abolitionists sacrificially dedicated themselves to building black schools and training black leadership for subsequent generations. At the same time, some northern black leaders also promoted the cause. For instance, one of the most effective black educators of the day was Daniel Alexander Payne (1811–83), bishop of the African Methodist Episcopal (AME) Church. Born free in Charleston, South Carolina, Payne was driven out in the 1830s for organizing education of blacks. After the Civil War, he returned to South Carolina for the first South Carolina Annual Conference of the AME Church. Payne's principal leadership role, however, was as the first black president of a black-controlled college, Wilberforce University in Ohio. Payne's leadership at Wilberforce was an important model for building other black institutions. By the end of the century, black Christians had established some two dozen black colleges and benefited from other black institutions that had primarily northern white support.

Despite gratitude for white support, dependency was not a comfortable position. Some black leaders called for strengthening their own black institutions and thus establishing true independence. This tension was complicated by deteriorating race relations in the latter decades of the century.

The dominant African American spokesperson to emerge in the era was Booker T. Washington (1856–1915), a Baptist and head of Tuskegee Institute in Alabama. Washington promoted the middle-class work ethic of the day, proclaiming that if blacks were to escape from their poverty, they would have to work their way out. The first step in this process was learning practical industrial and agricultural skills. In the meantime, Washington proclaimed that blacks should accept their secondary status in society and cultivate all the white help and goodwill they could get. Of the two races, he proclaimed in a famous speech in Atlanta in 1895, "in all things purely social we can be as separate as the fingers, yet one as the hand in all things essential to mutual progress." Not only was this position music to the ears of white segregationists and even to white progressives who had given up on resolving America's race problem, but it was accepted by most blacks.

Unlike the experience of contemporary immigrant groups in America, integration and assimilation into American society were proving to be illusory and frustrating options for African Americans. Washington's compromise thus seemed to most to be as far as they could go at the time. As in other communities, however, there were dissenters. During the early decades of the twentieth century, these black leaders demanded that blacks again pick up the agenda of full participation in American society, or at least that they should be demanding their civil rights. Such demands did not come so much from the churches as from extra-ecclesiastical organizations, most notably the National Association for the Advancement of Colored People (NAACP), founded in 1909. W. E. B. DuBois, who abandoned his earlier Christian faith, was the most prominent spokesperson, calling for more radical demands to go beyond the status quo.

Within the black churches, a parallel tension developed regarding the degree to which they should affirm the distinctive African American traditions of worship. Northern blacks who had New England mentors before the war and northern white supporters who wanted to raise black educational standards generally thought that the black churches should move beyond the patterns of folk religion that had developed during the time of slavery. In the twentieth century, black sociologists, beginning with DuBois, uniformly said the same thing.

Nonetheless, many black Christians developed a distinctive style of worship that was truly their own and that they were not willing to give up. This style combined elements of evangelical revivalism with ecstatic African patterns of worship. Spirituals as a creative dialogue within the congregation, a form of music which anticipated the development of jazz, were particularly meaningful and uniquely black religious expressions. These patterns of worship, and the theologies they entailed, had served African Americans well during times of intense hardship by giving them hope. Therefore, these patterns persisted in the vast majority of black churches. As historian Lawrence Levine summarizes contemporary reports of black worship during the three-quarters of a century after emancipation:

> All the traditional trappings were there: the ecstasy, the spirit possession, the shouts, the chanted sermons, the sacred sense of time and space, the immediacy, the feeling of familiarity with God and the ancient heroes, the communal setting in which songs were created and recreated.[15]

This African-influenced black-American style proved to be not only a preservation of the past but also a building toward the future. When the Pentecostal movement emerged in America at the beginning of the twentieth century, perhaps its most influential early leader was a black pastor, William J. Seymour, principal preacher at the famed Azuza Street revivals in Los Angeles that began in 1906. Modern Pentecostalism, which developed out of a number of traditions in white evangelicalism, also incorporated substantial elements of black styles of ecstatic worship. In their early decades, Pentecostal churches and worship were, remarkably, often integrated; soon, however, the movement separated out into black and white denominations. The largest black Pentecostal group was the Church of God in Christ.

Like the white American communities, African Americans, despite their flourishing churches, faced strong currents of secularization as they entered the twentieth century. By the turn of the century, this secularization was signaled by the emergence alongside the spirituals of new forms of black musical expression—jazz, ragtime, and the blues. Although jazz and the blues sometimes incorporated religious elements, they also marked the development of a black culture outside the churches.

Such secularizing tendencies were accelerated in the early twentieth century by massive African American emigration to northern cities. There they founded churches, both traditional Baptist and Methodist, and newer storefront Pentecostal and sectarian ones. At the same time, the forces of highly differentiated urban life were causing a compartmentalization of the role of the church that would have been impossible in a southern town. Perhaps even more sharply than in most other ethnic communities, church was largely a special activity or Sunday affair for blacks, divorced from highly secular everyday realities. The black communities, like most of America, were both intensely religious and intensely secular. The biggest difference for the black communities was that for a disproportionate number of blacks, the expressions of these polarities were limited to ghettoes perpetually kept impoverished by a discriminatory social and economic system.

White Protestant Religious Outsiders and Protesters

American culture has always included a strong democratic, populist impulse. One of the areas of American life, perhaps *the* area, where this impulse has most often been expressed is religion. Historians of American democracy have been most interested in the rise of liberal politics and have not much noticed the democratic tendencies in religion, which they often regard as reactionary. Nonetheless, some of the most frequent protests against the authority of elite power structures have been populist religious movements. Religious dissent is, of course, easier to organize and carry out than political protest and perhaps is sometimes a substitute for it. Still, the protests are real and substantial. They are protests against those who define the values and the valuing of persons in a community. The first Great Awakening of the eighteenth century generated some such populist and sectarian movements and the extended second Great Awakening of the first half of the nineteenth century generated even more. The Christianity of enslaved Africans and much of African American Christianity were also largely people's movements. As the United States entered the twentieth century, such anti-elite movements continued to offer to white Protestants significant numbers of alternatives to the dominant denominational structures.

The issues involved in the formation of new sects were primarily spiritual issues rather than class issues, but the two were often intermixed. New groups invariably developed out of a conviction that the mainline denominations were not sufficiently spiritual. Though such opinions could have appeal to people in any social class, most of the new movements that offered a more radical spirituality and new, conspicuously distinctive communities of faith were likely to flourish among people who, for one reason or another, felt on the fringes of society.

The Holiness Movement

The best example of these dynamics is in the development of a striking number of holiness sects growing out of Methodism during the nineteenth century. Methodism during this period was America's largest and most typical Protestant denomination. From 1865 to 1920, the Methodist Episcopal Church (Northern) grew from one million to four million members, and its Southern Methodist counterpart grew from half a million to two million members. Methodism, like the other large denominational group, the

Baptists, remained a popular and largely evangelical movement during this period. In the nineteenth-century South, the saying was "A Methodist is a Baptist who wears shoes; a Presbyterian is a Methodist who has gone to college; an Episcopalian is a Presbyterian who lives off of his investments." By the late nineteenth century, especially in the North, such denominational stereotypes would not have applied for either Baptists or Methodists. Methodism was still the denomination of the modest middle classes, but it had also acquired considerable sophistication. Methodists, for instance, were becoming leaders in higher education, maintaining scores of colleges and a number of universities. Such gains were signs of respectability acquired over generations. Inevitably, this meant that despite vitality that fostered continued growth, the intensity of the early days of the movement was often missing.

Holiness movements, quite simply, called for a renewal of this intensity. These movements especially called for renewal of emphasis on personal holiness, such as in Methodist founder John Wesley's teachings. Already, these themes appeared in midcentury evangelicalism. Charles Finney, although he was a Presbyterian and Congregationalist, preached holiness doctrines. Phoebe Palmer taught them in her holiness meetings. The Wesleyan Methodist Church (1843) and the Free Methodist Church (1860) split from the parent denomination since they extended personal holiness to include radical views condemning slavery.

The example of Phoebe Palmer, a doctor's wife who held her holiness meetings in her spacious home, illustrates that the holiness protests were not necessarily related to social class. In the latter part of the nineteenth century, the movement continued to have well-to-do advocates, including some educated women leaders who took advantage of the movement's openness to spiritual authority regardless of gender.

Nonetheless, as the movement grew into something of a revival within Methodism, it spread furthest among simpler folk attracted to an old-time religious intensity. The principal expression of this movement was in "holiness camp meetings," which were organized into a national movement in Vineland, New Jersey, in 1867. By the 1880s, this had grown into numerous regional holiness associations on the edge of Methodism. Holiness teaching reemphasized the separation of the Christian from the world, saying that a dramatic conversion experience of being born again was not enough. Rather, one should also expect a "second blessing" of being filled, or baptized, by the Holy Spirit, which involved the eradication of "inbred sin." In addition, holiness teachers stressed two other doctrines not typically emphasized in mainline Protestantism: the power of miraculous healing and the expectation of Jesus's return at any moment to set up a millennial kingdom on earth. The holiness emphases were sometimes summarized as a fourfold or "foursquare" gospel of Christ as savior, as baptizer with the Holy Spirit, as healer, and as coming King.

By the 1890s, the holiness teachings led to splits within the Methodist denomination and the formation of a number of small holiness denominations, most of which formed into either the Church of the Nazarene or the Pilgrim Holiness Church. In the meantime, other holiness groups also emerged. The best known is the Salvation Army, founded by William Booth (1829–1912) in England in 1865, which soon flourished as an evangelistic ministry to the poor in the United States. The English origins point out a trans-Atlantic connection that still could be found in almost every evangelical development. The ministry to the poor both through charity and evangelism illustrates that such evangelistic movements were not concerned only with saving souls for the next life. Other new holiness organizations were the Christian and Missionary Alliance and the Church of God (Anderson, Indiana), one of a number of groups called the Church of God.

Pentecostalism

This quest to be set apart by spiritual intensity, a dramatic experience of the Holy Spirit, miraculous powers and expectations, and a holy life produced not only new holiness groups but also what by the later twentieth century became their much larger worldwide offspring—modern Pentecostalism. We have already noticed black contributions to Pentecostalism, or at least affinities of black traditions to emerging Pentecostalism, in an ecstatic style of worship. However, the main roots are clearly traceable to the turbulent holiness revivals of the late nineteenth century.

Many of the late-nineteenth-century holiness revivals were referred to as Pentecostal outpourings, which it was believed marked a new age of the Holy Spirit. Occasionally at revival services, people spoke in strange tongues, but such phenomena were not considered to have unusual doctrinal significance.

Modern Pentecostalism is usually dated, conveniently enough, from the first day of the twentieth century, January 1, 1901, when tongues-speaking broke out at a holiness revival service in Topeka, Kansas, as predicted by its leader Charles Fox Parham (1873–1929). In 1906, William J. Seymour, a black man who heard Parham teach, carried the new views to the Azuza

Street revivals in Los Angeles, which sparked a nationwide movement. At first, speaking in tongues often was interpreted as speaking actual foreign languages, such as Chinese. Later, it was usually regarded as speaking in unknown tongues that required an interpreter.

Early Pentecostalism appealed to disproportionate numbers of the economically poor, both white and black. During its formative stages, many competing doctrines emerged and literally hundreds of small denominations eventually formed. The largest Pentecostal groups to emerge were the predominantly black Church of God in Christ, the Church of God (Cleveland, Tennessee)—both organized earlier as holiness groups—and the Assemblies of God (organized in 1914).[16] This complex movement accentuated many developments that flourished first and best in the American environment. Lack of effective centralized church authority, and the ideal of equality for all people in the Spirit, opened room for spiritual innovation and enterprise among all classes.

One sign of the new age of the Spirit was believed to be the fulfillment of the prophecy in the book of Joel (2:28, KJV), repeated in the book of Acts (2:17, KJV) in the account of the first Christian Pentecost: "I will pour out my spirit upon all flesh; and your sons and your daughters shall prophesy." Holiness and Pentecostal groups accordingly had fewer inhibitions about women's leadership than did most Christian groups. Prominent among women leaders was Aimee Semple McPherson (1890–1944), who organized and ran the International Church of the Foursquare Gospel, a holiness-Pentecostal denomination headquartered in Los Angeles. McPherson, who had a magnetic appeal something like that of a Hollywood star, was one of the most successful women leaders of the era, the best-known woman preacher, and the head of a thriving urban church organization with many programs for service as well as evangelism.

Despite these accomplishments, McPherson's career also underscored the tensions that have often troubled some free-enterprise religious movements in which the leadership is subject to no ecclesiastical authority. McPherson was plagued by rumors of scandal, including in 1926 a dramatic "disappearance" into the sea, reported to be a cover for a rendezvous with her radio announcer. Once McPherson returned to Los Angeles, she was subjected to one of the most sensational trials of the century. Eventually, after months of newspaper headlines, all charges were dropped for lack of conclusive evidence. McPherson reestablished her ministry and continued her often-controversial work until 1944 when, while on an evangelistic campaign, she died of a barbiturate overdose. The denomination she founded,

The International Church of the Foursquare Gospel, continued to carry on her work.

Perhaps the most interesting cultural question suggested by the rise of holiness and Pentecostal movements in the late nineteenth and early twentieth centuries is why such teaching began to spread widely just at the period when industrialization and new technology were revolutionizing the world. A parallel question is why the doctrine of miraculous healing spread among Protestants just at a time when modern medicine finally began to make some real progress in healing people. Part of the answer to these questions must be that many people were reacting against the growing materialistic definitions of reality in the modern world. Middle- and upper-class people at this time often turned to romantic and idealistic philosophies that affirmed the primacy of the spiritual. Holiness and Pentecostal teachings, although not restricted to any class, and though (as in all religion) not always followed consistently by their adherents, provided another strongly spiritualistic alternative with which to define reality. In addition, growing individualism, and even the growing successes of modern medicine and health regimes, may have contributed to a turning away from fatalistic acceptance of disease as simply God's will. In a more modern and individualist setting, the alternative message had great appeal: Christians should expect supernatural interventions to overcome illnesses and other misfortunes.

Premillennialism

One of the four dogmas of the foursquare gospel of many holiness and Pentecostal groups was that Jesus would return to earth at any moment to set up a kingdom in Jerusalem for a millennium (a thousand years). This belief, known as premillennialism—that Jesus will return prior to the millennium—was in the late nineteenth century becoming popular among a wide variety of renewal movements on the revivalist side of American Protestantism. The view became so widespread, especially among those who were unhappy with the moderate or liberal drift of mainline Protestantism, that its rise becomes important for understanding many twentieth- and twenty-first-century religious movements.

Recall that in the mid-nineteenth century, millennial views were common within mainstream northern Protestantism. The dominant view then, however, was postmillennial, teaching that Jesus would return only *after* a golden age that would grow out of current cultural and social progress. Postmillennialists were thus optimistic about culture and fit with the dominant mood of nineteenth- and early-twentieth-century America. As observed earlier, the social gospel movement was a theologically liberal version of this hope to Christianize the social order.

Premillennialism was an older Christian belief, but its most common modern form, found in holiness, Pentecostal, and later fundamentalist and charismatic groups, grew out of a number of trends particularly strong in revivalist Christianity. Probably the strongest impulse was one found in all these renewal movements, a heightening of emphasis on the supernatural dimensions of Christianity. At the same time that moderate and liberal Protestants were blessing natural cultural and ethical developments and stressing adjustment to modern secular ideals, these other Protestants were reemphasizing the supernatural.

Integral to this view was a strongly supernaturalistic interpretation of the Bible, once more going against the modern scholarly trends of looking at the Bible as only a historical product. Premillennialist interpreters insisted that the Bible was truly the word of God and, therefore, accurate in every detail. Earlier Christians had usually taken for granted something like that view, but it was not until the rise of biblical criticism that some traditionalist interpreters began to insist on the "inerrancy" (freedom from error) of Scripture as a test of the faith. The rise in prominence of this teaching paralleled the assertion of papal infallibility in the Roman Catholic Church in 1870. In each case, as long-standing supernaturalist Christian beliefs were being challenged by modern views, one conservative reaction was to assert more strongly than ever that the traditional doctrines stood on infallible foundations.

For interpreters of Bible prophecies, the inerrancy of the Bible was especially important, since they believed that the prophecies contained accurate, even if mysterious, predictions about the future. For them, it was crucial that the thousand years of the millennium be an actual thousand years during which Christ would literally rule in Jerusalem, not a symbolic reign of Christ, as postmillennialists would say. Other of their interpretations of prophecies hinged on literal interpretations of biblical numbers.

Such interpreters of Bible prophecy did not regard themselves as rejecting sciences as a basis for biblical interpretation. Just the opposite—they saw the Bible as a book of reliable facts and themselves as applying scientific principles to arranging and understanding those facts. For instance, the most common premillennial view, called dispensationalism, divided world history into seven eras, or dispensations. Correct scientific reading of the Bible, they insisted, could demonstrate that modern people were living at the end of the sixth dispensation of the church age. This age, they said, had been predicted to be marked by a decline of the large established churches and of so-called Christian civilization. Only a remnant of the churches would have true, born-again and sanctified believers. At any moment, they predicted, Jesus would return to inaugurate a series of dramatic events. These events would begin with the secret rapture of the church, in which true believers would suddenly disappear from earth. Then seven years of wars and tribulations would follow, during which the Jews, returned to Palestine, would be converted to Christianity. These events would culminate with the return of Jesus and the saints, his victory over the Antichrist in a literal battle at Armageddon (in Israel), and his thousand-year rule in Jerusalem.

One major factor contributing to the success of dispensational premillennialism was that it appealed to the primitivist impulse in much of popular American Protestantism. Converted Christians could live as though they were in New Testament times when people could look for Christ's return any day. As an alternative to the disenchantment of modern scientific-technological culture where all change was explained by impersonal natural processes, one lived with an expectant sense that it was God who controlled historical change by dramatic interventions, as he had in each of the dispensations of earlier biblical times.

Mainstream America: Loving It or Leaving It?

Such views, widespread among revivalists, naturally created some tensions as to how Protestants were viewing their American heritage. On the one hand, they inherited the tradition, going back to the Puritans, that America was a Christian nation with a special destiny in history. On the other hand, premillennial views invited pessimistic readings of so-called Christian culture. Revivalists often wavered between these two views. Dwight L. Moody (1837–99), for instance, was a premillennialist, and many of his associates were the most prominent teachers of dispensational doctrines. With Moody's blessing, they founded Bible institutes, where the new doctrines were taught, to train an army of lay Christian workers. At the same time, Moody was a loyal believer in the American way of life and a friend to the optimistic liberal Protestants. Therefore, liberal and premillennial revivalists could cooperate under Moody's inspiration in the missionary efforts to "evangelize the world in this generation."

In fact, in the era before World War I, a serious crisis was building ominously in Protestantism concerning the proper relationship of converted Christians to American culture. Those who formed new holiness or Pentecostal sects were separating themselves from the dominant mainstream culture. Such separatists, however, were only a minority uneasy with the dominant trends. Many others, including some of the premillennialists, continued in mainline denominations but were beginning to be critical of liberal Protestantism's downplaying of some traditional supernatural aspects of Christianity and the liberal identification of spiritual progress with the advance of modern civilization. As in Moody's day, the more liberal and supernaturalistically oriented Protestants could still sometimes work together, as in the Prohibition campaign. Nonetheless, beneath such activism was the potential for an explosion at the center of the Protestant religious and cultural establishment.

New Religious Movements: Christian Science and Jehovah's Witnesses

One indicator of the religious tensions building in a culture is the types of new religious movements that spin off from that culture. In the late nineteenth century, the United States saw the development of two major religious groups that, while having Christian roots, departed significantly from traditional Christianity.

These groups, Christian Science and Jehovah's Witnesses, provide a revealing contrast. Sociologically, they have been at opposite ends of the spectrum. Christian Science had its most appeal among the wealthiest and best educated. Jehovah's Witnesses, on the other hand, flourished primarily among the economically and educationally deprived. Correspondingly, Christian Science might be seen as a radical departure from tradition in a liberal direction, while Jehovah's Witnesses are a similarly radical departure, but in a revivalist, millennialist direction. Both groups were responding to modern secularism and materialism by asserting the primacy of the supernatural. The types of supernaturalism were opposite, however. Christian Science, even more than liberal Protestantism, emphasized that all reality was spiritual. Discovery of such a principle would revolutionize human relationships and perceptions. Jehovah's Witnesses accentuated millennial Protestantism's tendencies of expecting spectacular supernatural interventions. Its revivalist moral regulations were strict almost to the point of being reactionary.

Christian Science went beyond liberal Protestantism in its tendency to use traditional Christian terminology but to give this terminology entirely new meanings. The particulars of the outlook grew from the experience of the movement's founder, Mary Baker Eddy (1821–1910). Eddy was a New Englander who intensely experienced the characteristic sense of loss that nineteenth-century New Englanders felt as Calvinism declined as the organizing principle that gave the dominant culture its meaning and direction. As we have seen, many well-to-do Anglo-Protestants of mid-century, especially women, turned to transcendental or other spiritualistic movements that regained spiritual intensity. Almost all of these movements emphasized the primacy of spiritual reality over the material. Many people from the same mid-nineteenth-century middle class were also preoccupied with new programs for promoting health.

The experience of Mary Baker Eddy incorporated all these tendencies. In 1862, after years of poor health and suffering, she was dramatically cured by mind-cure specialist Phineas Parkhurst Quimby (1802–66). Eddy adopted Quimby's views and reinterpreted them in terms of traditional Christian language. She taught that God constituted all reality, which was spiritual. One's recognition that empirical experience of the material world was illusory allowed God through Christ to transform and regenerate one's being. Recognition of the illusory character of the material world would also lead to physical health, without resorting to doctors or conventional medicine.

Eddy's Church of Christ (Scientist) was chartered in 1879, and by the later decades of her life, she achieved wide success and fortune, if not total freedom herself from physical suffering. Most notably, she attracted a devoted following and established a prosperous mother church as the headquarters of her movement in Boston. While the movement never gained much more than perhaps a quarter of a million adherents in the United States, because of its affluence, it had influence disproportionate to its numbers.[17] After the mid-twentieth century its membership numbers steadily declined.

The Jehovah's Witnesses were founded about the same time by Charles Taze Russell (1852–1916), a small-time merchant from Pennsylvania. Like many nineteenth-century Christians, he was preoccupied with the ideal that one should use scientific means for a personal study of the Bible, not relying on the authority of others. Russell concluded that the "millennial dawn" had already occurred in 1874, although the end of all things would not come until 1914. "Millions now living will never die" was his watchword. In these respects, his movement was similar to Seventh-day Adventism. However, Russell's biblical studies also led him to a number of unique doctrines that diverged from most Christian orthodoxy. For instance, he rejected the traditional doctrine of the Trinity, seeing Jesus, instead, as wholly distinct from God the Father. He also, like some of the liberals of the day, did away with the doctrine of hell, substituting an elaborate scheme of an era of probation or second chance for salvation, with annihilation as the alternative. Even though the literal end of the age apparently did not occur in 1914, the doctrine was reinterpreted, and the movement was successfully reorganized under the leadership of "Judge" Joseph H. Rutherford (1869–1942). As did most American-born millennial movements (such as Adventists, Mormons, Pentecostals, and fundamentalist groups), they promoted vigorous evangelistic and missionary efforts and established constituencies in many parts of the world.

One feature that has distinguished Jehovah's Witnesses from most other millennial groups is that they specifically reject allegiance to the state. Almost all American millennial groups have proclaimed that modern civilization is corrupt and that Christians must radically separate themselves from it. Few, however, have carried such doctrines to their logical conclusions. Therefore, when the chips have been down, most of these groups are willing to put their country first and to be intensely patriotic in supporting the nation's wars. Before World War I, some dispensationalist premillennialists questioned whether Christians could fight in wars, and a good many Pentecostals refused military service prior to World War II; however, few such millennialists have retained that heritage. Jehovah's Witnesses, on the other hand, have consistently taken literally the teaching that Christ's kingdom is not of this world. Accordingly, they have refused military service and refused to pledge allegiance to the American flag. Many suffered imprisonment for their unpopular stances during both World War I and World War II. In 1942, some Jehovah's Witnesses were granted recognition as conscientious objectors, and in 1943, the Supreme Court ruled that their children could not be excluded from public schools for refusing to salute the flag.

Peace Churches

Ever since the Pilgrims arrived on American shores, American Protestants have wrestled with the question of what allegiance they should give to the prevailing political establishment and in what ways they should separate themselves from the "world," or the dominant culture of their day. To what extent should the church be a sect separated from the world, based strictly on the model of the early church of the New Testament? Would too strict a separation destroy the church's influence?

The usual response to these questions has been essentially the same as that suggested by the Puritans—keep the church pure by retaining strict membership requirements but at the same time try to dominate and transform the culture, building a Christian civilization. By the early twentieth century, in mainline Protestant churches, one dimension of this solution (strict membership requirements) was beginning to recede, and the churches were increasingly blending in with the dominant culture.

Another tradition was represented early in America by Roger Williams, who denounced the possibility of a Christian civilization, emphasizing the separateness or sectarian nature of churches based on the New Testament pattern. Positions much like Williams's had already been developed during the Reformation by the Anabaptist sects, who insisted on adult baptism as a symbol of separation and who established Christian communities separate from the rest of society. Anabaptists insisted that allegiance to Christ superseded allegiance to any earthly rulers and were, therefore, strict pacifists. Quakers (also called the Religious Society of Friends), arising out of the English Civil Wars of the 1650s, took a similar view.

Eighteenth-century America, especially Pennsylvania, became a haven for radical sectarian groups. The two best-known Anabaptist groups to establish communities in America were the Mennonites and the closely related Amish. These groups often divided into subgroups. Typically, they have lived in separate communities and have been pacifists. However, as they developed in the United States, their internal differences divided them into a spectrum of views from the strictest separatism to considerable assimilation into the mainstream culture. The strictest groups are the Old Order Amish, who live in tightly closed, but internally very supportive communities and reject all outward signs of modernity. They dress plainly in a style from early modern times; reject the use of modern conveniences, such as electricity and automobiles; and retain their own German dialect. Some other Amish allow for modern conveniences. Mennonites are divided by similar patterns. Some are strict separatists; most, however, have become much more like other American denominations, using the English language and giving up all distinctive dress and communal practice. Most, but not all, remain pacifist.

Other peace groups in America have experienced similar tensions regarding how strictly they should remain as separate sects or how fully they could participate in the wider society as just another denomination. To be a sect meant to separate themselves and to try to remain pure.

The Quakers probably have experienced these tensions most sharply. Although founded as a radical sect, they became the first families of eastern Pennsylvania and among the wealthiest and most influential. Still, they attempted to remain distinctive, even if not living in separate enclaves. Not until the 1830s, for instance, did they give up their scruples against higher education; they then founded a number of outstanding colleges, beginning with Haverford College in Haverford, Pennsylvania, in 1833. Like other distinctive immigrant groups, they were becoming acculturated. Some became evangelical, while others became liberal in their religious views. Eventually, Quakers around the country covered a wide spectrum of religious opinion. Many were still pacifists, though not so much because they were sectarian as because their social-political views were so progressive. Others gave up their pacifism. America's two Quaker presidents, Herbert Hoover and Richard Nixon, were not especially known for their pacifism.

A Common Heritage in a Pluralistic Society

For almost every group in America, whether ethnic, sectarian, or both, the central theme in their development has been much the same—how does the group retain its identity but still participate in society? Almost every variation on this theme has been played out somewhere in America. Differences among groups as well as differences within them, often heightened by religious overtones, have separated Americans. Yet at the same time, this common dilemma has given many Americans some commonality of heritage.

CHAPTER 6

Keeping the Faith in Modern Times

Our Country is filled with a Socialistic, I.W.W., Communistic, radical, lawless, anti-American, anti-church, anti-God, anti-marriage gang, and they are laying the eggs of rebellion and unrest in labor and capital and home, and we have some of them in our universities. . . . If this radical element could have their way, my friends, the laws of nature would be repealed, or they would reverse them; oil and water would mix; the turtle dove would marry the turkey buzzard; the sun would rise in the West and set in the East, chickens would crow and the roosters would squeal; cats would bark and dogs would meow; the least would be the greatest, a part would be greater than the whole; yesterday would be after tomorrow if this crowd were in control.

Billy Sunday (1925)

Both our practical morality and our emotional lives are adjusted to a world which no longer exists.

Joseph Wood Krutch, *The Modern Temper* (1929)

Traditional Protestantism, Cultural Dominance, or Both?

During the early twentieth century, while outsider groups of Protestants were debating how much to assimilate with mainstream American society, insider Protestants were struggling over how to relate to a *changing* American society. Even if one belonged to a long-established Protestant church, such as Methodist, Baptist, Presbyterian, or Congregationalist, and were from long-Americanized British, or perhaps German, ethnic stock, one was still confronted with the issue of how Christians should relate to an increasingly pluralistic and secular society. For the leadership in such groups, one practical question was whether these groups could continue to dominate American life. If so, could they retain their traditional Protestant beliefs? Or would they have to modify and broaden those beliefs both in order to remain current with prevailing opinion and to continue their cultural influence?

The reason this was an either-or choice was simple. Traditional Protestantism, like almost all other Judeo-Christian religions, is exclusivist. It teaches that some people will be saved for eternal life and some will not. Moreover, differences regarding morality are not simply matters of preference but reflect the perceived will of God. The total dominance of such views in a society would lead to an exclusivist, God-centered society like early Puritanism. In the United States, however, Protestant views had a more informal dominance. They retained an impact on public life through some concessions to a limited pluralism. That is, within the boundaries of a broadly Judeo-Christian moral consensus, some alternate views were tolerated and civil government was not based explicitly on religion. So long as the national heritage was predominantly homogeneous and Protestant, religious and secular views could be easily blended together without great conflict. The public schools, for instance, could teach generally Protestant viewpoints mixed with American Enlightenment ideals.

By the early twentieth century, when the United States was one of the most pluralistic nations on earth, this stance was becoming awkward. Especially awkward were Protestantism's exclusivist claims. If these were replaced with inclusive teachings, for instance, saying that Christianity is just one of the ways by which humans can find God, then such a broadened Protestantism could retain its cultural leadership. Such broadening was fostered also by the intellectual outlook of the time, which challenged all claims to absolute truth and explained differences in belief in terms of differing historical circumstance.

A second alternative to Protestantism's exclusivism, especially for those who retained some form of the traditional supernaturalism, was to move in a separatist or sectarian direction, giving up aspirations of controlling the whole society but remaining pure within one's own group.

A third alternative was to give up neither traditional Protestant belief nor its aspirations for cultural dominance. Rather than withdraw from mainline churches into separate groups, Protestants might continue to fight for traditional Protestant values in the culture and against liberal theologies. The presence of such people, the first to be called fundamentalists, in some of America's most influential denominations led to some of the twentieth century's most dramatic conflicts regarding the role of religion in culture. Such conflicts have continued in a variety of forms into the twenty-first century.

Prelude to Conflict: Southern Conservatism

Most of the issues that divided mainline Protestantism in the twentieth century were fought in the North, but these conflicts were anticipated by religious antagonisms between South and North arising from the Civil War. As white southerners began reentering national life, especially after 1900, many of them contributed significantly to mainline conflicts.

When the white South tasted the bitter dregs of defeat in the Civil War, its people determined that they would still win the peace. They had fought for an ideal civilization, for what they considered a Christian civilization. A mere military defeat could not take away that ideal. The principles of the lost cause, which they considered morally and spiritually superior to Yankee civilization, could be preserved in the hearts and minds of the people. Preserving the lost cause meant romanticizing pre–Civil War southern culture as a model for civilization. Any deviation from that model would be a decline. This outlook meant that a strong motif in dominant southern thought was a resistance to post–Civil War modernity.

This stance had important religious implications. Preserving the ideals of pre–Civil War culture meant preserving the dominant religious outlook of the 1850s—essentially, revivalist evangelicalism. Since mainstream American Protestantism was changing rapidly in the late nineteenth century, this stance immediately put most white southerners on the conservative side of the current theological debates. Furthermore, the southern sectors of the largest Protestant denominations, such as the Methodists, Baptists, and Presbyterians, had separated into their own organizations and remained separate after the war. To justify such continued separation, they asserted their superiority to their northern counterparts. Yankees, they said, were turning toward theological liberalism, while southerners remained true to the faith. Such conservatism was reinforced by continuing revivalism in the South. During the Civil War, there were remarkable revivals among the southern troops, and revival religion remained in style.

A significant minority of southern Protestants resisted all these trends and worked toward building a new South that would be as progressive in its views as the North. Conservative influences, however, remained dominant. Conservatism was supported by the relative homogeneity of the white southern population. Immigration to the South, which was largely rural and not prosperous, was slow. The white population of most of the region, therefore, remained overwhelmingly Anglo-Protestant.

One helpful way to look at the white South since the Civil War is as a new American ethnic group.[1] Like other ethnic groups, it was shaped by a common heritage but also by a very strong sense of national identity—in this case, with the short-lived Confederate nation. This identity continued to be strong as southerners found themselves in a partly alien environment in the decades after the Civil War. As in other American ethnic communities, some argued for more assimilation with the dominant culture, while others argued for preserving their heritage. Much as it did for other ethnic groups, religion played an important role in defining southernness, and a sense of southernness helped preserve religious conservatism. Southerners were preserving the ways of the "old country"—in this case, the antebellum South. The result was that as the South entered the twentieth century, its dominant religion still had almost all the traits that were characteristic of American evangelicalism generally in the mid-nineteenth century. It was strongly biblicist and revivalist, putting emphasis on traditional theologies and on individual conversions.

Whether such traits were superior or inferior to the more progressive Protestantism arising primarily in the North was a matter of debate. A cultural explanation of why some trends prevailed in one part of the country and others prevailed in another does not settle such issues. For the people involved, traditional revivalism or progressive Protestantism was attractive for the merits of what was taught.

As with many issues in the South, religious issues were mixed with beliefs about race. Most white southerners in this era were firmly committed to keeping the South a white man's country. The churches were no exception. White churches welcomed the exodus of blacks after the Civil War and supported the strict segregationist society. Typically, white churches professed to hold to the doctrine of the spirituality of the church, by which they meant that churches should stay out of politics. This doctrine arose in opposition to northern church support of abolitionism. The doctrine, however, was far from a declaration that the church should not be tarnished by involvement with a cultural system. Rather, it was a doctrine for those who already dominated the culture politically. The social functions of being nonpolitical are apparent in a revealing statement by the Southern Methodist bishops in 1894:

> Our Church is strictly a religious and in no wise a political body. The more closely we keep ourselves to the one work of testifying to all men repentance toward God and faith toward our Lord Jesus Christ, the better shall we promote the highest good of our country and race.[2]

For most white, southern Protestants, the spirituality of the church was selective, not keeping the church from speaking out on what they considered moral issues as opposed to purely political issues. On questions of traditional evangelical morality, such as Prohibition or Sabbath observance, they were quite ready to support political action.

Among southern Protestant churches in the early twentieth century, therefore, the dominant mood was both theologically and culturally conservative. An important segment of white southerners did speak out for progressivism and for a social gospel; the region was, therefore, never all of one mind. Nonetheless, in the battles emerging over modernist theology and more secular and pluralist culture, southerners were more likely to be on the side of the antimodernists.

The Last Crusade for Protestant Civilization

The impending crisis within the dominant American Protestantism was partially obscured by Protestants' common evangelical heritage and, hence, by their continuing ability to follow a common cause.

The most remarkable instance of the power of concerted Protestant effort was the campaign to prohibit the sale of alcoholic beverages. In the age of crusades prior to World War I, this was the Protestant crusade par excellence. Liberals and conservatives, social gospelers and evangelists, and northerners and southerners joined together in the cause. Some of the more progressive, Americanized Catholic leaders also joined the campaign. Overall, however, Prohibition was the result of mobilizing the political potential of Protestant Christians. It was the high-water mark for the usually elusive ideal of a unified evangelical civilization.

The reasons for the wide support are not hard to find. First of all, excessive consumption of alcohol was the first major drug problem of modern America. Many people today speak as though the whole idea of Prohibition was preposterous, but they should note that the United States today prohibits the use of all sorts of drugs and, as in the case of prohibition of alcohol, has had immense problems enforcing such laws. The more problematic question is whether alcohol is an appropriate drug to put on the list of substances prohibited. At the time, it seemed plausible to many that it was a good candidate for this list. Its use to excess seemed to be encouraged both by frontier conditions and later by the tensions of the new urban industrial society. The extent of excessive use was sufficient that one later historian could appropriately characterize the United States as "the alcoholic republic."[3] Such excess undermined evangelical religion and other strict evangelical mores. Early nineteenth-century evangelicals accordingly latched onto alcohol as a chief vice to eradicate. They demanded total abstinence among their converts and worked to set a similar standard for society at large. By the late nineteenth century, alcohol was a primary symbol of secular civilization, and opposition to it was a chief symbol of evangelical civilization.

Some theological liberals, Catholic Americanizers, and progressive social gospelers also adopted this cause, since alcoholism was a major urban problem as well. Clearly, excessive use of alcohol broke up families and contributed to other urban vices. The situation was complicated, however, by the insistence on total abstinence from alcohol—a demand almost unique to American Protestantism. Recent immigrants, regardless of their Old World religious traditions, were unfamiliar with that ideal and typically consumed some alcohol regularly. Prohibition thus involved an attempt by dominant Protestants to impose their standards on immigrants.

Often their efforts were deeply resented. Those who opposed Prohibition pointed out that alcohol had been around since the dawn of civilization, had been consumed routinely in Puritan New England, was a benefit when used in moderation, and was not condemned by Scripture or tradition (Jesus turned water into wine and instituted the use of wine as a holy sacrament); they also pointed out that its abuse could be limited by voluntary moderation rather than by legislation.

The campaigns for Prohibition became a formidable political force with the formation in 1895 of the Anti-Saloon League, a largely Protestant organization. The two largest Protestant religious groups, the Methodists and the Baptists, both in the North and the South, fervently supported the campaigns. This zeal was mobilized by effective political organization, directed by the Anti-Saloon League. Attacking the issue on a state and local level, champions of Prohibition won five states to their cause by 1900 and twenty-six by the outbreak of World War I in 1917. Many other localities were also "dry." Wartime fervor provided the last great impetus to put the crusade over the top. Legislation made the country virtually dry by the end of the war. Meanwhile, Congress adopted the Eighteenth Amendment, which went into effect in 1920, banning the commercial manufacture and sale of alcoholic beverages throughout the country. The millennium had not been brought in, but the dominant Protestants had gained what seemed, for a brief time, an important symbol of moral progress.

War and Campaigns for Peace

Perhaps the most difficult issue in relating churches to culture has been the issue of war and peace. The Christian church was initially an outsider sect in the Roman Empire and was largely pacifist. After Constantine's conversion and later the establishment of Christianity as the official state religion in the fourth century, the church almost always supported state war efforts. St. Augustine, one of the early church fathers to face the new situation, proposed criteria for "just wars"—the only wars, he said, that Christians could support. The cause, for instance, had to be just, and the means of achieving that goal had to be proportional to the goal itself. Just wars should be fought by armies only and should not involve intentional killing of civilians.

Such just-war policies have been the theoretical standards for most churches up to the present. However, nations have always claimed that their causes were just, and churches have usually gone along. This has been especially true in the case of churches officially established by the state. These churches, almost as a matter of course, have supported state policy. Sectarian groups reacted to such complicity by insisting on strict pacifism for their members.

The mainline Protestant churches in the United States stood in a peculiar position on such issues. Almost all of them had a sectarian heritage that demanded at least some symbolic separation from the world and encouraged some criticism of the state. Baptists, for instance, particularly prided themselves on being champions of "the separation of church and state." On the other hand, these denominations constituted a sort of informal church establishment for the republic. Their members, like other Americans, were among the supporters of prevailing state policy. In times of war, with a few exceptions, American churches have almost always been swept along by the enthusiasm for the cause.

Protestants, who saw themselves as the conscience of the nation, were sometimes troubled by such Christian enthusiasm for violence in the name of the Prince of Peace. In almost every era, thoughtful people agonized over this anomaly. Was it proper for one to kill a member of one's own religious group for the cause of the nation? The brotherhood of the Masons could point to cases where military officers, seeing that a captive gave a Masonic sign, had refused to order a firing squad to fire upon that prisoner. Why could not Methodists or Baptists do the same?

Author Mark Twain, having departed from his evangelical upbringing but retaining its underlying moral sensibility, was free to state the paradox more sharply than most Americans. In his "The War Prayer" (1904), he presents a stranger who appears in a church and prays:

> Lord our God, help us to tear their soldiers to bloody shreds with our shells; help us to cover their smiling fields with the pale forms of their patriot dead; help us to drown the thunder of the guns with the shrieks of their wounded, writhing in pain; help us to lay waste their humble homes with a hurricane of fire; help us wring the hearts of their unoffending widows with unavailing grief; help us to turn them out roofless with their little children to wander unfriended the wastes of their desolated land in rags and hunger and thirst. . . .

Twain added with his typical irony: "It was believed afterward that the man was a lunatic, because there was no sense in what he said."[4]

Though indeed most pious Americans would have shouted down any wartime suggestions that Christianity and the national cause were at odds, some nineteenth-century Protestant leaders did agonize over how the brutality of war betrayed their high hopes for Christian civilization. Without going to the sectarian alternative of the peace churches, they had one recourse left—to work for reform from within the culture. This was the great hope for nineteenth-century American Protestants—that they could bring in the millennium by reform. This golden age would, among other things, be a time of perpetual peace. One of the reform movements of that era, accordingly, was a campaign for peace. Champions of the cause founded the American Peace Society in 1828. Consistent with the establishment stance but trying to reform it at the same time, this campaign was not totally pacifist but rather an effort to promote peace whenever possible. Such efforts were overwhelmed by the Civil War, which captured the enthusiasm of almost all the reformers who championed peace. Even that war, however, was viewed as perhaps the bloody birth of a new age in which both peace and justice would prevail. Soon after the war, however, disillusion set in.

Yet peace reform continued. Frances Willard, for instance, in the 1880s persuaded the Women's Christian Temperance Union to include peace advocacy among its causes. As in other areas, however, it was in the Progressive Era that the crusading spirit of the pre–Civil War days was revived. Just before World War I, campaigns to work for world peace and arbitration reached their peak. Andrew Carnegie (1835–1919) generously funded the leading American peace organizations, and in 1911, the Federal Council of Churches formed a Commission on Peace and Arbitration.

Growing international peace efforts were interrupted, however, by the outbreak of the Great War in Europe in 1914. The United States at first resolved to stay out of this conflict. Nonetheless, the nation was drawn inexorably toward the war. The US Secretary of State, William Jennings Bryan (1860–1925), was caught in the middle. Bryan, three-time Democratic presidential candidate, was both an ardent evangelical and an ardent champion of progressive causes, including the peace campaign. In 1915, after the German sinking of the *Lusitania*, a British ship with over a hundred Americans among its almost twelve hundred lost passengers, President Woodrow Wilson sent a sharp note to Germany demanding an apology and reparations. Fearing this act would lead to war, Bryan followed his conscience and resigned from the cabinet.

When Wilson finally did bring the United States into the war in 1917, most of the peace advocates, including Bryan, supported the decision. Universal peace, they reasoned, might be possible only by the victory of those who were principled and ultimately champions of peace. Wilson himself was a champion of arbitration and carefully provided a just-war rationale for entering the conflict. Consequently, peace advocates could join with Wilson in yet another millennial hope that this would be "the war to end all wars."

As Wilson recognized, the champions of restraint do not prevail in a time of war, when many people's relatives and friends are being killed. Even before Americans saw action, the wartime enthusiasm reached a height never surpassed in the nation's history. In 1918, Congress passed the Alien Act and then the Sedition Act, which gave the government sweeping powers to suppress disloyal, profane, or scurrilous remarks about the US cause or even the flag. Civil religion, in the sense of popular and legally enforced demands for total loyalty, reached a peak. In Oregon in 1918, one Methodist clergyman told the Portland Rotary Club:

> There is no place on the top side of American soil for a Pacifist. . . . If you have one, shoot him. Don't talk peace to me; I don't want peace, I want righteousness.[5]

Any meetings, including church services held in foreign languages, especially in German, were suspect and in some places outlawed. Towns with German names, such as Berlin, were changed to more patriotic ones. Stories circulated concerning German atrocities, rape, and pillage. So misleading was such propaganda that twenty-five years later during World War II, many thoughtful people were skeptical of reports of Nazi atrocities toward the Jews, thinking them repetitions of World War I exaggerations.

America's churches, along with their constituents, were swept along by this wartime fervor. Clergy were probably no more or less extreme than most other Americans, which meant that some were cautious about unrestrained nationalism, while others endorsed the American cause with abandon. Some of the latter virtually draped the flag over the cross so that one could no longer tell the difference between the two. The consensus regarding the war was simply stated by Frank Mason North, president of the Federal Council of the Church of Christ in America: "The war for righteousness will be won! Let the Church do her part."[6]

The patriotic enthusiasm, although only sometimes explicitly religious, nonetheless had causes closely related to the nation's religious heritage. The enthusiasm for the war was of the same ilk as the simultaneous enthusiasm for Prohibition, progressive reform, or world missions. All these were part of an increasingly popular zeal for an American democratic way of life, a somewhat secularized form of the old ideal of a Christian and republican civilization.

The difference was that, unlike in most earlier American crusades, nearly every group of Americans except peace churches lent their support to the secularized ideal of "making the world safe for democracy." Rather than drive insiders and outsiders apart, the war temporarily brought them together. Immigrant groups, Catholic, Protestant, Eastern Orthodox, and Jewish were all especially eager to demonstrate their patriotism and dispel any aspersions on their loyalty and foreignness. African-Americans, though severely discriminated against, retained a firm faith in the American way. White southerners were reentering the mainstream and could point to one of their own in the White House—Wilson was from Virginia. World War I marked a major step for many conservative southerners in their transfer of loyalty from the Confederacy to eventually becoming among the nation's most fervent champions of national patriotism.

Conflict in the Mainstream: Fundamentalists Versus Modernists

Wars are catalysts for social change. They speed up the processes of social development and conflict. While World War I temporarily brought most of the nation together in an orgy of patriotism, the morning after revealed open antagonisms that could not be healed. In the long run, none of these antagonisms was culturally more significant than that between fundamentalists and modernists in the mainline churches. At first, many observers thought this highly publicized conflict was a temporary aberration in the overall story of building consensus. Instead, it was the first uncovering of a major fault line that ran through that center. Only in the second half of the twentieth century would it become apparent that major cultural conflicts were coalescing around two competing moral visions of American life. These moral visions were grounded, to a large extent, in the nation's religious history.

Since Protestant Christianity stood so close to the centers of power in nineteenth-century America, one of the strong impulses for Protestants was to keep up with whatever changes were going on in the culture. This impulse was a major component in theological liberalism, or modernism, which believed that Christianity should provide leadership for modern cultural and intellectual change by reinterpreting Christian traditions to fit with modern ideals. Modernism, although by its nature having many varieties, thus could be very compatible with fervent wartime patriotism. Building a progressive, democratic, worldwide civilization based on the brotherhood of all people under the fatherhood of God was close to the essence of the hopeful vision of liberal Protestants.

Premillennialists, on the other hand, taught that the hope for humanity was not in building a liberal civilization but in the dramatic return of Jesus to set up a millennial kingdom. The more extreme premillennialists, such as Jehovah's Witnesses and some Pentecostals, following the implication of this view that America was not the hope of the world, remained pacifists. Most of the premillennialist Protestants, however, such as those associated with Dwight L. Moody, were more moderate. The majority of these still remained in mainline denominations and, while occasionally entertaining pacifist views before World War I, became ardent American patriots once the war broke out.

Despite this essential commonality regarding the war itself, the sense of cultural crisis that the war precipitated turned growing conflict over theological questions into major debates over the nature of American civilization itself. Premillennial revivalists with mainstream Protestant connections, as well as other mainline conservatives, had been sniping away at modernist theology in their denominations for some years. From 1910 to 1915, these revivalists published a twelve-booklet series called *The Fundamentals*, in which conservative authors defended the traditional Protestant faith against theological liberalism and higher criticism of the Bible.

Billy Sunday, a Showman-Evangelist

Such serious-minded attacks were amplified by revivalists, who increasingly turned to the techniques of modern show business as a means of drumming up support. The most famous evangelist of this era was Billy Sunday (1862–1935). Sunday provides a revealing continuity and contrast to the great evangelists of previous eras—George Whitefield during the Great Awakening, Charles Finney during the Second Great Awakening, and Dwight L. Moody in the late nineteenth century. Each of the previous evangelists, to some degree, stood against the religious establishment of his day, but eventually each evangelist's ideas were largely accepted. Sunday, although ordained a Presbyterian, remained more of an outsider. This was partly a matter of style. Sunday combined Finney's concern for technique with Moody's disinterest in deep theological discussion. A former major league baseball player, Sunday was essentially a showman, who used shouting and well-timed acrobatic gestures, including sliding into the podium as though it were a base or, in a frenzy of patriotism, planting a flag on top of the pulpit. "I'd stand on my head in a mud puddle," he once quipped, "if I thought it would help me win souls to Christ."[7] His evident sincerity, as well as his showmanship, won him a wide audience. In fact, in 1915 a *New York Tribune* drama critic playfully compared Sunday to the great vaudeville actor of the era, George M. Cohan. "George Cohan has neither the punch nor the pace of Billy Sunday," he wrote. "It is true that Cohan waved the flag first, but Billy Sunday has waved it harder. . . . All in all we believe that Sunday has more dramatic instinct than Cohan."[8]

Sunday's gospel can be best described as a combination of popular Americanism and revivalist Christianity. He preached for moral cleanness and "real manhood" (occasionally adding "real womanhood"). The saloon was a favorite target of Sunday's. Likewise, during the war, his patriotism was second to none: "If you turn hell upside down," he said, "you will find 'Made in Germany' stamped on the bottom."[9] Despite this fusion of Christianity and Americanism, which he had in common with liberal Protestantism,

Sunday did not hesitate to lambaste the liberals he thought had forsaken the old gospel message of sin and salvation. Such attacks and such a message ensured that he would remain an outsider to the mainline religious establishment, reaching audiences who, although largely white Protestants, for one reason or another also felt like outsiders. With the world changing rapidly, popular prophets such as Sunday could easily alarm their followers about ominous new trends.

The Postwar Cultural Crisis

The immediate aftermath of World War I increased the sense of cultural crisis. In 1918, the actual engagement of American troops in the war brought the nation to a fever pitch of patriotism. In November of that year, the war suddenly ended, leaving many Americans with undirected zeal to fight for a holy cause. Immediately, some saw an enemy within. The Bolshevik communist revolution in Russia in 1917 and major labor strikes in America in 1919 led to the "red scare" and what became in some circles a permanent fear of a communist takeover. Revivalists such as Sunday, while not primarily responsible for such fears, fanned the flames as Americans added bolshevism to the threats to national morality.

At the same time, however, hopes for a better future ran incredibly high in mainline Protestant denominations. The war effort brought them together and obscured theological differences of earlier times. The war was won. Prohibition was passed. Leaders talked of uniting all major American Protestant groups. In 1919, Protestants also launched the Interchurch World Movement, which was to be a colossal effort for worldwide Protestant cooperation in benevolent missions. This was the Protestant equivalent to the League of Nations, which was to ensure world peace.

As with the League of Nations, intense opposition to such idealistic efforts set in during 1919 and 1920. Though some old denominational antagonisms were forgotten by progressive church leaders, new ones were widening the fault line that separated theological liberals from conservatives and revivalists. These new antagonisms were exacerbated by a widespread, though ill-defined, sense of cultural crisis, a sense that things were changing too rapidly and that America might be losing its heritage. The plans to unite Protestantism and the Interchurch World Movement both soon collapsed.

Meanwhile, conservative Protestants and revivalists were providing a strong dissenting analysis of the perceived cultural crisis. The problem, they said, was primarily theological and moral; America was founded on the Bible. Liberal Protestants and secularists attacked the authenticity of the Bible, offering evolutionary-based philosophies as an alternative. Evidence of the consequences was a dramatic change in moral attitudes, sped up by the war. America was moving rapidly from the Victorian era to the age of the flappers, or young women who defied "lady-like" proprieties. Conservative church leaders deplored the new dances and short dresses, or as one critic put it, the transition from "the bended knee to the bared knee." Such changes, said conservatives, were just a few signs that America was losing its morality. Liberal theology and secularism, they said, were to blame.

Darwinism as Symbol

These views gained popularity when in 1919 one of the nation's best-known politicians, William Jennings Bryan, entered the fray. Bryan and a number of other conservative leaders concluded that evolutionary philosophies were at the root of the crisis in Western civilization. This theme emerged during the war as Americans sought to explain how Germany had turned to the barbarism that American propaganda described. One explanation was that German culture adopted the "might is right" philosophy of German Friedrich Nietzsche (1844–1900). Conservative Christians immediately tied this to the fact that liberal theologies and higher criticisms of the Bible were based on evolutionary views of how religions and the Bible itself evolved as cultural products. Liberal theologies were often "made in Germany" and imported to the United States.

The symbolic center for such views was Darwinism, or biological evolution. Such views, Bryan and others pointed out, led people to believe that humans were nothing more than higher-order animals. Hence, there would be no basis for morality. Bryan was particularly impressed by a study published in 1916 by James H. Leuba which showed that well over half of American biologists did not believe either in God or immortality.[10] Some conservatives also believed biological evolution contradicted their literal interpretations of the creation account in Genesis. Bryan and others insisted that it was better simply to trust God and the Bible than what he saw as the speculations of modern science. "It is better to trust the Rock of Ages," he said, "than to know the ages of rocks."[11]

Evolution thus became a symbol that tied many things together to explain the cultural crisis. On the one side, traditionalists could say, was civilization founded on the Bible and the belief in the Creator of the moral order. On the other side were atheistic and purely naturalistic explanations of the human condition, such as evolutionary sociologies and psychologies, which made values relative to time, place, and individuals and offered schemes for reform or revolution with no firm foundations for a moral order. Astoundingly, according to the traditionalists, liberal theologians were more open to the evolutionary views than to the old-time biblical view.

This complex set of sociocultural issues could be boiled down most easily in public debate to the issue of biological evolution. Even though biological evolution was as much a product of the broader evolutionary outlook as its cause, it served as a handy symbol for the whole package. Opponents of traditional Christianity for some time used the prestige of evolutionary theory as such a symbol. It also served particularly well as a symbol for many, including biblical literalists such as premillennialists, southern conservatives, many revivalists, and certain ethnic Protestant conservatives. Genesis, they insisted, excluded the evolutionary origins of humanity. In 1919, William Jennings Bryan and others began campaigning to stop the spread of teaching biological evolution in America's public schools. In the same year, William B. Riley (1861–1947), the premillennialist Baptist pastor of a large church in Minneapolis, founded the World's Christian Fundamentals Association to support this and other militantly conservative, revivalist Protestant causes. Major battles were brewing on a number of fronts.

Defending Fundamental Doctrines

In 1920, the word *fundamentalist* was first used to describe this coalition of militantly conservative Protestants who were trying to preserve the nineteenth-century revivalist Protestant establishment. The term was coined by a conservative Baptist editor, Curtis Lee Laws, to designate his party in a battle in the Northern Baptist Convention (the major Baptist denomination in the North). Defending fundamentals implied being willing to fight for certain essential doctrines that liberals denied. Lists of these doctrines varied, but usually they included beliefs in the inerrancy of the Bible, the virgin birth of Jesus, the authenticity of his miracles, atonement for sin through the death of Christ, Jesus's resurrection, and his coming to earth again.

Fundamentalists were distinguished from other Protestant conservatives by their willingness to fight for these doctrines. Typically, they saw the world through images of warfare. The war was on two fronts: fundamentalists were fighting against modernist theology in their denominations and against some of the conspicuous trends toward secularism in their culture.

The denominational wars were fiercest in the Northern Baptist Convention and in the Presbyterian Church in the USA, two of the major northern denominations where militant conservatives and moderates were of roughly equal strength. In 1922, the most famous liberal preacher of the day, Harry Emerson Fosdick, became the center of the denominational struggles. A Baptist, but serving a large Presbyterian church in New York City, Fosdick preached a widely publicized sermon—"Shall the Fundamentalists Win?"—pleading for tolerance in the denomination. Presbyterian conservatives counterattacked, eventually forcing Fosdick to leave their denomination.

In 1923, the fundamentalist cause was strengthened by the appearance of J. Gresham Machen's *Christianity and Liberalism*. Machen (1881–1937) was a New Testament scholar at Princeton Theological Seminary, a stronghold for dignified Presbyterian theological conservatism. Machen did not like to call himself a fundamentalist and his emphasis on the intellect did not fit with popular revivalism. The difference in style was indicated, for instance, when he once spoke at Billy Sunday's Bible conference at Winona Lake, Indiana, complaining privately that his lectures were preceded by the "singing of some of the popular jingles, often accompanied by the blowing of enormous horns or other weird instruments of music."[12]

Nonetheless, in *Christianity and Liberalism*, Machen provided fundamentalists with their strongest defense. He argued that liberal Protestantism, despite using traditional terminology, was a new religion since it denied the most essential traditional doctrines, such as that Jesus died as an atonement for human sins and literally rose again. Liberals, he said, should be perfectly free to start their own churches, but since their religion was different from traditional Christianity, they should not remain in denominations that were based on traditional creeds. "A separation between the two parties in the Church," he declared, "is the crying need of the hour."[13]

Though some influential outside observers agreed with Machen's argument that extreme Protestant liberals believed in a religion other than traditional Christianity, most Protestants were not concerned enough for doctrine of any sort to have the stomach for grim theological warfare. Conservative and fundamentalist efforts to purge denominations of liberals, while creating a sensation for a few years, met with little success.

Keeping the Faith in Modern Times

Bryan and the Scopes Trial

In the meantime, more Americans seemed ready to rally to the cause on another front in the battle to save America from the alleged threat of secularism. Here, in the public arena, symbols were more effective than substance, and evolution became the chief symbol for a whole set of social changes that conservatives found ominous. The success of the antievolution crusade owed a lot to the leadership of William Jennings Bryan, who was always an effective orator. His campaigns had the most success in the South, where a number of state legislatures passed laws banning the teaching of biological evolution in public schools. Many other states were also considering such action. The scientific community, many secularists, liberal religionists, and champions of the freedom of expression were deeply alarmed at a sweeping national trend that looked to them like a return to the Dark Ages.

In the summer of 1925, the crisis came to a head in a scene that could not have been staged better to dramatize the tensions between the old evangelical culture and the new, more secular outlook of the twentieth century. John T. Scopes (1900–70), a young high-school teacher in rural Dayton, Tennessee, with the support of the American Civil Liberties Union (ACLU), volunteered to defy a recently passed Tennessee law banning the teaching of the biological evolution of humans. The ACLU supplied skilled lawyers, including the most famous trial lawyer of the day, Clarence Darrow (1857–1938). The prosecution countered by accepting the services of William Jennings Bryan.

This was at the height of the age of ballyhoo and media-generated national crazes, as well as controversies over changing moral standards, jazz, new dances, styles of dress for women, and sexually suggestive Hollywood movies. Proponents of the new, more lenient culture were already deeply antagonistic toward defenders of the old-style Victorian moral standards, and so they made the most of a drama in which science could be pitted against religion, urban against rural, and North against South.

The setting of the trial in rural Tennessee accentuated the urban versus rural theme. To sophisticated observers of the day, fundamentalism seemed to be a function of the countryside. As Richard Hofstadter later observed of this era, "The United States was born in the country and has moved to the city."[14] Cities were considered more secular than small towns because they were more impersonal and provided many organized alternatives to the life of piety. Because cities were ethnically diverse, they were also less evangelical than the more Protestant countryside. Moreover, sociological theory reinforced the assumption that traditional religion went with traditional, rural culture. Education and life in a sophisticated, modern, urban, industrial society were supposed to disabuse people of the pieties of a more primitive, agrarian time.

William Jennings Bryan, who rose to fame in the election of 1896 as "the boy orator from the Platte," representing agrarian and populist impulses, could easily be fit into the bumpkin stereotype. H. L. Mencken, the acerbic critic of American foibles, wrote of Bryan at Dayton: "Making his progress up and down the main street of little Dayton, surrounded by gaping primates from the upland valleys of the Cumberland Range, his coat laid aside, his bare arms and hairy chest shining damply, his bald head sprinkled with dust—so accoutred and on display he was obviously happy."[15] The antithesis to Bryan was the urbane, sophisticated Darrow, representing modern, urban culture and right thinking.

Their actions amplified by unprecedented press coverage, the actors played their roles. The local judge, openly sympathetic to evangelical religion, allowed Bryan to testify on the Bible as an expert witness. Bryan's expertness consisted of years as a popular Sunday-school lecturer. Darrow subjected him to withering and sarcastic cross-examination with village atheist-type questions such as where Cain, the oldest son of the Bible's first humans, Adam and Eve, got his wife. The outcome of the trial itself was indecisive. Scopes was found guilty but given a token fine. The drama was heightened, however, when Bryan, who felt he performed well, suddenly died in Dayton five days after the trial. The trial and Bryan's death marked a symbolic turning point in the drama. Fundamentalism was still alive and well, but the trial provided ammunition for its critics. H. L. Mencken wrote that "we can thank the inscrutable gods for Harding, even for Coolidge. . . . Dullness has got into the White House, and the smell of cabbage boiling, but there is at least nothing to compare to the intolerable buffoonery that went on in Tennessee. The President of the United States may be an ass, but he at least doesn't believe that the earth is square, and that witches should be put to death, and that Jonah swallowed the whale. The Golden Text is not painted weekly on the White House wall, and there is no need to keep ambassadors waiting while Pastor Simpson, of Smithville, prays for rain in the Blue Room."[16]

The Image of Fundamentalist Defeat

The most important impact of the Scopes trial, one of the few twentieth-century religious events reported in most American history texts, was the image that it created. Fundamentalism, indeed all conservative Protestantism, it became easy to believe, had been thoroughly routed and discredited. That was not so apparent immediately after the trial, since the Tennessee law and others like it still stood and fundamentalists seemed strong. Yet within the next few years, it became apparent that fundamentalism had been put on the defensive. Some conservative Protestants who had been initially sympathetic to fundamentalist concerns now were reluctant to endure the risk of ridicule that went along with being tagged "fundamentalist." Soon critics seized on the idea that fundamentalism was in decline and would gradually disappear, especially as education spread and the nation urbanized.

In mainline denominations, fundamentalist and conservative hopes for control indeed declined precipitously after 1925. Moderates who tolerated liberals took the counteroffensive. J. Gresham Machen, for instance, was denied promotion at Princeton Theological Seminary and left to found his own theological school in 1929. A few years later, when he refused to support Presbyterian missions that included liberals and set up his own mission board, he was defrocked from the ministry and so started his own tiny denomination. Northern Baptist fundamentalists and conservatives experienced similar defeats.

Such events created the impression that conservative evangelical Protestantism was dying out. In fact, during the 1930s, mainline observers spoke of an "American religious depression" since there was some decline in mainline church membership. However, mainline Protestantism was not synonymous with American religion, not even with American Protestantism. Fundamentalists and other conservative and revivalist elements were regrouping. Many local congregations left mainline denominations to found independent Bible or Baptist churches. The Southern Baptist Convention, an overwhelmingly conservative group that intentionally remained outside mainline Protestantism, was growing rapidly and was becoming one of the nation's largest denominations. Smaller Pentecostal, holiness, and other sectarian evangelical groups were also growing, although few at the centers of American life were paying attention. Such groups were building networks of Bible schools for training leaders and strong senses of identity that would serve them well in the latter half of the twentieth century.

In the wake of the fundamentalist-modernist controversies of the 1920s, however, such continuing evangelical strength seemed, to most secular and mainstream Protestant observers, not the wave of the future but the vestige of a formidable, but dying, order.

A Growing Catholic Presence

While American Protestants were debating each other on how to respond to modernizing trends, they also had to face the reality of a growing Catholic presence. That became most vividly apparent when Al Smith, a Catholic, was nominated in 1928 as the Democratic candidate for president. The Democratic Party had long been primarily an alliance of groups outside the mainstream Protestant, Republican business establishment. Its two most loyal constituencies were southerners and Roman Catholic immigrant communities—two groups that had very little in common except that they opposed mainstream Protestant Republicans. In fact, the South was far more overwhelmingly Protestant than most of the rest of the country, and anti-Catholic prejudices were strong there.

These prejudices contributed to the revival of the Ku Klux Klan after World War I. Although antiblack racism was the chief interest in the Klan, opposition to Catholics, Jews, and other immigrants was also strong. The Klan, in fact, fit the image that critics attributed to fundamentalism. It appealed primarily to relatively poor or small-town, white Protestants, both in the South and the North, who unabashedly opposed the growing religious and ethnic pluralism in America. The Klan was an organization of Protestants with some religious ceremonies, but its cultural concerns were far more important than its ecclesiastical or theological interests. Many fundamentalist and conservative Protestant leaders denounced the Klan, although the Klan had cordial relations with some churches, especially in the South. By 1924, the Klan was a formidable political force, but the power of the Klan declined sharply after 1925. Despite the decline of the organization, the racist and nativist attitudes that it reflected remained strong.

Though most white southerners did not belong to the Klan, the overwhelming majority were ardently for racial separatism and were at least moderately anti-Catholic, thus making their alliance with the northeast, Catholic immigrant wing of the Democratic Party highly artificial. Only the strong, white, southern loyalty to the memory of the Confederacy, rendering them indelibly anti-Republican, kept them solidly in the Democratic ranks. The nomination of the Catholic Smith as the Democratic candidate for the presidency severely tested this loyalty and provided another symbolic moment in the contest between two definitions of Americanism emerging in the twentieth century.

Anti-Catholicism was by no means confined to the South or to conservative Protestants. Liberal Protestants, who sometimes virtually equated the Kingdom of God with the advance of democracy, were also fearful that Catholic influences in politics would lead to authoritarianism. Most liberal Protestants, however, were already Republican.

Smith was the popular governor of New York. Like almost all Catholic politicians in America, he was a Catholic and a politician, rather than a Catholic politician who explicitly related his religious faith to his political outlook.[17] In the United States, such a stance was almost a prerequisite to Catholic political activity. This was so not only because of the traditional American distancing of religion and politics, but because of anti-Catholic prejudices compounded by international Roman Catholic policy. International Catholicism was premised on its being the official state religion and that Catholic rulers should accept moral guidance from the church hierarchy. Moreover, the papacy, despite the loss of almost all its lands, continued to operate as a civil power as well as an ecclesiastical one. When Protestant critics pointed out these factors, local Catholic politicians could reply quite accurately that these ancient Catholic policies had no effect whatsoever on their political behavior in America. Al Smith captured the attitude perfectly during the 1928 campaign when he quipped in reply to a question about the latest papal encyclical, "What the hell's an encyclical?"[18]

Catholics also had an effective counterattack to Protestant criticisms. One Catholic author, for instance, asked the question, "Are Protestants Americans?" He argued that if Roman Catholics were not qualified to run for the presidency because of their alleged allegiance to the papacy, then Protestants were violating the Constitution by, in effect, imposing a religious test for office.[19]

The Catholic issue was a delicate one that no national politician could afford to say much about; it was complicated, however, by a campaign debate over Prohibition, a major concern of most Protestants, whether liberal or conservative. Smith was avowedly a "wet" candidate, favoring the repeal of Prohibition. The largely Baptist and Methodist white South had been strong in supporting Prohibition. Especially for Methodists, who emphasized piety and practice more than theological debate, Prohibition was a counterpart to theological fundamentalism. Virginia Methodist Bishop James A. Cannon Jr. led the southern campaign against Smith and for Prohibition. Anti-

Catholicism and support for Prohibition were strong also in most Protestant areas of the North, where they helped cement the old Protestant-Republican alliance.

Neither the Catholic issue nor the Prohibition question was decisive in the election. Smith was overwhelmingly defeated, but probably any Democrat would have been in the prosperous Republican days before the stock market crash of 1929. Smith lost in his home state of New York by approximately one hundred thousand votes. Remarkably, Republican Herbert Hoover broke into the "solid South" and carried the states of the upper South. The Catholic issue and Prohibition, no doubt, were significant factors in these states. Nonetheless, the only region Smith carried entirely was the Deep South, the very region where one would expect Protestant and Prohibition forces to be the strongest. Distinctly religious issues were factors in modifying the election patterns, but typical of American politics, they were only a few factors among many.

Building a Catholic Identity

While in politics Catholic Americans were moving into the mainstream, the Catholic church itself was building a strong, distinct identity. As always, ethnicity was a primary factor. The era spanning the two world wars was the golden age of the urban, Catholic, ethnic neighborhood. Not everything was golden, of course. Every urban ethnic community had poverty and crime. Differing ethnic neighborhoods often developed strong rivalries and resentments of each other, which a common religion did little to quell. Nonetheless, ethnic neighborhoods offered many of the compensating features of close-knit communities in which family and church played major roles. For most Catholics, religion was connected to location. Unlike most Protestants who *attended* churches, Catholics *belonged* to a parish. To the question, "Where are you from?" the Catholic might answer with the parish name.

This was a great era of popular devotional Catholicism in America. Such activities would often be deeply connected with preserving old-world ways and reinforcing family ties. For instance, one event that has been studied closely is the annual *festa* of the Madonna of Mount Carmel on 115th Street in Italian East Harlem, New York. This religious festival was imported from southern Italy and extravagantly celebrated in East Harlem every July during this era. It was a time of family gatherings, food, dancing, partying, and fireworks. The central event was a great parade following the image of the Madonna through the streets. The Madonna was believed to have powers of healing, and the celebration, mixing what might seem like the sacred and the profane, reflected the preservation of an old-world sense that the spiritual and the mystical penetrate into everyday existence.[20]

Catholics were building strong religious identities in many other ways, as well. Despite continuing ethnic rivalries, the national church organization was becoming more centralized and unified. One of the strongest forces was the parochial school system, which was now almost universal in areas of concentrated Catholic settlement and which ensured that Catholics would not become too homogenized into secular Americanism or forget their distinctive religious teachings and identity. Catholic higher education, concentrating mainly on liberal arts colleges, offered a church-controlled avenue for entry into American middle-class life. In some ways, these institutions marked the entry of more Catholics into the mainstream. Catholics could take pride in Notre Dame football, coached by Knute Rockne during this period, as the best in the nation. Catholic academic thought, too, was quite distinctive, centering on neo-Thomism, the revival of the views of the great medieval thinker Thomas Aquinas. Arguing that reason provided a solid foundation for faith, neo-Thomists sharply challenged the prevailing secular assumptions of this positivist era that science and reason would conflict with classic Christianity. A formidable system of Catholic presses, likewise, provided the population with materials that reinforced their sense that Catholics, because of their religious commitments, were different. At all levels of sophistication, Catholic magazines and books cultivated a separate identity. Catholic charitable institutions and hospitals provided a Catholic context for all of life's major activities from birth to death and beyond.

The sense of Catholic identity was also reinforced by continuing Protestant nativism, as seen in the anti-Catholicism of the revived Ku Klux Klan. The strict immigration quotas adopted in the 1920s also transparently reflected an attempt by the Anglo-Protestant establishment to limit further Catholic growth. In the state of Oregon, there was even a law that required all children to attend public schools; the statute was finally struck down by a Supreme Court ruling in 1925.

While American Catholics after World War I were victims of the reactionary conservatism of the time, the same national trends were reflected within the Catholic community itself. The general Catholic conservatism of this era paralleled and drew from some of the same cultural trends as Protestant conservatism and fundamentalism. Strongly religious people of all sorts were alarmed at cultural trends in modern America. In Catholic churches, however, the leadership included no real modernist party. In part this reflected immigrant conservatism, and in part it reflected the conservatism of the beleaguered international church. Catholics worldwide, for instance, were strongly anticommunist and tended to be so in America also.[21]

American Catholicism, in fact, generated its own brand of political fundamentalism, borrowing Protestant revivalist techniques of enterprising evangelism. In the early 1930s, the most famous radio preacher in America was Father Charles E. Coughlin (1891–1979) of Royal Oak, Michigan, a Detroit suburb. In some Catholic communities, Sunday afternoon ball games were halted to hear Coughlin's broadcast. People could remember walking down the street and "hearing out of every window the voice of Father Coughlin blaring from the radio." A person could walk for blocks, they recalled, and never miss a word.[22] Coughlin's message was a strange mixture of anticapitalism and anticommunism. At first, he adamantly favored the election of Franklin D. Roosevelt (1882–1945). Soon, however, he turned on Roosevelt and attacked him as part of a Jewish and communist conspiracy. Eventually, his anti-Semitism and favorable views of Hitler forced him from public life in 1942.

Coughlin was only one of the extreme anti-Semitic, anticommunist, anti-New Deal preachers of the 1930s. Most of the others were Protestant fundamentalists, or simply demagogues, who were moving toward an American fascism. Coughlin, for instance, made common cause in 1936 with Gerald L. K. Smith, a Disciples of Christ preacher who had been a close associate of Louisiana's Huey Long, who was assassinated in 1935. In 1936, Coughlin and Smith's Michigan-based Union Party gained nearly a million votes in the popular election. It marked, however, the high point of organized American political reaction, which quickly declined after 1936 as many Americans became alert to the real dangers of European fascism and Nazism.

"The Acids of Modernity"

The sensational reactions that marked the era between the two world wars reflected the tensions of rapid cultural change. These reactions also sometimes obscured the significance of the changes, since they helped create the impression, eagerly promoted by media, that anyone who would express alarm at the transformation must be a bigot or fanatic.

Nonetheless, some sober observers recognized the revolutionary nature of the developments taking place within American society itself. One of the most astute of these observers was the famed journalist Walter Lippmann (1889–1974). In *A Preface to Morals*, appearing in 1929, Lippmann observed that the "irreligion of the modern world [is] radical to a degree for which there is, I think, no counterpart."[23] Modern Americans, he later said, had "defied the Methodist God and have become very nervous."[24] Lippmann, a secular Jew himself, was not recommending a return to old-time religion. Even though he thought that J. Gresham Machen had "the best popular argument produced by either side in the current controversy," he was convinced that anti-intellectual popular fundamentalism and extremism had irremediably discredited traditional Protestantism among thinking people in the community.[25] Civilization, however, could not go on without a shared morality. Lippmann's solution was to base such a moral consensus on a new humanism. "When men can no longer be theists, they must, if they are civilized, become humanists."[26]

Building a new humanist moral consensus was, of course, more easily said than done. Likewise, "the acids of modernity" that Lippmann described had sources that went beyond ideological or even religious change.

Perhaps most basically, the United States was increasingly becoming what the sociologist Pitirim A. Sorokin described a few years later as a "sensate society."[27] That is, the operative values for most Americans most of the time were increasingly defined by satisfaction of the senses—materialistic, hedonistic, or sensuous. This accentuated the trend that Henry Adams had pointed out at the end of the nineteenth century, namely that the United States was preeminently a materialistic civilization. It was materialistic philosophically in that it was built on a science and technology that regarded the material, empirically observable world as the "real" world. America was practically materialistic in its efficient commercial and technological management of material culture.

The change in morals was closely related, then, to the rise of consumer culture. In the nineteenth century, the United States had been more a producer culture, emphasizing virtues such as self-discipline, self-denial, and hard work. By the 1920s, it had become more of a consumer culture in which relentless advertising pushed Americans toward definitions of themselves in terms of things that they owned and pleasures they could enjoy. Freedom of choice was among the highest values, and one of the greatest freedoms was to buy what one wanted. In the 1920s, the wide promotion of such outlooks was relatively new. Commercial advertising was just emerging in its modern form. Inevitably, such a commercial system glorified self-indulgence as a great good. The commercial possibilities of sexual suggestion, for instance, were just being developed. During the Victorian era, sex was a subject to be avoided in public. Once that taboo was broken, around World War I, advertisers made the most of it. As one observer put it, "Advertising, once pristine, began the transition which . . . was to transmute soap from a cleansing agent into an aphrodisiac."[28]

The commercial value of sexual suggestion also became a major force shaping much of American popular culture. Although relatively tame by later standards, popular songs celebrated "hot lips" or "burning kisses" or proclaimed, "I need lovin'." Hollywood movies, though threatened with censorship, made sex their leading motif with films like *Up in Mabel's Room, Her Purchase Price*, and *A Shocking Night*. The new dances, complained Southern Methodist Bishop James Cannon, brought "the bodies of men and women in unusual relations to each other."[29] Cannon and other traditionalists could do little, however, about the rumble seats of automobiles, which were subject to similar objections.

The sexual revolution found its intellectual rationale in the new popularity of the psychological theories of Sigmund Freud (1856–1939) in the 1920s. Freud, who developed his theories in nineteenth-century Vienna while working with patients who had upbringings in which sexuality was strictly suppressed, built his analysis around theories of broadly defined human sexuality. Americans of the 1920s, who typically had similar upbringings, eagerly latched onto popular versions of Freud's views as a rationale for open sexual expression. Freud provided the aura of scientific authority for new "healthy" standards of human behavior, radically different from the so-called "bluestocking Methodist" standards (or equally strict Catholic norms) typical in nineteenth-century America.

The revolution, of course, did not take place overnight. It had many precursors, and the battle between the two standards continues even to the present. In the 1920s, however, the encounter between the two moral ideals was probably as sharp as it ever was. In many ways, the culture was still remarkably straight-laced. Buying alcoholic beverages was illegal. Strict observance of the Sabbath, a form of true asceticism in which children would be forced to renounce their daily games and pleasures and spend long afternoons in quiet, pious reading, was still the experience of most Americans who were reared as Protestants and had not receded in some parts of the country, especially the South. Many in Catholic immigrant communities retained similarly strict religious disciplines and sexual moral standards, reinforced by regular confessions to priests and appropriate acts of penance. In small-town America, young women who dared to be seen in the swimwear of the day (excessively discreet by later standards) were liable to be warned by guardians of the old order that they were risking the flames of hell. Many strict evangelical groups, including many Pentecostals, fundamentalists, Southern Baptists, and Southern Methodists, banned mixed bathing. The cultural change, however, was more complex than merely a conflict between the new sensate culture and the old-time religion. The changes were ones that internally were altering American Protestantism itself.

Such concessions were not so much to the new sensuality, which liberal Protestants generally condemned, as to a new view of human nature. Essentially, the belief growing within both wings of American Protestantism was that humans were free and largely in control of their destinies. Such changing views were reflected in the continuing decline of Calvinism, which emphasized that humans were ultimately neither free nor in control of their destinies. These latter doctrines had disappeared in liberal churches and were played down in much of revivalism, at least since the time of Moody. The new revivalism emphasized instead the importance of individual choice and the ease with which it could be made. Simple decisions for Jesus made by raising a hand at the end of a revival service increased both the numbers of converts and the sense that human will was in control. Billy Sunday's ethical message to "be strong and show yourself a man" had similar import.[30] For both liberal and conservative Protestants, Christianity was increasingly a matter of building character through self-discipline.

The ideal of character challenged the dominant American cultural trends only partly. Perhaps because so many Protestants concentrated on symbolic behavioral issues such as Prohibition, they directed little critique towards the larger dimensions of the cultural revolution. The social gospel, which had been vigorous before the war, declined in the Republican 1920s. Relatively few mainstream Protestants questioned in any basic way the commercial character of the culture and the material and competitive values it was promoting. For instance, the best-selling nonfiction book in 1925 and 1926 was Bruce Barton's *The Man Nobody Knows* (1925). Barton, an advertising executive, presented Jesus as a master businessman who built an organization of only twelve men into the world's most successful enterprise. The book's epigraph was the boy Jesus's statement to his parents after he remained teaching in the temple: "Wist ye not that I must be about my Father's *business*?"[31]

Disillusion

In the meantime, important literary figures of the generation of Americans coming of age were thoroughly disillusioned with the churches. Perhaps the most effective critique was novelist Sinclair Lewis's *Elmer Gantry* (1927). Gantry was a partly self-deceived, sometimes sincere and sometimes shallow, religious enterpriser and charlatan. A clergyman moving through a variety of church posts and sexual liaisons, he could be a modernist, a fundamentalist-revivalist, or a civic reformer as the occasion demanded. His own success was paramount. Many in this time of sophisticated disillusion readily saw Gantry as representing the phoniness of the churches.

H. L. Mencken captured the cynicism of the era with his suggestion that municipalities build giant stadiums in which clergymen could be turned loose on each other as a public display.

Many saw the crisis as a deeper illness in Western civilization itself. Young men had died, wrote poet Ezra Pound after World War I:

> For an old bitch gone in the teeth,
> For a botched civilization.[32]

People spoke knowingly of German author Oswald Spengler's *Decline of the West* (1918), though few read through his involved arguments. American writers fled what they regarded as the stifling "Puritan" atmosphere of Prohibition America, setting up their own expatriate colony in Paris. Ernest Hemingway, for instance, represented well the outlook of this "lost generation." Subjected to a strong evangelical upbringing by his grandmother, Hemingway seemingly detached himself entirely from the traditional ideals and concerns of so-called Christian civilization.[33] Rather than moralize, his writing reflected a deep appreciation of style and sensitivity to the experience of the moment.

Joseph Wood Krutch, whose *The Modern Temper* (1929) was widely read at the end of the decade, addressed the philosophical issues behind this disillusion. True to his generation, he saw the findings of natural science, particularly evolutionary science, as the great challenge to traditional belief. Krutch, however, went beyond the commonplace claim that natural science undermined Christian faith to point out that it undermined humanism as well. If humans were truly no more than higher-order animals, as modern science proclaimed, then humanistic ideals such as love, beauty, and moral standards were all illusions, simply pleasing survival mechanisms.[34]

Perhaps the most powerful analysis of such pessimistic themes came from historian Carl Becker. In his book, *The Heavenly City of the Eighteenth-Century Philosophers*, published in 1932, Becker argued that educated moderns were as far away from the worldview of the eighteenth century as they were from the Middle Ages.[35] The most enlightened eighteenth-century thinkers, such as Jefferson and Franklin, believed in reason as a sure guide to finding truth. They had such faith in reason, Becker pointed out, because they presumed that there was a Creator and therefore an order of natural and moral laws to be discovered. Truly modern people had no basis for such a belief in a purposeful and ordered universe. In a brilliant summary of the modern predicament, Becker, who like so many Americans had been reared in evangelical Protestantism, wrote:

> Edit and interpret the conclusions of modern science as tenderly as we like, it is still quite impossible for us to regard man as the child of God for whom the earth was created as a temporary habitation. Rather must we regard him as little more than a chance deposit on the surface of the world, carelessly thrown up between two ice ages by the same forces that rust iron and ripen corn, a sentient organism endowed by some happy or unhappy accident with intelligence indeed, but with an intelligence that is conditioned by the very forces that it seeks to understand and to control. The ultimate cause of this cosmic process . . . appears in its effects as neither benevolent nor malevolent, as neither kind nor unkind, but merely as indifferent to us. What is man that the electron should be mindful of him![36]

Most Americans, even most intellectuals, were not willing to follow the naturalistic worldview to conclusions so consistent with its premises. It was one thing to profess such a worldview; it was another to live consistently with its implications.

Pragmatic Secularism: John Dewey

More typical was an effort to reconstruct meaning on a thoroughly naturalistic basis, such as that offered by John Dewey (1859–1952). Dewey was *the* representative American secular thinker of the first half of the twentieth century. According to historian Henry Steel Commager, who lived through the era, Dewey "became the guide, the mentor, and the conscience of the

American people: It is scarcely an exaggeration to say that for a generation no major issue was clarified until Dewey had spoken."[37]

Dewey advocated pragmatism, the most typical philosophy of the day, and offered the most plausible alternative to traditional religion for constructing values. Pragmatism was built on essentially naturalistic evolutionary principles. Rather than design a philosophy by first asking abstract questions about God or the nature of ultimate reality, the naturalistic worldview declared such questions to be ultimately unanswerable. Therefore, pragmatism starts with what science can still observe and describe about human thought: how the mind works. Dewey's version of pragmatism regarded the human mind as essentially an "instrument" that functioned for purposes of survival. In a famous summary, he declared that "ideas . . . become true just in so far as they help us to get into satisfactory relation with other parts of our experience."[38] That is, people should not waste time worrying about whether their ideas correspond to some absolute truth in the real world. Rather, they should consider how their beliefs actually function.

Such an instrumental view of belief, said Dewey, reveals that our ideals and values are shaped by our social settings. Various religious beliefs, for instance, were generated by societies to legitimize their social, political, and ethical order. Such religious beliefs, evolving over the centuries, were typically irrational, however, and therefore not always the most healthful adjustments to reality.

In the light of modern science, then, Dewey continued, new religious beliefs ought to be constructed that more healthfully advance the human species. Defining religions functionally as people's highest ideals and values, Dewey proposed, in *A Common Faith* (1934), humanistic values on which people from all traditions ought to be able to unite. These were principles that promoted ideals like human community, justice, security, art, and knowledge.[39]

Dewey's widest impact came from applying similar principles to American educational theory. Education, Dewey emphasized, should promote a social environment that allows the full development of each individual's potential. A fixed body of knowledge, although not irrelevant to education, was less important than learning that built character. Democratic values, such as those outlined in *A Common Faith*, provided the ideals that individuals should internalize. Thus, Dewey, having a functional definition of religion, was in effect promoting the public schools as the functional established churches of America in which common ideals promoting human growth would be taught.

Dewey is important both because of his wide influence and the way his thought illustrates an important transition in dominant American public philosophy. He was a New Englander and, like so many of his nineteenth-century contemporaries, was reared in an evangelical environment. During his early adult career as a professor, until the 1890s, he was active in church work and even taught Sunday school. Then, once again like so many of his academic contemporaries, he abandoned Christianity entirely. Nonetheless, Dewey retained the evangelical and old New England Calvinist zeal in transforming the social order. Like the liberal Protestants and some of the conservatives, he concentrated on building character. He offered twentieth-century Americans a secular faith that promised to yield the highest moral ideals. Through such a faith, Dewey and many of his contemporaries hoped that a scientifically based civilization could usher in an era when people of all traditional religious heritages could be brought together. The millennial dreams still persisted.

The Neo-Orthodox Critique

By the 1930s, influential liberal Protestant spokespersons were questioning the degree to which their churches were identifying the cause of Christianity with increasingly secular American civilization. Because this critique was influenced by a neo-orthodox European reaction to liberal theology, beginning just after World War I, the American movement also became known as neo-orthodox. The American movement, however, did not necessarily repudiate theological liberalism as thoroughly as did the European movement.

European neo-orthodoxy was identified primarily with the work of the Swiss theologian Karl Barth (1886–1968), who in massive and impressive theological tomes reemphasized traditional doctrines such as the sovereignty of God, the depravity of humans, and the centrality of salvation in Christ, uniquely revealed through the witness of Scripture. Though Barth did not claim the historical and scientific accuracy of the Bible the way fundamentalists did, he asserted that there was a great gulf between what humans could learn by unaided reason and true knowledge of God, which could be learned only through Christ.

The leading spokesmen for American neo-orthodoxy were the remarkable brothers, H. Richard Niebuhr (1894–1962) and Reinhold Niebuhr (1892–1971). Reared in a conservative Protestant German-American community in the Midwest and coming of age just when World War I placed German Americans in an awkward position that demanded strong loyalty from them, the Niebuhrs both became intensely interested in questions concerning the relationship of Christianity to culture. Coming from outside the mainstream, they saw more vividly than their Anglo-Protestant counterparts the ambiguities and paradoxes of identifying Christianity with any national cultural norm.

H. Richard Niebuhr argued in the early 1930s that American Protestant churches had fallen into bondage to a corrupt civilization, one dominated by capitalism, humanism, liberalism, and nationalism. All these were human-centered doctrines. Christianity, he emphasized, must be centered on God. American Protestantism, he claimed in a famous statement, had detheologized itself. As a result, it preached that "a God without wrath brought men without sin into a kingdom without judgments through the ministrations of a Christ without a cross."[40] To be truly the church, Christians must stand against the world. "If the church has no other plan of salvation," H. Richard proclaimed, ". . . than one of deliverance by force, education, idealism or planned economy, it really has no existence as a church and needs to resolve itself into a political party or a school."[41]

Reinhold Niebuhr was more concerned with politics than his brother and, perhaps for that reason, became better known in the twentieth-century world, when politics was often the operative religion. Like many intellectuals of the generation between the world wars, he leaned toward socialism. Under the influence of neo-orthodoxy, however, his principal contribution to Christian social thought was a Christian realism that warned against identifying the kingdom of God with any political ideology. In his classic volume, *Moral Man and Immoral Society* (1932), he pointed out that we cannot apply the same moral standards to social and political institutions that we can to individuals. Governments, businesses, and labor unions are constructed essentially to promote self-interests. Hence, the impact of Christian ethics on them, although potentially important, will always be limited. Often in public policy, one will have to settle for the lesser evil. Therefore, the kingdom of God cannot be identified with any social-political proposal.[42]

Theologically, Reinhold Niebuhr's major contribution was to revive the doctrine of original sin. This doctrine, which was a leading motif in early American Protestant thought, had been increasingly denied in the optimistic and romantic era of the nineteenth and early twentieth centuries. Humans, Americans were coming to believe, were capable of doing anything. They believed this especially when they thought they had science and technology on their side. John Dewey's philosophy was a good example. Liberal churches, however, were just as optimistic about human nature.

Reinhold Niebuhr argued that there was an essential flaw in human nature, which he equated with original sin. Because humans had the freedom to be creative, they rose above the animals. Their freedom and creativity, however, also led them to overestimate themselves. They thought of themselves as the creators of their own destinies. The very virtues that made them great became their vices. The righteous man Jesus, Niebuhr observed, was crucified through the combination of the two great human achievements up to that time—Jewish religion and Roman law. Thus it was with all individuals and nations. Humans overestimate their virtues and turn them into vices. Only from the perspective of the Divine Creator can humans see themselves in their true, limited perspectives.[43]

Neo-orthodoxy, which in America often meant something like "chastened liberalism," had a significant impact on mainstream Protestant thought for the next generation. Because of its sophisticated nature, it found its strength primarily in seminaries, through which it influenced many pulpits. Nonetheless, its subtle emphases on the ambiguities and paradoxes of the application of Christianity to the world prevented it from becoming a widely popular movement. Most twentieth-century Americans, if they were looking for religious answers, wanted simpler formulas. Nevertheless, the neo-orthodox critiques tempered theological liberalism for a generation. Liberal preacher Harry Emerson Fosdick, for instance, declared in a much-noticed sermon of 1935 that "the church must go beyond modernism." Modernism as a theological self-description went out of style, though various forms of liberalism continued to be popular among Protestant leadership and in mainline seminaries.

A Secular New Deal

One reason why the neo-orthodox prophets were calling their mainline churches to stand against the world was that the world was becoming more overtly secular, even in the relatively religious United States. During the Progressive Era, when the only slightly secularized New England reforming culture experienced a triumph, it was still easy for Protestants to believe that progressive reform was essentially an expression of Christian civilization. By the 1930s, an increasing number of leading American figures, especially in the arts, entertainment, and education, were openly secular, and the idea of Christian civilization was becoming more problematic.

The New Deal under Franklin Roosevelt was an important symbol of public secularity. Although Roosevelt himself was an active Episcopal layman and sometimes referred to God in his public utterances, his administration was presented frankly as an effort in pragmatism versus dogmatic moral principle. The immediate end of Prohibition helped provide a secular tone. More pervasive, however, was a pragmatic style. While the key words exciting social action in the Progressive Era (as Richard Hofstadter had identified them) had been *soul, morals, service, duty, shame, disgrace, sin,* and *selfishness,* during the New Deal, the key words were *needs, organization, humanitarian, results, technique, institution, realistic, discipline, morale, skill, expert, habits, practical,* and *leadership.*[44]

Progressivism had embodied two major impulses. The dominant impulse was to apply moral fervor to politics, and the secondary theme was an emerging pragmatism, as represented, for instance, in the legal thought of Oliver Wendell Holmes Jr. The New Deal represented the triumph of this latter ideal. It was, most simply, the triumph of technological principle applied to government. The technological principle states that the bottom line is finding the most efficient means to get the job done.

This view was articulated most clearly by one of Roosevelt's cabinet members, Thurman Arnold, in a widely read volume of 1937, *The Folklore of Capitalism.* Arnold argued that the principles of modern business should be applied to government. Businesses are not run by ideologues with creeds; they are run by experts with slogans. Efficient organization is the goal. To keep public support, the principles of advertising should be applied to government.

What Arnold was promoting was a relatively benign American version of the principles of modern propaganda, being so skillfully and sinisterly promoted in Stalin's Russia and in Hitler's Germany. The big difference, though, was that the totalitarian propaganda was used in the cause of rigid ideologies, while in America, the government had a long tradition of non-ideological pragmatism that the New Deal was accentuating. At the same time, the American heritage also included a strong tradition of moral review of the government and scrutiny by the press and public. Some culturally built-in restraints, therefore, limited how far the government could depart from taken-for-granted moral principles. Moreover, pragmatic organization has to be directed toward some goals. The New Deal, therefore, despite playing down overt moralism, could draw on a heritage of shared humanitarian and democratic goals.

From the longer perspective of American cultural development, however, the rise of large, bureaucratic, pragmatic government was, for better or worse, another step toward the secularization of modern public life.

CHAPTER 7

A Return to Faith
and the Quest for Consensus: 1941–63

Now the trumpet summons us again—not as a call to bear arms, though arms we need—not as a call to battle, though embattled we are—but a call to bear the burden of a long twilight struggle, year in and year out, "rejoicing in hope, patient in tribulation"—a struggle against the common enemies of man: tyranny, poverty, disease, and war itself. . . . With a good conscience our only sure reward, with history the final judge of our deeds, let us go forth to lead the land we love, asking His blessing and His help, but knowing that here on earth God's work must truly be our own.

President John F. Kennedy, Inaugural Address (1961)

World War II marked another major turning point in American cultural history. Its impact was, however, almost the opposite of that of World War I. Whereas the First World War brought to the United States a temporary wild enthusiasm for its international mission, it soon led to disillusion and a period of cultural pessimism. The Second World War, on the other hand, led not only to America's role as a world leader but also to a widespread revival of faith in America and America's religions.

Looking back in broad overview at the twentieth century, we now can see that World War II and the optimism of the 1950s marked an interruption of the sense of cultural crisis that emerged in the 1920s and 1930s. In the Vietnam era of the 1960s and early 1970s, the sense of crisis resumed. The Reagan years of the 1980s then reflected an attempted return to the ideals of the World War II era. However, so much changed in the meantime that the return was only partial and a sense of new and often bitter cultural divisions only intensified. The roots of these divisions were often deeply intertwined with the patterns of American religion.

World War II and American Faith

Between the world wars, many of America's Protestant leaders thought they had learned an important lesson about religion and culture. They endorsed the American cause in the First World War, sometimes with extravagant enthusiasm, only to find out afterward that they had been taken in by war-time propaganda. Looking back, it was difficult to see the war as the forces of light versus those of darkness. Therefore, they organized for lasting peace. These peace concerns paralleled optimistic international efforts, most notably the Kellogg-Briand Pact of 1928, in which fifteen major nations agreed to renounce warfare as a national policy. Thousands of clergy, especially from mainline Protestant denominations, signed pledges vowing never to support a war again.

Clerical opposition to American military intervention in the ever-worsening international situation continued right up to the bombing of Pearl Harbor in December 1941. That event brought a dramatic reversal and an almost universal willingness to support a war that seemed to be for the survival of democratic civilization itself. Compared with the ideal, American liberal culture seemed to many thoughtful people to be deeply flawed; compared with the alternatives—especially that presented by Adolf Hitler, who combined modern technology with a horrible lack of moral principle—the American way of life seemed worth fighting and even dying for.[1]

American church leaders and politicians and even President Roosevelt himself sometimes spoke of the war as a struggle for "Christian civilization." Totalitarianism had suddenly spread worldwide and appeared poised to destroy democratic civilization. Most Americans saw the combination of republican government and a popular willingness to play by the rules as one of the great accomplishments of the British and the Judeo-Christian cultural heritage. The myth of a Christian republican heritage, although usually exaggerated and often used crassly, had some basis in reality.[2]

Nonetheless, the old paradoxes of fighting a war for a seemingly righteous cause crept up. As theologian Reinhold Niebuhr frequently observed, a too-confident sense of justice often leads to injustice. One did not have to look far from home to exemplify that point. An outstanding instance was that many Americans feared disloyalty from Japanese Americans in their midst and so raised little objection to the expulsion of over one hundred thousand Japanese Americans into concentration camps for most of the war.

While these camps were benign places compared with Hitler's incredibly sinister death camps for Jews and others in Europe, Americans and their allies were reduced to Hitler's standards on another score with more permanent consequences. One of the traditional criteria for a just war was that it be fought by armies while reasonable efforts were made to exempt civilian populations from the killing. With the bombing of Dutch and British cities, Hitler violated this principle on a scale unprecedented in modern times. The allies soon retaliated in kind. Americans at first were reluctant to engage in indiscriminate bombing of German cities but by 1944 had lost their compunction. With the British, the United States engaged in horrifying firebombing of German cities, killing in the bombing of Dresden alone on the night of February 13–14, 1945, well over twenty thousand men, women, and children. Since it was Shrove Tuesday, or Mardi Gras, the night before the Christian observance of Ash Wednesday, many of the children killed were dressed in festival costumes. Even if Hitler was more barbaric, war barbarizes everyone, and the juxtaposition of the ideals of Christian civilization and the realities of human use of technology were now appearing starkly on both sides.[3]

When firebombing became routinely accepted, Western civilization abandoned an ancient principle and entered a new age, considering it almost normal that war included terrorism against civilians. Another technical advance, the invention of the atomic bomb, came to symbolize this turning point of mindset. In August 1945, Americans used two of these to destroy the civilian populations of the Japanese cities of Hiroshima and Nagasaki. Thus, they brought the war to a close but introduced a new meaning for war.

The atom bombs underscored anew the dilemmas of war, peace, and justice among clergy. The pope condemned the bombings and so did some Catholic and liberal Protestant clergy. Others justified it as a lesser evil since it saved lives by ending the war. Theologically conservative clergy more often tended toward this latter view. Fundamentalists often added that the atom bomb should remind everyone of the fragile character of all human civilization and that God would soon bring history to an end.

Despite the paradoxes, international tensions, and instabilities created by the wartime destruction, most Americans emerged from the contest with renewed idealism. They believed especially in themselves as the last, best hope for the world. America was less scathed by the war than other major nations, and Americans now took seriously the nation's role as an international power. This again marked an important turning point, since from then on the United States would be defined, in part, by a consciousness that it was an integral part of the world community. The founding of the United Nations in 1945, with its headquarters in New York City, signaled this new role. American Protestant clergy followed the lead, playing a major part in founding the World Council of Churches in 1948. The American sense of world leadership was based in part on its economic and technological superiority after the war. But it also included a strong sense of mission in providing economic aid as well as leadership in restoring justice and establishing democracy throughout the world. Many people from all faiths believed that religious values were important for promoting such goals.

The dark side of the picture was the overshadowing presence of the cold war in a nuclear age. World War II ended with political power in the world divided primarily between the United States—allied with Britain and France—and the Soviet Union. At the end of the war, the Soviet Union consolidated a vast empire, which included Eastern Europe. Stalin's Russia was no better than Hitler's Germany when it came to employing modern technologies for the ruthless extermination of its enemies and for total suppression of dissent. To make matters more alarming, in 1949 an extended civil war in China ended with a Marxist victory. The Soviet Union and the People's Republic of China became allies, and in the United States, international communism was widely believed to be one concerted force. By 1950, expansion by communist North Korea into South Korea drew the United States, fighting under the official auspices of a United Nations peacekeeping force, into another war. Until this war was settled indecisively in 1953, a threat of a third world war, with nuclear weapons on both sides, seemed particularly imminent.

Under a real threat of communist expansion, the imagined powers of the international movement were magnified. Led by Senator Joseph R. McCarthy (1908–57), worried political conservatives attempted to rid the land of supposed communist sympathizers. McCarthy was a Catholic from Wisconsin with a strong, conservative Catholic constituency. Protestant fundamentalists and conservatives also tended to support militant anticommunism, but in the South, Protestant conservatives did not have much of a political base. One of the most colorful of the politically oriented fundamentalists was Carl McIntire (1906–2002). McIntire had a daily radio broadcast, carried on some six hundred stations at its height, which emphasized anticommunism. McIntire argued that the mainline National Council of Churches (formerly the Federal Council of Churches) and the World Council of Churches, which included representatives from the Russian Orthodox Church, were hotbeds of communist subversion. According to McIntire, as well as many fundamentalists and other conservative Protestants, the turn of mainline churches to modernist theology was leading to a relativistic world church and world government that would essentially be in sympathy with "godless communism." J. Edgar Hoover (1895–1972), head of the Federal Bureau of Investigation, and a strong foe of communist subversion, was a conservative Protestant who held similar views.

The Irony of American History

Such strong views from the religious right helped make more moderate Protestant outlooks welcome in the cultural mainstream. In particular, neo-orthodox theologian Reinhold Niebuhr reached the height of his popularity in the postwar era. Although not a media figure, Niebuhr was apparently the last major American Protestant theologian to be taken seriously outside of the churches. Some of his academic admirers called themselves "atheists for Niebuhr."

In *The Irony of American History* (1952), Niebuhr pointed out the ironic similarities between the United States and the dreaded Soviet Union. The two nations were similar in their enlightened confidence in human ability to use scientific analysis to create an ideal society. Each had ultimately similar goals: humans should be masters of their own destinies. Each country proposed similar means for reaching these goals, essentially through an economic system. Both tended to define humanity in terms of property—either the ownership of it or the lack thereof. Each revered a scientific elite. Each nation had similar mythologies asserting its own innocence and the corruption of its opponents. Ironically, for instance, while Americans took their economic prosperity to be evidence of their virtue, much of the rest of the world took it to be evidence of vice. Finally, each nation used the myth of the virtue of its intentions to justify the vices of its policies in reaching its goals.

Niebuhr was not endorsing the Soviet Union as being just as good as America. Rather, he supported a realistic foreign policy that would stand up to the Soviet threat. However, at the same time, he pointed out the irony that the Soviet vices Americans criticized—especially materialism and the belief that one could build a better society based simply on human mastery of science, technology, and economics—were in effect the same principles that Americans most believed in. Moreover, to double the irony, Americans used their religious heritage simply to endorse this humanism and materialism. Rather than see themselves in the light of a transcendent God who laughs at all human pretension to manage their own destinies, Americans used their religion to rationalize for themselves unlimited powers and rights. By contrast, Niebuhr urged maintaining a sense of human limitations, even when people were sure they were in the right. Abraham Lincoln epitomized such modesty when he observed, in his second inaugural speech, that both sides in the Civil War prayed to the same God and that the prayers of neither would be fully answered since "the Almighty has his own purposes." Such a stance, Niebuhr added, can proceed only from a "broken spirit and a contrite heart."[4]

The Postwar Revival

The United States from the 1940s until the early 1960s was in the midst of an extensive religious revival, but many observers, such as Niebuhr, questioned its depth. Religious groups of nearly all sorts were growing and prospering. A national survey, conducted shortly after World War II, revealed that two out of three Americans attended religious services at least once a month and that 42 percent attended every week. Other polls revealed that nineteen out of twenty Americans believed in God, nine out of ten said they engaged in prayer, six out of seven viewed the Bible as the divinely inspired word of God, and three out of four believed in life after death.[5] These figures were all substantially higher than in any other major industrialized country. On the other hand, lack of depth to some of these commitments was suggested by a poll revealing that over half of the adults could not name any one of the four Gospels—Matthew, Mark, Luke, and John.[6]

Whatever the depth of the commitments or knowledge of the faith, unprecedented numbers of Americans were joining religious groups, with memberships rising from about 50 percent to over 60 percent of the population in the decade after the war.[7] As usual, when most people talked about the revival, they thought first about the mainline northern Protestants who still regarded themselves as representing a sort of all-American religion. Probably the beliefs of most laypeople within such churches were traditional Protestant ones, but critics were noticing how often those beliefs were vague and how many of them were mixed with seemingly secular Americanism. As historian Martin Marty observed at the time, more and more people seemed to have faith in faith itself. They were in favor of "religion-in-general" and believed in a God who was understandable, manageable, comforting, and ultimately a good-natured "man upstairs." Bible-believing actress Jane Russell, for example, described God as a "livin' Doll."[8] Apparently bland, suburban religion was reinforced by a marked increase in public piety. President Dwight D. Eisenhower, who took office in 1953, came to be a symbol of American spiritual values. During this time, prayer breakfasts, special church services, and back-to-God-and-values crusades were conspicuous Washington activities.[9] With the government reflecting now more broadly and vaguely than ever the old Republican agenda of uniting the nation under a moral-religious ideal, people were encouraged to go to the church of their choice and to pray for peace. The words "under God" were added to the hitherto secular Pledge of Allegiance. President Eisenhower encapsulated the prevailing view that religion was a "good thing" with his famous remark: "Our government makes no sense, unless it is founded in a deeply felt religious faith—*and I don't care what it is.*"[10]

The outlook of faith in faith was embodied by Norman Vincent Peale's *The Power of Positive Thinking* (1952), a runaway bestseller of the Eisenhower years. Peale (1898–1993), one of New York City's leading mainline Protestant preachers, proclaimed positive thinking as the "secret to success." All that was necessary was to "believe in yourself! Have faith in your abilities!" The book was filled with rules and formulas for overcoming negative attitudes, and it promised happy and productive lives.[11]

The most widely heralded analysis of this sort of popular American religion was Will Herberg's *Protestant-Catholic-Jew: An Essay in American Religious Sociology* (1955). Herberg, a Jewish scholar, argued that despite the differences among America's three major traditions, these were not the real religions of most Americans. He made a distinction between professed religion and "operative religion," the latter defined as the highest values that people actually live by. The operative religion of most Americans was faith in the "American Way of Life." This religion involved a faith in democracy, individualism, optimism, idealism, humanitarianism, nationalism, and tolerance of other Americans.[12]

For instance, almost all Americans believed that one should love one's neighbor as oneself, and over half believed they did follow this rule "all the way" in their lives. This in itself was a remarkable assertion of their own virtue for people formally professing religions that traditionally emphasized human sinfulness. Moreover, 90 percent claimed they truly "obeyed the law of love" toward people of other religions and 80 percent toward those of other races. Yet, Herberg observed, many of these same Americans did not extend the law of love to communists or to enemies of one's country. So, said Herberg, "Where the American Way of Life approves of love of one's fellow man, most Americans confidently assert that they practice such love; where the American Way of Life disapproves, the great mass of Americans do not hesitate to confess that they do not practice it, and apparently feel very little guilt for their failure."[13]

The United States, Herberg was pointing out, was simultaneously professedly religious yet very secular. For instance, even of those Americans who said that religion was "very important" to them, well over half said that their religious beliefs had no real effect on their ideas or conduct in politics or business.[14] Catholics and Jews, indeed, had been largely absorbed into an essentially Protestant Anglo-Puritan tradition, but the resulting American cultural value system severely limited the functions of traditional religions.

One could read this as the outcome of liberal religionists' programs of tolerance. The opinion was coming to prevail that religion, though valuable for personal fulfillment, should not interfere with being a good American. Hence, traditional religions were in danger of losing their identities in a blend of secular and religious humanitarian ideals. Though Americans spoke much of God, they often seemed to trust more in human abilities to solve humanity's problems.

Billy Graham: From Fundamentalist to Evangelical

Not all of the religious resurgence of the era was so broadly liberal. Many more conservative groups also flourished. The best-known figure in the postwar revivals was a young evangelist named Billy Graham (1918–2018). Graham began as a fundamentalist but soon became the leader of a new style of evangelicalism that shed some of the hard edges of its fundamentalist heritage. The story of Graham's rise to fame illustrates the differences between fundamentalism and the new evangelicalism.

Although defeated in the mainline northern denominations, fundamentalists in the 1930s and 1940s were building their own institutions, especially evangelistically oriented local churches and other evangelistic agencies. Even if fundamentalists were not much noticed by the dominant media and power structures, they remained numerous. For instance, at some times during World War II, the radio program with apparently the largest audiences was not one of the popular comedy or entertainment programs but Charles E.

Fuller's (1887–1968) "Old Fashioned Revival Hour." Fuller preached a simple, homey, but dignified old-time gospel of conversion. Despite his popularity, the three major networks, NBC, CBS, and ABC, would not carry Fuller. The only religious broadcasting these networks allowed was free Sunday morning time for Catholics and Protestants. The Protestant broadcasts were controlled by the Federal Council of Churches, anathema to the fundamentalists. Harry Emerson Fosdick (1878–1969), famed opponent of fundamentalism, was the principal, officially recognized Protestant radio preacher.

Despite such problems in gaining recognition (they had similar difficulties in keeping the Federal Council from controlling the military chaplaincy), fundamentalists were sparking a wartime revival. In impressive youth rallies in many American cities, they were filling famed sports arenas, such as New York's Madison Square Garden and Chicago's Soldier Field. A major outgrowth of such young people's revivalism was the organization in 1945 of Youth for Christ. Billy Graham was the national organization's first full-time evangelist.

In 1949, during a tent revival in Los Angeles, Graham gained the notice of the media establishment through support from newspaper publisher William Randolph Hearst (1863–1951), who told his editors to "puff Graham." The thirty-year-old evangelist immediately hit the big time. Much of Graham's message made America sound more like Babylon than Israel. He tied anxieties about the threat of nuclear destruction in with biblical warnings of judgment for sin. He preached for conversions and for traditional American values. Though he stayed away from public involvement in politics, he spoke often of the communist threat and the dangers to America of such atheistic and materialistic values.

Graham was part of a larger effort of many fundamentalist Protestants who, having found themselves now as cultural outsiders, were working to become insiders again. Their overriding motive was to convert people to Christ; but to do this, they needed to regain respectability. Graham encouraged conservative scholars, seminaries, and publications to defend the integrity of biblical revelation and oppose liberal Protestant thought, but in intellectually sophisticated ways. He also used his immense popularity to cultivate the friendships of major political leaders and became a regular visitor to the White House through many administrations. The evangelical movement had considerable financial support from conservative business leaders who hoped to exercise political influence, mostly through lobbying and personal connections rather than in grass-roots mobilization. At the same time, Graham began moving toward the ecclesiastical center in his revival campaigns. Originally, his evangelistic crusades were sponsored largely by fundamentalists or other conservative Protestants who would not be associated with mainline churches. In 1957, however, at a major crusade in New York City, Graham accepted the sponsorship of the local council of churches, which included Protestant liberals.

This move brought a sharp break between Graham and more militant fundamentalists, who insisted on strict separation from religious liberals. John R. Rice (1895–1980)—later a mentor of Jerry Falwell (1933–2007)—whose weekly newspaper, *The Sword of the Lord*, was influential in fundamentalist circles, took the lead in breaking with Graham. Bob Jones Sr. (1883–1968), founder of the strictly separatist Bob Jones University, soon followed suit. After 1957, "fundamentalism" as a self-designation meant those who totally separated from mainline churches. The larger group of conservative Protestants, who still held to the traditional fundamentals of the faith but were trying to reenter or stay in the mainstream, came to be called "neo-evangelicals" or simply "evangelicals."[15] Though Graham himself could not be ignored, establishment Protestants and the secular media still did not pay much attention to this large group. Some people did, however, begin to speculate about conservative Protestants as a third force in Christendom beside mainline Protestants and Catholics.[16]

Pentecostal Healing

An important part of this third force was the Pentecostal movement, which was still small (its largest denominations were still under half a million members) but growing. Paralleling the other revivals of the time was a Pentecostal revival, which concentrated particularly in healing ministries. The period from 1947 to the early 1960s was the great age for a remarkable number of sawdust trail healing-tent evangelists. Oral Roberts (1918–2009) was the best known of these, but he was only one of many colorful figures, some more and some less reputable. Roberts himself was born into the home of an Oklahoma Pentecostal preacher and grew up in the rural poverty of the Depression. Before his birth, his mother later told him, she was informed by God that he was to have a special ministry. After a dramatic healing from tuberculosis when he was a teenager, he began preparing to become a Pentecostal preacher himself. After World War II, Roberts followed some others into healing-tent evangelism and soon became its leading practitioner. Like other healers, he claimed miraculous powers, such as a "word of knowledge" about people's lives or their hidden illnesses. Like others of the early healing evangelists, Roberts also sent his followers anointed prayer cloths that reputedly had healing powers.

Popular responses to Roberts's crusades, especially among the poorer and less educated, were immense, and his claims grew even larger. During a three-year period in the late 1950s, he claimed to have won ten million converts, though perhaps a more accurate gauge of his following was the circulation of six hundred thousand copies of his magazine. Roberts also gained national fame with television broadcasts during which he performed healings.

In addition to preaching for conversions and performing healings, Roberts promised success and prosperity in his messages. He developed a "seed-faith" principle, proclaiming that the more one gave to God, presumably via the Roberts ministry, the more one would be blessed by God. In effect, Roberts's messages amounted to a mix of revivalist Protestantism, Pentecostalism, and a poor person's version of Norman Vincent Peale's "power of positive thinking," each of which proclaimed a gospel of success.

During the 1960s, Roberts also began to move toward greater respectability. While not giving up Pentecostal doctrine, he left his Pentecostal denomination for the mainline Methodist Church. He also started Oral Roberts University, which included a medical center that would supposedly provide an unusual combination of advanced technology and openness to spiritual powers.[17]

The Pentecostal movement in general was moving toward greater social respectability. After World War II, many of its constituents were freed from their desperate poverty of the Depression years. At the same time, some Pentecostal leaders planned a major effort to reach into the American cultural establishment. In 1951, Demos Shakarian (1913–93), a wealthy California businessman who was supported initially by Oral Roberts, founded the Full Gospel Businessmen's Fellowship International. Partly through the efforts of this group and the leadership of David Du Plessis (1905–87), a Pentecostal minister, by the early 1960s, Pentecostal teachings began to make some inroads into mainline denominations. This was the beginning of the charismatic revival, which during the next decades had a tremendous impact in spreading Pentecostal influence beyond the traditional, specifically Pentecostal denominations.

The Mainstream Widens

From before the founding of the American nation until the mid-twentieth century, the default religion in the cultural mainstream was one or another kind of Protestantism. Public ceremonies often included Protestant prayers. Every president of the United States had been at least nominally a Protestant. That did not seem remarkable, since Protestants dominated most other aspects of American public life. Then in the mid-twentieth century, in the wake of World War II and the emergence of America as a world power, the cultural mainstream gradually widened and became at least somewhat more open to persons of other faiths.

Jewish Identity and the American Way

Between the world wars, the central feature of American Judaism seemed to be its rapid secularization. Large numbers of the second generation of the massive Eastern European immigration turned from religious practice, often adopting overtly secular outlooks.

Nonetheless, during the time between the wars, most American Jews retained a strong sense of Jewish identity. This was a matter of both choice and necessity. While the United States was more hospitable to Jews than most other nations were, anti-Semitism was a constant fact of life. Between the wars, which were decades of international racism and fascism, some virulent anti-Semitism sprang up in America. Beginning in 1920, Henry Ford widely publicized the *Protocols of the Elders of Zion*, forged documents that claimed to expose an international Jewish conspiracy to rule the world. Populist preachers, such as Father Charles Coughlin (1891–1979) and a number of Protestant counterparts, also attempted to fan anti-Semitic flames.

For most Jews, however, the most tangible effects of discrimination were those of everyday life suffered at the hands of the Anglo-Protestant establishment. Prestigious neighborhoods often had covenants that kept Jews, as well as blacks, from buying homes there, and most major country clubs routinely banned Jews as members.

In higher education, Jews also often ran into major roadblocks. A much greater percentage of Jewish young people, compared with other ethnic groups, attended universities, but only a few schools, like City College of New York, were fully open to them. Whereas Harvard, for instance, accepted Jewish students on the basis of merit before World War I, when the number of Jewish students threatened after the war to go over 15 percent, the administration, despite some protests, maintained an informal quota. Most other schools had unpublicized quotas as well. Some schools, even though they were almost entirely secular in what they taught, still talked about maintaining a "Christian" ethos.[18] In 1941 at Princeton, less than 2 percent of the students were Jewish. Prior to World War II, prejudice against Jews in most prestigious university faculties was strong enough to prevent Jewish appointments to their ranks, except in rare instances.[19]

Jews were accepted in some areas of national life, including some significant government and court appointments, especially by Democrats, whom Jews overwhelmingly supported as the party of assimilation. The best-known Jews in America, however, were on the stage and in comedy, fields that remained open to them. Comedians such as Jack Benny, George Burns, Fanny Brice, and the Marx brothers were loved across the nation; it was significant, however, that many of these comedians dropped their Jewish names and were entirely secular in their styles. Secularized Jews, such as L. B. Mayer and the Warner brothers, created most of the Hollywood film industry and from it projected an image of America as both more glamorous and more secular than the WASP (White Anglo-Saxon Protestant)-dominated realities.[20]

World War II drastically changed the mood of Jews in America. Two events were overwhelmingly crucial. First was the ruthless slaughter of some six million Jews in Hitler's death camps. The total horror of this unforgettable genocide made the issue of survival central for Jews. The other world-shaking event was the establishment of the Jewish state of Israel in 1948. During the preceding seventy-five years, American Jews had been divided in opinion over Zionism, or the establishment of a Jewish state. With its actual establishment, however, Israel became a powerful religious symbol, eventually gaining the support of the overwhelming majority of American Jews.

Their close identification with the state of Israel put the American Jewish community into a peculiar position regarding religion and culture. On the one hand, they had established a firm stance in the United States favoring the secularization of the culture. The residual Christian establishment often was discriminatory toward them, so it was in Jewish interest to help dismantle that establishment. Hence, Jews were often active with liberal Christians and secularists in the American Civil Liberties Union, which, among other things, opposed all religious discrimination and religious observances and teachings in public schools. In the 1950s, for instance, some states still required reading from the Bible and recitation of the Lord's Prayer as part of their schools' opening exercises. Not until 1962 did the Supreme Court of the United States strike down, in a symbolically important case, the use of a prayer composed by the Board of Regents for the New York State public schools.

At the same time that most Jews supported such secularization at home, much of their deepest commitment was to the state of Israel, which in addition to being a secular enterprise was a profound symbol of the Jewish religion. This loyalty to Israel became particularly intense during the Six Day War of 1967, when the continued existence of Israel seemed threatened. Such dedication to Israel meant that most American Jews saw the strong political implications of their faith—but only for a distant land. Jacob Neusner, one of the most astute and prolific internal observers, makes the point forcefully with some rhetorical overstatement: "How can American Jews focus their spiritual lives solely on a land in which they do not live?"[21] Such a question relates to a larger issue much discussed in the American Jewish community: "What does it mean to be Jewish?" To what extent does Jewishness mean ethnic identity, to what extent does it mean religious practice, and to what extent does it involve a political stance about Israel?

By no means was all of American Jewish religious energy directed toward the state of Israel. Following World War II, observers noted a marked upsurge in Jewish religious observance and a correspondingly wider inclusion of a religious component in people's definition of Jewishness. Weekly attendance at religious services remained relatively low (under 20 percent) in the 1950s and 1960s, but attendance at services celebrating high holy days was over 50 percent, comparable to regular observance in other major American religious groups.[22]

At this same time, the Jewish community became proportionally more affluent than any other American religious-ethnic group and was moving to the suburbs. As with other religious groups, this move from close-knit urban centers took its toll on religious and ethnic identity. Ironically, the marked acceptance of Jews by other Americans and the virtual end of public discrimination by the 1960s were also taking their tolls. While as late as the 1950s, only 6 percent of Jewish marriages were with persons of other faiths, by the early 1960s, this figure rose to 17 percent, and by the late 1960s, to 32 percent. Since Jewish identity was formed dually by ethnicity and religious practice, this secularizing trend was undermining one of the foundations of the community. In the subsequent decades there was, however, an increase in religious observance that seemed to reflect concerns by some in the community to reclaim identity that was otherwise eroding. A rise in distinctly Jewish education and day schools was also part of an effort to preserve Jewish identity.[23]

The American Jewish community, however, remained more deeply ambivalent toward the religious and the secular than any other major American group. Both the Holocaust and the state of Israel reinforce the point that religion can have profound implications. Moreover, despite the strong experiences of secularity that Jews have had along with other urban-oriented Americans, most Jews have also been exposed to deep reverence for tradition both in the family and in their religious education.

The tensions in the juxtaposition of the modern and the traditional views are engagingly portrayed, for instance, in novels such as *The Chosen* (1967) and *The Promise* (1969) by Chaim Potok, where modern sensibilities are contrasted with the strict observance and distinctive dress of the fervently orthodox Hasidic Jews.

Less reverently, one can see the ambivalence in the films and writings of Woody Allen. Unlike the Jewish comics of the 1930s, Allen, who experienced eight years of Hebrew school, constantly dealt with religious themes. He wrote facetiously that at New York City College he was attracted to courses such as "Death 101," "Intermediate Truth," and "Introduction to God." In the movie *Love and Death* (1975), set in Russia with mock Dostoevskian themes, the hero, Boris Grushenko (Woody Allen) suggests to Sonya (Diane Keaton) that there may be no God. Sonya replies, "But if there is no God, then life has no meaning. Why go on living? Why not just commit suicide?" Boris quickly replies, "Well, let's not get hysterical. I could be wrong. I'd hate to blow my brains out and then read in the papers they found something." Later in the movie, an angel appears to Boris and tells him not to worry because he will be rescued from a firing squad. After he is not, the deceased Boris appears in an epilogue and says: "If it turns out that there is a God, I don't think he is evil. I think that the worst thing you can say about him is that he is an underachiever."[24]

Catholics Move into the Mainstream

At the end of World War II, both interreligious and interracial hostilities still ran high. One impact of the Holocaust, nevertheless, was that it alerted people to the dangers of such prejudices and it strengthened the resolve of those who were working to bring about changes. The dramatic changes that eventually came, however, should not obscure historical memories of how deep the antagonisms were until recently.

Particularly dramatic has been the revolution in the relationships between Protestants and Catholics. Immediately after World War II, Protestant spokespersons still often equated Catholicism with authoritarianism and, hence, with totalitarianism. One popular and influential book of the era was Paul Blanshard's *American Freedom and Catholic Power* (1949), which reiterated the old theme, commonplace in America since colonial times, that Catholics were threatening to take over and would bring an end to American freedoms.[25] The same year as the publication of this book, Bishop G. Bromley Oxnam, one of the most influential bishops in the Methodist Church (America's largest Protestant denomination), spoke in a nationally distributed radio interview of

> the striking parallel between the organizational structure and method of the World-Wide Communist political party and the World-Wide Roman Catholic political party. Both are totalitarian. Both seek control of the minds of men everywhere. Both practice excommunication, character assassination, and economic reprisals. Neither Rome nor Moscow knows what tolerance means.[26]

For religious liberals such as Oxnam, who still looked for a world dominated by Christian principles, Catholic authoritarianism seemed to subvert their Protestant and democratic ideals. In 1951, President Harry S. Truman attempted to appoint an ambassador to the Vatican, but a public outcry, led by mainline Protestant church leaders, forced him to abandon the attempt.

Feelings regarding Catholicism ran deep. For instance, after the war, a Presbyterian magazine warned against marrying Catholics, noting among other things that "it is Protestant theology, not Roman Catholic, which has provoked men to demand free government and the overthrow of tyrants."[27] The Episcopal Church passed a strong resolution against mixed marriages with Catholics in 1949.[28] The feelings, of course, were mutual; Catholic leaders discouraged mixed marriages at least as vigorously as did Protestants.

Catholicism, like other religions, was flourishing after World War II, although it was remaining fairly stable in size relative to Protestantism. In the early 1950s, about 20 percent of Americans were Catholic, as compared to about 35 percent Protestant church members (plus many nominal Protestants).[29] However, Catholicism also had vast and well-ordered organizations and educational systems.

Popular piety was also flourishing. Since Catholicism was a massive coalition, such piety was expressed in wide varieties that in Protestantism would have been manifest in denominational and social class division. Devotion to the Virgin Mary was particularly popular during this period. In the ten years from 1948 to 1957, ten thousand Marian titles were published. Devotion to *Our Lady of Fatima*, inspired by a Marian apparition in Fatima, Portugal, in 1917, flourished in post-World War II America. Popular devotion also was often associated with anticommunism and prayers for the conversion of Russia.[30]

A somewhat different style of popular Catholicism was indicated by the vogue in the 1950s of Bishop Fulton J. Sheen's television show, *Life Is Worth Living*. As the title intimates, Sheen was the Catholic counterpart to Norman Vincent Peale. He skillfully provided Catholic commentary on contemporary society and offered an essentially upbeat message.

Perhaps most important was the growing sense within the Catholic community of being a full member of America's three-faith pluralism or "triple melting pot," as Will Herberg has put it. Catholics were then, by and large, confident and comfortable with their status as one major faith in an essentially democratic and pluralistic society. Conservatism in Rome, as well as American Catholic clannishness, had long kept most Catholics relatively isolated in America. However, there were glimmers of more openness in the church and certainly signs that Catholics were ready to assume a role as full partners in the American enterprise.

A number of devout Catholics were highly regarded cultural figures. Thomas Merton, who after his conversion in 1938 became a Trappist monk in Kentucky, was renowned for his inspirational and mystical piety, especially as expressed in *The Seven Storey Mountain* (1948), a best-seller of the 1950s. Another convert, Dorothy Day, founder of the Catholic Worker movement in the 1930s, although more controversial, was also one of the most respected religious writers and workers of the era. Publishing her views in her daily newspaper, *The Catholic Worker*, Day promoted a pacifist, non-Marxist, Christian socialism. She and her coworkers founded dozens of hospitality houses that helped the poor throughout the country. She also nourished a small, politically radical wing within the church.

Of the mainline Catholic establishment, Father John Courtney Murray, SJ, was the most effective and respected spokesperson for Catholicism's full reconciliation with democratic pluralism. Murray faced squarely both Protestant and conservative Catholic critics and argued that the Catholic tradition itself included principles of democracy and religious freedom. Murray not only won Protestant respect, but his views eventually became the basis for the Vatican's redefinition of the relationships between the church and society.

Nothing, however, signaled so greatly the new status for Catholicism in America as the election in 1960 of John F. Kennedy as the first Catholic president. Although there was still some significant anti-Catholic opposition and the vote was unusually close, the election of Kennedy showed that overt anti-Catholicism was eroding. His assurances that he would keep his faith and his politics in separate compartments, and his actually doing so while in office, did much to allay any fears of influence on America by the foreign power of the Vatican. The oldest theme in American religious and political history—Protestant versus Catholic rivalries—was virtually at an end.

At almost the same time, the Catholic Church began its own revolution. The elderly Pope John XXIII, of whom little was expected when he assumed the papacy in 1958, convened the Second Vatican Council, which from 1962 to 1965 suddenly brought sweeping reforms to the church, including a much more open attitude toward Protestants and toward cultural pluralism. Differences between Protestants and Catholics and their virtual isolation from each other were suddenly and drastically diminished, thus reinforcing trends begun in the Kennedy years.

Though during his brief presidency John Kennedy freely used the symbolism of American civil religion on state occasions, his administration, like most Democratic administrations, set a slightly more secular tone for the nation. Kennedy's view of America resembled that of Reinhold Niebuhr, who indeed was much admired by many of Kennedy's "New Frontiersmen."[31] On the one hand, Kennedy could be critical of the United States and recognized some of its limits and imperfections; he was also a political realist who could play hardball. On the other hand, his firm opposition to international communism was also based on American idealism, and he effectively preached a new vision of the American way of life built on justice for all people. The Peace Corps, which he initiated to send Americans overseas to aid third-world nations, was transparently a secularized version of the American missionary movement. Enthusiasm for mainline Protestant missions, which long had been an important source for American presence and image abroad, had been declining since World War I. The Peace Corps, however, provided new opportunities for American young people to present the world with the tradition of service that was indeed part of the national heritage. Kennedy was no Woodrow Wilson Puritan, especially in his personal conduct, but there was in him a touch of national moral idealism as well as political realism.

In retrospect, Kennedy's administration had much more in common with the 1950s than with the later 1960s. He still represented the ideal of building a consensus in America. Just as Protestants and Catholics were becoming more alike, so were the two political parties. The melting pot was still the ideal in which Americans would be brought together through the promotion of a consensus of American values. Despite lingering tensions, as over the race issue, WASP America and other ethnic groups seemed to be successfully blending into a common meld.

Secularism

When Will Herberg talked about Protestants, Catholics, and Jews as representing three major faiths, he was pointing out that these faiths were all to some degree secularized in that they all supported the American way of life. Many Americans, however, did not subscribe to any formal religion but held to a thoroughly secular value system. Some commentators of the era designated such a secular value system as simply a fourth faith. John Courtney Murray, for instance, explicitly added "secularist" to "Protestant, Catholic, and Jew" to describe the dominant American religions.[32] Protestant Martin Marty followed Murray's lead in speaking of the fourth faith as "secular humanist" or "secular and humanistic."[33] This "religion of democracy," as Marty also called it, had "an 'established church' in the field of public education." Other commentators made the same point.[34] Such religious observers perceived the actual situation in America to be much like that which secularist John Dewey had earlier recommended.

Despite its support from the three major traditional faiths, consensus America, of which John Kennedy was the last great symbol, was based on a largely secular ideology. This did not mean that America was being overrun by avowed atheists and agnostics. Rather, it meant that most Americans held to two faiths, or some amalgam of the two: one traditional and one largely secular. In public life, however, it seemed that the secular style was triumphing. The absence of substantive religion, after all, seemed to provide the best hope for bringing people of various faiths together.

The unanswered question was what such mutual tolerance might do to religion itself. Would it open the door for the ideological triumph of an aggressive relativism that would undermine all the traditional faiths? Would it drift into a bland relativism that would no longer please anyone? Or would it provide an atmosphere in which distinctive faiths could flourish?

For the time being, however, the secular faith still provided the basis for a hopeful American idealism, even a secular millennialism. Secularism had indeed appropriated much of the rhetoric and the hope of the religious traditions.

Civil Rights

The United States, however, was not, in fact, nearly as secular as its public philosophy might indicate. All sorts of subgroups in the culture retained vital and distinctive religious traditions. Only rarely, however, did these religious traditions impinge directly on public affairs. One place in which they did was the civil rights movement, where the inclusiveness of the progressive American democratic faith converged with the millennial hopes of African-American Christians.

The civil rights movement was also the best illustration that Puritan moral idealism was not dead during the Kennedy years. During the Roosevelt era, blacks shifted their long-standing Republican allegiance to the Democrats, who were doing more for the poor. Partly out of political self-interest, but just as certainly out of the religious and secular moral idealism of the traditions that supported them, liberal Democrats took over what had been the classic Republican reforming agenda—the cause of African Americans. While liberal Democrats preached that it was the duty of all Americans to accede to the principles of elementary justice, conservative Republicans joined the old chorus of conservative southerners who said that "morality cannot be legislated."

Morality was legislated, or at least in the 1950s and 1960s some behavior and attitudes were drastically changed, largely through court and legal action. At the same time, however, as in the antislavery crusades, the churches played a significant role in providing the moral leverage necessary to change popular opinion. Liberal Protestant leadership, which had a basically Republican heritage, now shifted to the Democratic Party in this moral campaign. The earlier social gospel had not made racial equality a prominent issue. Now liberal Protestants joined with secularists, progressive Catholics, civil rights-oriented Jews, and others for the new crusade.

The most important religious contribution to the cause, however, came from black churches themselves. In black communities, long denied political power, clergy had remained the chief community spokespersons and organizers for political concerns. Even the formally secular civil rights organizations, such as the National Association for the Advancement of Colored People (NAACP), founded in 1909, depended heavily on church support.

Clergy leadership in the efforts of African Americans to gain their civil rights meant that black political thought retained an explicitly Christian prophetic tone that had disappeared in most other places in American politics since the mid-nineteenth century. In this respect, blacks were responding to their outsider status in a way almost the opposite of Catholics. While successful Catholic politicians typically presented a secular public image, blacks could appeal to themes that were close to the heart of the dominant British-republican heritage, especially those who connected true Christianity with the spirit of political liberty.

Although the explicit appeal to Christianity was an anomaly in mid-twentieth-century American politics, it was arguable that, for a group who had no political power or prospect of power, it was appropriate to appeal to a higher authority. One of the major dangers in mixing religion and politics is that, if it is routinely done, those who have power or who aspire to revolutionary violence will use religious rationales in combination with force to promote deadly, and often unjust, programs. The black civil rights movement, at least in its early stages, was hardly in danger of such an abuse of power.

Martin Luther King Jr.

Martin Luther King Jr. (1929–68), who became the great leader of the civil rights movement, not only understood such principles but put them into practice. Graduating from Morehouse College at age nineteen, King went on to study at northern liberal Protestant schools—Crozier Theological Seminary (for a divinity degree) and Boston University (for a doctoral degree). King's own thought reflected influences of liberal theology, such as in Walter Rauschenbusch's social gospel. Nonetheless, he succeeded where liberal optimism about gradual progress toward eventual acceptance of human rights had failed. That success grew in part from combining the principles of peaceful nonresistance of Mahatma Gandhi with the realism of Reinhold Niebuhr that helped him recognize that people's minds would be changed only by coercion, even if the coercion was in the form of peaceful protests.

These intellectual ideals, however, would have been useless to King had he not drawn on and mobilized the spiritual intensity of the African-American religious heritage.[35] Rather than become a seminary professor, he chose to be a pastor of a southern black Baptist church. He later wrote in *Ebony* magazine, "I am fundamentally a clergyman, a Baptist preacher. This is my being and my heritage, for I am also the son of a Baptist preacher, the grandson of a Baptist preacher, and the great-grandson of a Baptist preacher. The Church is my life and I have given my life to the Church."[36]

In 1955, early in his career as pastor in Montgomery, Alabama, King gained national prominence for his involvement in promoting the Montgomery bus boycott. In January 1956, threats on his life and family brought him to a religious crisis and a spiritual experience that strengthened his resolve to renew the black church and community.[37] In 1957, he led in organizing the Southern Christian Leadership Conference to mobilize forces for protest. Not all the clergy leadership in the black community, however, favored King's approach. Some opposed protests, felt that the church should be more purely spiritual in its activities, and believed that the black communities would do better to build their own strength and internal discipline than to engage in confrontational politics. Because of such objections, King and others felt it necessary in 1961 to secede from the largest black denomination, the National Baptist Convention, and form a smaller Progressive National Baptist Convention with about five hundred thousand members.[38]

King, however, eventually won a large following in the black communities, primarily by his abilities as an eloquent preacher who could appeal to elements in their heritage as African-American Christians. If the African-American communities had a weakness in political outlook, as its more radical black critics said it did, it was that it often exemplified too well some of the cardinal Christian virtues. Black Christians had preserved better than most other twentieth-century Americans the nineteenth-century Christian teaching that one should expect suffering and should grow from the reality of suffering to find higher spiritual meanings to life. The African-American communities had also been, on the whole, remarkable exemplars of the principles of the Sermon on the Mount. Despite much deep-seated resentment against their white oppressors, they often treated them with remarkable charity. Theories of violent revolution never found wide appeal in American black communities, despite the presence of all the economic and racial factors that were supposed, inevitably, to breed revolutionary attitudes.

King mobilized these long-standing Christian virtues in the black community, turning the power of love and the principles of the Sermon on the Mount into an active force. King hoped to bring social change by the power of love and nonviolence. One of the rare qualities of King's activism was that he made a clear distinction between the sin and the sinner. One should hate the sin, he repeatedly urged, but love the sinner. He observed, early in his career, that most of the southern white racists who thwarted and threatened him "are not bad men."[39] Rather, they were often upstanding citizens in their community but victims of that community's tradition of racist definitions of right and wrong.

All the elements of King's essential message, as it stood when he was at the height of his influence, are present in his famous "I Have a Dream" speech, delivered at the Lincoln Memorial for the March on Washington, August 1963. Recordings of King's words are still heard today, though often as though they were background music for television spots, so that it has become difficult to hear their message. Nonetheless, King reiterated that the new black militancy must not degenerate into hatred of all white people or into violence. Rather, "we must rise to the majestic heights of meeting physical force with soul force." Central to the speech was the combination of American republican and biblical themes. The dream, he was not ashamed to say, was the "American dream." "We hold these truths to be self-evident, that all men are created equal." It is a dream, as the final, often heard, per-oration elaborates, that "My country 'tis of thee, sweet land of liberty, of thee I sing. Land where my fathers died, land of the pilgrims' pride, from every mountainside, let freedom ring." Yet the appeal to the republican, and even the Puritan, themes is interspersed with quotations from the Bible, which was always the heart of King's preaching:

> I have a dream that one day every valley shall be exalted, every hill and mountain shall be made low. The rough places will be plain and the crooked places will be made straight, "and the glory of the Lord shall be revealed, and all flesh shall see it together."[40]

The American dream was for King, ultimately, the dream of the millennial themes that inspired blacks and whites alike in the mid-nineteenth century. It was the dream to be "free at last." King was demanding that this tradition be faithful to its own claims.

King's ideal for black people was integration into the mainstream of American society. He was calling on the mainstream to be true to itself, asking that African Americans might be absorbed in the consensus. This consensus integrationist outlook, which was shared by the vast majority of the liberal leadership of the day, reflected trust in the American Christian and republican tradition and an ultimately optimistic view of human nature and society.

King's outlook changed dramatically between his "I Have a Dream" speech in 1963 and his assassination in 1968. American culture changed rapidly in those years marked by riots in African-American urban ghettoes and by widespread protest over America's involvement in the Vietnam War. King gave up on simply joining in the "American dream." He regarded America's Vietnam policy as genocidal and white people as oppressors. Though disillusioned in many respects and increasingly confrontational, King did not give up on nonviolence as the key to effecting change.

Alternatives for Black Power

Not all black activists, especially in King's later years, were happy with his nonviolent approach. They also appealed to another tradition that had been represented by a minority in the black community over the years. This was the tradition of separatist black nationalism. It was expressed early by Bishop Henry McNeal Turner (1834-1915) of the African Methodist Episcopal Church. With the collapse of Reconstruction and efforts for black civil equality, Turner promoted an African colonization movement, though he gained little following. More successful, but also more controversial, was the Back to Africa movement of Marcus Garvey (1887-1940) after World War I. Though his movement was not explicitly religious, Garvey was a flamboyant cult figure who attracted hundreds of thousands of followers before he was convicted for mail fraud in 1925 and deported to his native Jamaica in 1927.

Although not explicitly nationalist, a number of distinctly African-American alternatives to Christianity sprang up in the ghettos of the North between the wars. The best known of these were the movements founded by Father Divine and Sweet Daddy Grace, both messianic figures who followed long-standing American traditions of combining extravagant religious interests with creative free enterprise.

Of more lasting impact was the Black Muslim, or Nation of Islam, movement, organized principally in Detroit by Wali Farad Muhammad (formerly Wallace D. Fard) in 1930. This highly disciplined black nationalist movement was strongly anti-white and anti-Christian. Although because of its racial doctrines, it was not recognized by other Muslims, it followed Islamic practices, and so demanded a puritanical ethic. The movement grew to some hundreds of thousands after World War II. Its best-known proponent was Malcolm X (1925-65), who, after experiencing interracial Muslim brotherhood during a pilgrimage to Mecca, broke with Elijah Muhammad (1897-1975), leader of the Nation of Islam. Malcolm X was assassinated in 1965, shortly before the appearance of his book *The Autobiography of Malcolm X*, which became a leading work promoting a sense of black identity based on the rejection of Christianity as the white man's religion. A number of leading sports figures, including heavyweight boxing champion Muhammad Ali, helped give the movement continued prominence.

Some others of the most vocal of black leaders turned from the nonviolence of Martin Luther King toward emphases on black power, black pride, and black liberation. Parts of the movement reflected the secular radicalism of the day. As always, however, the dominant black leadership was Christian. By 1966, black theologians such as James H. Cone were developing a theology of black power. Rejecting integration as a goal, they turned to the liberation themes of Christianity as normative in defining its essence. They rejected white theologies, which they saw as defining Christianity in such a way as to make it a justification of oppression. Nonetheless, in affirming a black theology, they were also retaining continuity with the black African Christian heritage.[41]

Even before the assassination of Martin Luther King in 1968, the black community was deeply divided on goals and strategies. Black consolidation and organization of effective African-American institutions were essential for black power, but ironically, massive gains for integration during the Lyndon B. Johnson years were undermining those very separate institutions. Black churches remained separate, but they were divided into several camps, ranging from those who found King too radical to those who found him too conservative. The inability to resolve this impasse of integrationism versus separatism, as well as continuing white racism, left the black community with important gains in legal civil rights but limited means for improving their economic, social, and educational situation.

The civil rights era coincided with the ongoing secularization of black communities, especially in urban centers. African-American culture involved striking contrasts between intense religion and intensely secular lifestyles. The continuing twentieth-century migrations to the cities strengthened these contrasts, fostering the growth of the secular aspects of the community, even while the churches remained as significant, if relatively diminished, counterforces. In the years after the gains in civil rights, the roles of the churches became more ambiguous as the community became increasingly dependent on government action. Though the community welcomed the government support it received, one side effect was that the community looked relatively more toward secular agencies to help resolve its problems.

As with other ethnic and racial groups in America, the central question for the black community was whether it would be a gain or a loss to give up its distinctive cultural religious heritage, to be absorbed into a wider American culture. For African Americans, this was an especially poignant question since they were as fully American as any of the Europeans who settled in the United States and had long been among the chief proponents of the nation's dominant religious heritages and political ideals. Yet those very ideals were contradicted by forces that kept most blacks from sharing in material promises that seemed so central to the American dream itself.

CHAPTER 8

The 1960s and Their Legacy—
A Fragmented Nation in Search of a Soul

. . . a nation with the soul of a church. . . .

G. K. Chesterton, *What I Saw in America* (1922)

The Great Divide

In the early 1920s, the perceptive British observer, G. K. Chesterton, made the famous remark, quoted above, that the United States was "a nation with the soul of a church." A visitor in the 1950s might well have said the same. Most Americans, despite deep and sometimes bitter divisions, shared a faith in the nation that seemed undergirded by a spiritual dimension, however vague that common faith might be.

By the end of the twentieth century, hopes for such national consensus had long disappeared and the nation seemed deeply divided as to what should be the essence of its moral vision. During the decades ushered in by the cultural upheavals of the 1960s, some long-standing ideological fault lines significantly widened, cutting across the traditional patterns of American religious and cultural life. Insider versus outsider issues receded in relative importance, while differences between conservatives and liberals regarding basic values gained prominence. As in the earlier conflicts among ethnic groups, religion played a significant role in defining the outlooks of the contending parties.

Traditional ethnic and religious differences, although still significant, were declining in intensity. Especially dramatic was the near disappearance of the longest-standing religious barrier dividing the American population:

that between Protestants and Catholics. Although the divisions between blacks and whites were far more persistent, major changes did occur in those relationships over the period as African Americans gained at least formal representation in most areas of American life. Jewish and Christian differences persisted, as well, but with considerably less antagonism than at mid-century. New outsiders included the rapidly growing Hispanic and Asian populations, but even so, most of the nation seemed more solidly committed to a cultural pluralism that was accepting of greater diversity with less antagonism along ethno-religious lines.

In the meantime, the gulf between liberal and conservative views on some basic principles of morality was widening to an extent that made many of the traditional divisions seem even less relevant. Among most Protestants, the reasons for old denominational rivalries were now largely forgotten; liberals from denominations such as Methodist, Baptist, Presbyterian, Disciples of Christ, or Episcopalian clearly had more in common with each other than they did with conservatives in their own denominations. Protestant versus Catholic differences, while more considerable, were likewise overshadowed by the growing ideological division between liberal and conservative. Similar lines of division were found within most American subcommunities, including the Jewish and Eastern Orthodox, who retained a strong sense of identity.

On the liberal side of the divide were those Americans who placed their strongest emphasis on the values of openness, pluralism, diversity, and mutual tolerance of differences. If these Americans were religious, they typically subordinated theology to ethical concerns. Their typical ethics emphasized love, relationships, peace, justice, inclusiveness, tolerance of minorities, and acceptance of varieties of lifestyles and expressions of sexuality. They generally did not speak in terms of an objective moral law, but they nonetheless spoke as though such moral principles were self-evident.

Various resurgent conservatives, on the other hand, tended to talk more of finding ethical absolutes, which reflected long-standing Christian and Jewish teachings concerning family, sexuality, discipline, and the importance of moral law. Often they saw these as implications of more-or-less traditional theological beliefs. They also tended to be patriotic toward America, firmly anticommunist, supportive of a strong military, and in favor of law and order.

These tendencies of liberalism and conservatism, roughly characterized though actually coming in many varieties and variations, could be seen as the opposed efforts of two groups who, as the old lines between insiders and outsiders blurred, each sought to establish themselves as the new cultural insiders and to define the nature of an American consensus.

Of course, divisions between liberals and conservatives in American religion were nothing new. Similar tensions can be seen, for instance, in eighteenth-century divisions between pietists of the Great Awakening and liberals influenced by the secular dimensions of the Enlightenment. The common cause of the American Revolution helped avert a deeper split, and in the nineteenth century, evangelical religion and liberal politics cooperated in building something of a dominant cultural consensus. During the first half of the twentieth century, liberal politics, supported by tolerant liberal Protestantism, sustained an increasingly secularized and tolerant version of this consensus. Now, however, avowed cultural conservatism with pietist and other conservative religious support was sharply challenging the directions to which the unchecked principles of tolerance seemed to be leading.

The Counterculture as a Moral-Religious Quest

The assassination of President Kennedy on November 22, 1963, was a critical psychological turning point in the history of the nation. Although Kennedy was deeply disliked by many political conservatives, his administration seemed to others to be a triumph of the liberal consensus that had been developing since Franklin Roosevelt's New Deal. The dominant mood of optimism and progress, which had characterized the Eisenhower years, still prevailed. Within a year or two of the assassination, however, the dominant national mood changed toward frustration and suspicion, and a new counterculture with radically unconventional values was beginning to emerge.

Although the emergence of a counterculture was not solely an American phenomenon, some immediate American developments contributed substantially to the American version. Among the early signs were the urban riots and fires of the summer of 1964, reflecting African-American frustrations with and suspicions of the New-Deal culture's true commitment to civil rights and equality of opportunity. The primary contributor to the growing mood of disillusion with the old establishment, however, was America's deepening involvement after 1964 in the Vietnam morass.

The widespread reaction of the growing youth culture to the United States' involvement in Vietnam was accentuated by the emerging baby boom generation, which, in turn, coincided with the rise of mass higher education in the 1960s. This combination of developments created large self-contained youth communities at universities. Moreover, the war directly threatened the self-interests of most males in this group, who had to face the military draft and the risk of killing or being killed for a cause they did not accept. Self-interest thus became a way of clarifying moral values.

The countercultural critique of the establishment also cut much deeper, however. This critique basically said that there was something fundamentally wrong with American culture itself. Part of the assessment focused on the technocratic aspects of society. The new generation of protesters saw science and technology as the gods of the culture and technical experts as the high priests.[1] They saw a culture that had systematically enthroned what Theodore Roszak, in his influential book, *The Making of a Counter Culture*, called the "myth of objective consciousness." That is, the structures of business, technology, and government favored dealing with problems by means of supposedly detached, objective observers or experts. Subjective human values were sacrificed to the mythologically neutral objective. In fact, the counterculture pointed out, American technical and scientific expertise was not objective at all. It was in the service of other, even higher, "religions" of the culture—business profit and self-interested nationalism. If anyone stood in the way of this expertise, whether it be black laborers or Vietnamese peasants, technical solutions would dehumanize or destroy them.[2] Hence, the vaunted declarations of American ideals of liberty and justice for all were riddled with deep hypocrisy.

The counterculture drew on a number of American heritages in its spontaneous and informal critique of the dominant culture. For one thing, it drew indirectly on the biblical heritage of moral imperatives, since its indignation was built upon an outrage that the American establishment served its own interests rather than those of the poor or non-Americans. In addition, the counterculture drew on the romantic tradition that had long provided a subjectivist counterbalance to scientific-technological objectivist trends. In some striking ways, in fact, the counterculture resembled the romantic radicalism in the decades before the Civil War. Each culture emphasized being true to self and finding truth intuitively. Each also emphasized finding the divine in nature rather than civilization. Each built radical communes and went back to nature. Each was influenced by Eastern religions. There were many differences, of course, but also these striking similarities.

The counterculture of the 1960s had many sides and no fixed or unified ideology (another American trait). It championed radical politics, largely hopeful until 1968, and then developed increasingly violent and revolutionary rhetoric. At the same time, some of their number advocated "dropping out" of society to pursue purely experiential solutions to the world's problems. The ubiquitous slogan "Make love, not war" suggested two sides of the movement—personal freedom and political concern. The drug culture, often mixed with Eastern and mystical religion and the occult, set up a value system at a polar opposite to the dominant technological culture and its conventional morality.

One way to view the counterculture is as a new religious worldview and value system. This millennial philosophy of a new age, or the "age of Aquarius," was built around "the monistic assumption that all life is united and all existence is one." Its truth system was built on trusting immediate intuitions. While its expressions of public morality were almost biblically prophetic, its private morality was built around individual expression and fulfillment. "Do your own thing," "let it all hang out," "express love and awareness for all beings," and "get the most good vibes" were typical moral maxims.[3]

While the counterculture was a major force on the liberal side of cultural trends, it was also a radical critique of old-style New-Deal liberalism. To the protesters, Democrats Lyndon B. Johnson and Hubert H. Humphrey did not look much different from Republican Richard M. Nixon. All seemed part of a corrupt, self-serving establishment. The critique thus opened the door for other doubts about the old liberal consensus that dominated American life from the 1940s through the early 1960s.

The Mainline Churches

Religious liberals in the mainline Protestant churches were caught in an awkward position by the emergence of the ever-more-radical counterculture of the 1960s.

At the outset of the era, mainline denominations had been flourishing near the progressive forefront of American life. Their leadership usually consisted of Kennedy liberals, whose major concerns were still integrative unification of American life. Central on the agenda of mainline denominations was the ecumenical movement, represented primarily by the National Council of Churches, but also hopeful for mergers that would bring most of the Protestant denominations into one group.

Essentially, these religious liberals were affirming American life. One of the best-selling books of the hopeful half of the 1960s was Harvey Cox's *The Secular City: Secularization and Urbanization in Theological Perspective* (1965). Rather than deplore the secularization of urban civilization, Cox celebrated it. "Urbanization," he wrote, "means a structure of common life in which the diversity and the disintegration of tradition are paramount." To the liberal, disintegration of tradition meant opportunity for unity or, as Cox put it in biblical language, "the transformation of 'strangers and outsiders' into 'fellow citizens and members of one another.'" In this view, there was no distinction between the nation and the church. In fact, as a popular slogan of the time put it, "the world should set the agenda for the church." In other words, as Cox said, "Theology . . . is concerned first with finding out where the action is. . . ."[4]

Even though portions of some of America's cities burned during riots in the summer of 1964 before Cox's words were published, old-style liberals plausibly saw themselves as staying in leadership by keeping up with secular trends and by bringing out their redemptive meanings. One constantly had to be freeing oneself of the traditional and of the outdated. A few theologians went so far as to say that God-language was no longer meaningful or relevant to "modern man." In 1966, this view got startlingly wide publicity when a *Time* magazine cover appeared with only the following three giant words on it: "IS GOD DEAD?" In fact, the so-called "God is Dead" movement to which the headline referred turned out to be an obituary for theology in public life; no longer would there be theologians, such as brothers Reinhold and H. Richard Niebuhr, who could command national attention.

At the time, however, it seemed plausible to see that the future of the church depended primarily on maintaining relevance to the culture. Some mainline church leaders, after all, were in the forefront of the civil rights movement and were among the most outspoken critics of the Vietnam War. They shared with the counterculture some of its critique of the materialism and nationalism of modern America. The strategy seemed to be to stay "where the action is." Campus ministers were putting on blue jeans, handcrafted shirts, and beads. They brought guitars and balloons into their worship services, hugged and "shared," and talked of "love." Playing down the exclusivism of any particular tradition or its practices, they hoped to include everyone.

As historian Leonard Sweet has observed, "The wildest miscalculation of many churches in the 1960s was their belief in the basic inhospitality of the 'modern mind' to traditional religious symbols and doctrines."[5] Just as segments of the counterculture were seeking more distinctive religious expression, some of the liberal church leadership was still trying to be relevant by being less distinctive. Eastern, cultic, and exotic religions began to flourish, and campuses became far more open to overt spiritual expression than they had been in the 1950s. By the end of the 1960s, many counterculture young people were being swept into the Jesus people movement, which had many radical countercultural traits, such as close communal living and simple lifestyles, but was based on a strict discipline and reverence for the Bible. Many more people, both young and old, Catholics and Protestants, were turning to the new charismatic movement, which likewise emphasized some traditional theology as well as ecstatic spiritual experience. Meanwhile, young people were beginning to stay away from liberal churches in droves. By the 1970s, liberal campus ministries had declined drastically. For many in a generation seeking authenticity, relevance to prevailing cultural standards, even progressive ones, held little attraction.

Of course, nowhere near all people in the mainline churches followed the most liberal trends. Since these denominations were always a mix of conservative, moderate, and liberal elements, it is hazardous to generalize about their messages, which were always partly traditional and moderate. Nonetheless, particularly conspicuous in the era, in almost all major groups, was the triumph of "therapeutic" religion, a development that reflected a synthesis of some traditional and countercultural themes. Therapeutic religion was, of course, not new to America and had flourished in the 1950s in the positive thinking of Norman Vincent Peale and others. During the 1960s, psychological solutions to human problems became increasingly popular, and many churches followed suit.

From a therapeutic outlook, questions of morality were no longer considered in terms of rules of right and wrong but rather in terms of relationships. Protestant ethicist Joseph Fletcher caused a stir with the publication in 1966 of his *Situation Ethics*, which argued that personal consequences were more important than rules. The triumph of psychological-relational definitions of values, however, was so widely based that it was not usually considered a matter for debate. In churches, it combined Christian teachings of loving one's neighbor with utilitarian ethics—"what promotes the greatest happiness"—and a middle-class version of expressive individualism—"feeling happy is a highest goal." Such an outlook counterbalanced a technological society of managers and experts who depersonalized life for technical efficiency. Personal relationships and feelings were put at the center. Sermons of the era thus often offered advice on promoting better personal relationships.[6] As one mainline critic of the trend later put it, "Our main message has been 'God is nice and we should be too.'"[7]

Perhaps the most serious problem facing the old mainline liberal denominations was that of identity. Very few people knew or cared what the difference was between a mainline Baptist, Methodist, Presbyterian, or Disciple of Christ. The traditions that once defined these differences had been largely jettisoned. Therapeutic religion, which often tended in an "I'm OK, you're OK" direction, further blurred differences. Evangelism, which would presume that religion had authority and that people needed to change, was often considered an embarrassment. Mainline foreign mission programs, which early in the century were the pride and joy of their denominations, were mere shadows of their former magnitude. Many mainline leaders believed that it was imperialistic to present their religion as superior to other traditions. This may or may not have helped America's image abroad, since the nation proceeded to unprecedented heights of economic and political imperialism without the benefit of mainline missions. The broader issue at home, however, was identity. If there was little reason to invite others to change to their religion, there was little reason to remain with that religion if an alternative presented itself.

The Catholic Revolution

The revolution for America's fifty million Catholics in the decades following 1960 was far more dramatic than that for most mainline Protestants. Catholicism of the 1950s had been, by and large, far more conservative than mainline Protestantism and far more insulated from the mainstream culture. The changes of the next decades were, accordingly, not necessarily in the direction of embracing liberalism. More essentially, the revolution involved a new openness within the church. At the same time, many Catholics were moving from old ethnic neighborhoods to the suburbs. The result was that growing up Catholic in the 1980s was far different from growing up Catholic in the 1950s. A whole way of life had almost disappeared.

By the 1950s, the American Catholic Church had, despite its ethnic diversity, developed a clear identity. It grew up within and among relatively isolated, self-contained communities that included their own educational systems, a relative uniformity in religious practice based on acceptance of church authority, and a strong patriotism. During the 1960s, all three of these supporting elements were removed simultaneously, creating a massive crisis in Catholic identity.

Like other urban Americans who were prospering in the 1950s and 1960s, Catholics were moving from urban and ethnic communities to the suburbs. This trend was especially disorienting for many Catholics because their parishes had provided them with a greater sense of place than most other American religious groups had received. For the same reason, conflicts in racially changing Catholic neighborhoods were often intense, despite the best efforts of the leadership to promote racial integration.[8] Catholic transitions to the suburbs were all the more disruptive because they coincided with a religious revolution as well as the cultural revolutions of the 1960s.

For Catholics, the religious revolution came suddenly and from the top down. The Second Vatican Council, inaugurated by Pope John XXIII in 1962, had, by its completion in 1965, drastically changed Catholic doctrine and practice. The reforms, called *aggiornamento*, were essentially efforts to bring the church up to date.[9] In effect, the council instituted many of the ideas that "Americanist" Catholics, before being suppressed, advocated in the late nineteenth century. For instance, the council followed American John Courtney Murray in declaring that religious freedom, rather than the universal establishment of Catholicism by law, was a desirable state of affairs. Furthermore, the Catholic Church now recognized Protestants as "separated brethren" and encouraged dialogue with them, which had been rare until that time. Vatican II also redefined the nature of the church. Rather than seeing the church primarily as an institutional hierarchy that dispensed justice and grace, the council emphasized that the church is the body of Christ at the service of humanity.

Of greatest practical consequence for most Catholics, however, were the remarkable changes in the liturgy. Consistent with the principle that the church was not simply an institutional hierarchy but the body of Christ including the laity, the reformers tried to relate the service more directly to the people. No longer was the mass said only in Latin by the priest facing the altar, while the people listened in silence. The reforms called for active participation of the congregation, with the mass and prayers in English, with the singing of hymns, and with more emphasis on sermons.[10]

Most Catholics welcomed these changes, which were introduced gradually. At the same time, however, the liturgical reform cut off the sense of continuity with the past, which is important to religious identity. Practices that seemed essential to Catholicism, such as when to say the rosary, were changed. Familiar saints whose historicity proved dubious were declared no longer saints. For instance, Saint Christopher, who was supposed to keep one safe in travel and whose image was often seen on Catholic car dashboards, disappeared, as did some other symbols of Catholic identity. Pious Catholics were always identifiable by their practice of eating fish instead of red meat on Fridays. Now that mark of identity suddenly disappeared as well.

For whatever reasons, Catholic practice dropped off sharply after the revolution. In 1974, only 50 percent of Catholics were attending church regularly, as opposed to 71 percent in 1963, and the rate of those not going at all doubled. Only 17 percent were now going to confession regularly, as opposed to 37 percent in 1963. An estimated ten thousand priests left the ministry between 1966 and 1978, and by 1984, the number of seminarians studying for the priesthood dropped to twelve thousand, only one-fourth of what it was in 1964.

Just as remarkable was the widespread disagreement among the laity with official church teaching, especially regarding sexuality. Here the leading issue, especially during the 1960s, was artificial methods of birth control, which the church continued to ban. In 1955, an estimated 30 percent of Catholic women defied the church and used such birth control. By 1970, the number defying the church had risen to two-thirds, and about nine of ten Catholics disagreed with the church's stand on birth control.[11]

Other changes were just as momentous. Attitudes toward divorce, on which the church took an officially strict stand, were changing as well. Most Catholics still agreed with the church's stand in opposing abortion and same-sex practice, although some dissenting voices were heard. The church, which was controlled by a male hierarchy, allowed little place for women's leadership, another source of discontent for many Catholics.[12] Membership in religious orders for nuns declined dramatically along with almost everything else in this era. The Catholic school system, which long depended on the sacrificial services of nuns, lost much of its distinctiveness. The teaching was taken over by laypeople, and the school's constituencies ceased to be so exclusively Catholic.[13]

In addition to the changes of moving from city neighborhoods to suburbs and the reforms from Rome, the cultural changes of the 1960s intensified this upheaval in American Catholicism. As in other subgroups, Catholics divided sharply on controversial cultural and political issues. Internal division and dissent thus further undermined a sense of identity.

One of the factors that bound most American Catholics together until the 1960s was their common patriotism. With the Vietnam era, that suddenly came into question as well. A number of leading Catholics were among the best-known opponents of the war. Dorothy Day of the Catholic Worker movement in the 1930s was still an outspoken antiwar advocate, as was the renowned Trappist monk Thomas Merton. As the national crisis of the 1960s mounted, other Catholic antiwar activists gained prominence. Two of the best known were the brothers and Catholic priests, Fathers Daniel and Philip Berrigan, famed and notorious for draft-card burnings and raids on draft-board records. More in the mainstream, two of the most effective spokespersons against American Vietnam policy were two Catholic laymen, 1968 presidential contenders Eugene McCarthy and Robert F. Kennedy, who was assassinated during the campaign. Catholics were, in fact, somewhat more likely than Protestants to oppose the war, although the majority in both groups supported it.

The breakdown in trust in America among some Catholics during the Vietnam era, together with the defection of many Catholics from traditional church teachings and practices, signaled a deep division developing within the Catholic communities. This division fell essentially across the same fault line that was dividing Protestants from the 1960s to the 1980s. By the 1980s, no longer were the most prominent divisions between Protestants and Catholics. Rather, they were between liberals and conservatives.

The dominance of progressive trends in the church hierarchy was reflected in two significant pastoral letters issued in the 1980s from the Council of Catholic Bishops. One on nuclear war carefully questioned whether nuclear war could be consistent with a just-war tradition. The other on the economy questioned whether Americans were doing enough to support the poor at home and abroad. Both received severe criticisms from Catholic conservatives.

In theology and biblical criticism, Catholics by the 1970s and 1980s were also divided on most of the same questions that had divided Protestants for many years. In the Catholic case, expressions of some of the most liberal views were still limited by the presence of a theologically conservative pope, John Paul II, elected in 1978.

Catholics also differed sharply with each other over liberation theology. These theologies typically fused Christian principles of concern for the poor with Marxist economic analysis. In predominantly Catholic Latin America, such theologies were influential in demands for political reform or revolution. Catholics, as well as Protestants, in both North and South America were divided on the issue. In the United States, the question was closely related to American foreign policy in deciding which regimes it would support in Latin America. Moreover, the rapidly growing Latino population of the United States was overwhelmingly Catholic. Some Latino immigrants came in reaction to communism and were aligned with the political right. Others inclined to the political left or, more often, were politically neutral. Correspondingly, among longer-established American Catholics, liberals typically supported the liberation cause while conservatives favored militant anticommunism.

Pope John Paul II took stances that did not neatly fit typical American patterns. On matters of theology; questions of sexuality, such as abortion and birth control; and on women's ordination to the priesthood, he was a staunch conservative. Yet on matters of economic justice and peace, his declarations would seem liberal by American standards.

American Catholics were deeply divided on all these issues, yet Catholics still differed from Protestants in at least one very important respect: Catholics still all belonged to one international, institutional church. Even though much of the traditional Catholic identity was lost, the church survived intact, and the opening up of the heritage provided some hopeful prospects for relating tradition to contemporary trends. Trying to relate the best of each of these to each other, however, was a massive challenge.

Feminism

The major transformations of old-line American churches came not only as changes from within that helped direct cultural change but also were responses to massive changes in the broader culture. Of these changes, none promised to have wider and more lasting effects than feminism.

While women reformers had been campaigning for over a century to end discrimination in American life, the cultural upheaval of the 1960s opened the door for a more popular feminism directed toward full equality. The new reformers demanded, and often got, formally equal opportunities and affirmative action in the workplace. They also widely promoted the ideal of the independent career woman, freed from subordinating roles of wife and mother, or at least from any obligations beyond what would be expected of males as well. These ideals raised questions about the structure of the family. The traditional view that the man was the head of the household came under heavy and often successful attack. However, even more fundamental was the question of whether the family was based on a temporary contract among equal individuals or whether its structure reflected a divinely sanctioned order, as Christians and Jews traditionally said. If essentially a voluntary contract, was it not then subordinate to the individuals who made the agreement and could therefore dissolve it at will? The prevailing trends in individualistic America were toward the latter view.

Churches not only had to face sharply divided opinions on these issues, but they also had to face the practical question of whether women would be granted fully equal roles in the churches themselves. In the Judeo-Christian tradition, churches and synagogues were almost exclusively governed by men. For Orthodox Jews, Catholics, and Eastern Orthodox Christians, groups who depended largely on the authority of tradition, the whole structure of authority would be threatened by ignoring ancient precedents. Bible-believing evangelicals and fundamentalists believed the apostle Paul's apparent ban on women in leadership roles in the New Testament church still applied to the church in modern times.

Liberal and moderate Protestants and Reform and Conservative Jews, who long had been frankly open to interpreting Scripture in the light of current trends, largely accepted new roles for women. The mainline Protestant constituency overlapped with the largest social group in which the women's movement took place—among the well-established, white middle class. In the late nineteenth and early twentieth centuries, in fact, mainline churches were some of the principal places where independent women's organizations were formed. Missionary and educational societies, run by women, played major roles in denominational life. With greater pressures for women's equality by the 1920s, mainline denominations typically integrated men and women in such societies and began opening positions for women in denominational bureaucracies. Although some women were ordained in mainline groups, the practice was still rare. Typically, by the 1920s, subordinate church offices, such as deacons, were opened to women, and by the 1950s, ministerial ordination was also allowed.[14]

Women clergy, however, were still a rarity until the feminist uprising of the 1960s. By the end of the 1970s, all mainline Protestant denominations were routinely ordaining women. Women were also attending mainline theological seminaries in large numbers. By the early 1980s, women constituted over 20 percent of all seminarians and over 50 percent in some mainline seminaries. Their presence took up the slack created by declining numbers of male seminarians that was part of the wider attrition of young people from mainline denominations. Nonetheless, even though increasing numbers of women were among the graduates of seminaries, they still often found difficulty in winning acceptance by congregations as equals with male clergy. People in the pews tended to be more traditional than the seminaries and the denominational leadership.

Women also developed feminist theologies to promote their cause. Such theologies were typically built around the themes of liberation for the oppressed and included challenges of theologies formulated by male oppressors.

Particularly important in forcing denominations to face the question of feminism was the practical revolution in religious language promoted by feminists. Both the Bible and its traditional English translations used male pronouns for references to both man and woman. By the 1970s, American feminists had already won the battle in much of the wider culture in using explicitly inclusive language when referring to male and female. Christian feminists pressed to have translations of the Bible do the same and also asked for new renderings of church hymns. Especially controversial was the insistence that God not be referred to only by male pronouns but rather that God be spoken of as female as well as male. Such practice had both liturgical and theological implications since reference to God as "Father" was prominent in the Lord's Prayer and in formulations concerning the Trinity as "Father, Son, and Holy Spirit." Once again, progressive church leaders pressed for the changes, while many mainline laypeople resisted.

The Gay and Lesbian Movement

Paralleling the women's movement was the remarkable advance of people who were avowedly gay or lesbian in American life after the 1960s. At the beginning of the period, persons who engaged in same-sex sexual activities were considered pariahs in most of American society. As late as 1973 the American Psychiatric Association listed homosexuality as a disorder in its Diagnostic and Statistical Handbook of Mental Disorders.[15] By the 1980s, gays and lesbians gained wide recognition as a minority group and significant legal protection against discrimination.

The most liberal wings of religious groups supported this revolutionary sexuality. Tolerance of gays and lesbians fit their ethic of personal fulfillment and love. Liberal Christians saw acceptance of the formerly outcast as an expression of the ethic of Jesus. They celebrated human difference and formed support groups. Some liberal Protestants ordained avowedly practicing gays and lesbians into the ministry. The issue also created bitter and protracted debates, especially within mainline denominations. Differences regarding the moral acceptability of LGBT (Lesbian, Gay, Bisexual, and Transgender) identities and practices, eventually including gay marriage, would remain a sharp dividing line between religious traditionalists and progressives.

New Age, New (and Old) Religions

Although a division between liberals and conservatives was the major motif in American culture and religion in the later twentieth century, the situation was more complex. One major manifestation of this complexity was the presence of a bewildering myriad of new religions that blossomed, especially in the 1960s and 1970s, and continued to be a major feature of the American scene for the years following. Growing largely out of the new spiritual openness of the counterculture era, these religions provided continuing alternatives to the dominant trends.

The United States has always included many alternative religions and religious practices. There have long been subcommunities in which non-Western ancient religions, such as Buddhism, Shintoism, Hinduism, and Islamism, have been practiced. Until late in the twentieth century, however, none of these religious subcommunities were large enough to have much impact on the larger American culture, although they attracted some converts and inspired American imitators. The presence of such religious subcommunities also forced other Americans to recognize the reality of world religious diversity. Awareness of world religions, especially since the late nineteenth century, played an important role in leading some Christians to question the exclusive claims of Christianity.[16]

In addition to these imported religions and practices, America has always added many homegrown varieties, and never more than in the era of the counterculture. In part, this reflects apparently innate human religious proclivities, but also it reflects remarkable qualities of the American environment, which might be thought of as analogous to a fertile bank described in a famous passage of Darwin's *Origin of Species*. There, in one small area, Darwin saw growing an immense variety of natural life. The United States likewise has long provided especially fertile ground for the growth of countless religions. Freedom of religion, a strong religious heritage, free enterprise and opportunity for any individual to succeed, and openness to new expressions as accentuated by the counterculture were all conducive to exotic religions.

To the extent that one can classify these, the non-Christian types fall into two major categories, each with a considerable American heritage. On the one hand there were groups, often called cults, that were variations on a Judeo-Christian heritage or worldview but yet were distinct new religions. Probably the best-known example is the Unification Church founded by the Reverend Sun Myung Moon (1920–2012), a Korean with a Christian background. Moon presented himself as the latest prophet of God, going beyond the work of Jesus and promising a coming millennial kingdom. Although the numbers of his strictly disciplined American followers were never large, they were conspicuous. Mammoth international business enterprises, publishing, and political campaigns gave the religion some prominence for a time in the later decades of the century.[17]

Most notorious of the religions of this Judeo-Christian type was the People's Temple community of the Reverend Jim Jones. Though he began his movement as a Christian sect, Jones soon proclaimed himself a prophet of a new religion. Accentuating authoritarian leadership even more than in most such groups, Jones moved his community to Guyana in South America. There, in November 1978, in a remarkable demonstration of cultic power, he led nine hundred people into an apparent mass suicide.

Fifteen years later, federal government efforts to control another cult brought almost as tragic results. In February 1993, the Bureau of Alcohol, Tobacco, and Firearms attempted to raid the heavily armed compound of the Branch Davidians near Waco, Texas, but were repulsed, leaving four agents dead. The Branch Davidians were a small, millennial group in the Adventist tradition who were led by an authoritarian, self-proclaimed prophet, David Koresh. In April 1993, after a tense two-month standoff, a second assault on the compound resulted in an explosion and fire in which eighty-six of the cult members died. Debate over how far the government should go in trying to control religious groups and over who was responsible for this deadly conflagration continued for years.

Other new variations of Judeo-Christian religion did not go to the extremes of the People's Temple or the Branch Davidians. Many smaller groups have prospered peacefully. So generalization should not be based on the most unusual cases.

The second, very different type of new religion, or variation on old religions, that flourished in America at this time typically turned to the East for alternatives to Christianity. These religions came in many varieties, including American Zen Buddhism; Hare Krishna; the followers of the Indian Guru Maharaj Ji, who briefly gathered a wide American following when he was an enterprising teenager in the early 1970s; the community of Bhagwan Shree Rajneesh, which took over a town in Oregon for a time in the 1980s; and followers of a number of other Hindu gurus. Occult or secret practices, including those of older groups such as Spiritualists, Theosophists, and Rosicrucians, were also popular. More a mix of Eastern and Western ideals than formal religions were groups that promised success through mind discipline, such as Transcendental Meditation, Erhard Seminars Training (EST), and the Scientology of L. Ron Hubbard.[18]

With so many varieties—and there are more—generalizations will not do justice to all. Nonetheless, Robert S. Ellwood Jr. offers some helpful characterizations of such religions. Typically, these religions look to a distant Eastern culture for inspiration, they sometimes involve feminine spiritual leadership, they usually advocate meditation or some sort of mind control that allows the spiritual to overcome the material, and they are monistic. Monism, which is a central characteristic, means that, unlike Judeo-Christian religions premised on the distinction between the Creator and the creatures, these religions are premised on the unity of all life, which is essentially spiritual. They are—again in contrast to Judeo-Christian religions—nonhistorical, that is, not based on historical claims but on methods by which the individual transcends history by entering into harmony with a spiritual realm.[19]

As a group, these religions may be seen as part of a general "new-age" culture that gained millions of adherents in the United States following the 1960s. Although involvement in new-age cultic communities, such as Hare Krishna, demands total commitment, contacts with new-age or occult practices by many middle-class Americans have often have been supplemental to continuing Christian practice.[20] Nonetheless, a significant new outlook, promoted by networks of publications and bookstores, was apparent. One notable cultural trait of the new-age movement is its inherently pluralistic and, hence, often ethically relativist nature. Whereas Judeo-Christian religions have been traditionally rule-oriented regarding morality, new-age practices, which open one up to the wisdom of many cultures and times, are experiential and expressive in their orientations.[21]

Such beliefs have not been new to America just since the 1960s. They had substantial precedents especially among mid-nineteenth-century refugees from New England Protestantism. Many such people learned of Eastern wisdom through the writings of Emanuel Swedenborg, an eighteenth-century Swedish sage. Ralph Waldo Emerson turned to Swedenborg and to Eastern religions for alternatives to Christianity, and in the later nineteenth century, spiritualist practices such as contacting the dead were popular. The Bahá'í faith, which originated in nineteenth-century Iran and proclaimed the oneness of major religions, also gained a following in the United States. Perhaps the most mainstream of American esoteric religions has been Free Masonry, practiced by a number of American founding fathers and by many other leading citizens since. While membership in Masonic lodges is not regarded as an alternative to Christianity, its secret mystical rituals and affirmations of universal brotherhood anticipated a few of the traits of later new-age religions. In each case, the appeal has been primarily to the American middle classes.

The new-age culture that flourished after the 1960s was in many respects thoroughly American, at least America in the individualistic, self-expressive, and nature-loving tradition of Ralph Waldo Emerson. For one thing, it accentuated the pluralist and inclusive impulses that have long been strong in American life. Moreover, it often included long-standing antitechnological sentiments, reinforced by the counterculture. Dominant American cultural values have often oscillated between two poles: one of immense trust in technologies and the other of extravagant assertions about the value of the individual and subjective experience. New-age religion, like much of American culture and religion, sometimes seems to assert as much trust in humanity as in the divine. It asserts that within each individual are the resources to find the divine.

Habits of the Heart

Such beliefs were not so far, either, from what many ordinary Americans already believed. During the 1980s, a team headed by Robert Bellah of the University of California at Berkeley took an in-depth look at the beliefs and values that are typical of the dominant American middle classes. The team's findings and analysis were published in *Habits of the Heart* (1985), one of the influential books of the 1980s. Among the important factors that have shaped twentieth-century American life, the authors observed, was the increasing compartmentalization of life. In a technological society, private life is, typically, sharply separated from work, and work itself is divided into separate sectors that require expert managers. The two major definers of American life, accordingly, are the managers and the therapists. The managers oversee the technological aspects of the society that tend to depersonalize life and treat individuals as interchangeable parts. In their work, Americans have often been driven by the ideals of "utilitarian individualism," which makes success paramount. This also can be dehumanizing. The therapists, whose ideals pervade mass media, counter with expressive, individualistic ideologies that emphasize fulfillment of the self as a unique individual.[22]

Whether Americans are dominated by the success orientation of utilitarian individualism or by the fulfillment of expressive individualism, society is remarkably individualistic and privatistic in its most modern style. Beliefs are considered to be private affairs, and most modern Americans have considerably less concern for the community at large than did their small-town forebears. The modern Americans, rather, seek people of their own kind in "lifestyle enclaves."[23]

These features of modern American life have important implications for religion. In the modern popular view and dominant in the media, values are determined subjectively on the basis of how they promote the fulfillment of the self. Religion, accordingly, is seen as an entirely private affair. One poll revealed that 80 percent of Americans would agree that "an individual should arrive at his or her own religious beliefs independent of any churches or synagogues."[24] In *Habits of the Heart*, the authors reported an interview they believed epitomizes much of American religion. The interviewee, named Sheila, said frankly that her religion was "Sheilaism." Sheila described it in the following way: "I believe in God. I'm not a religious fanatic. I can't remember the last time I went to church. My faith has carried me a long way. It's Sheilaism. Just my own little voice."[25]

Bellah provided sociological confirmation for a similar cultural critique developed by social philosopher Christopher Lasch, who described the dominant outlooks emerging in American life as "The Culture of Narcissism" in a 1979 book of that title. In the nineteenth century, Lasch observed, the cult of success involved "an abstract ideal of discipline and self-denial." In the twentieth century, by contrast, people increasingly defined success as victory over one's competitors, so that they "wish to be not so much esteemed as admired. They crave not fame but the glamour and excitement of celebrity." At the same time this narcissistic culture is not entirely individualistic. It also depends on bureaucratic capitalism regulated by experts. In order to gain the freedom to be able to design one's "lifestyle" from the consumer goods and entertainments the culture provides, modern people in their work need to submit to bureaucratic regulation based on the demands of technological efficiency.[26] As many other critics of American cultural trends have observed, such a combination of narcissism and bureaucratic regulation leaves unanswered questions regarding personal meaning or principles for building a moral order.[27]

Evangelical Resurgence

While conflicts between conservatives and liberals are nothing new, in the late twentieth century, they seemed to signal a realignment that cut across

older religious divisions. On the conservative side, one of the most remarkable developments during the era following the 1960s was the resurgence of
evangelicalism.

Evangelicalism is a very diverse movement. It long has been a very loose
coalition of Christians who have in common a traditional "gospel" message—evangelical means "gospel"—of salvation, often called "born again,"
based on Christ's atoning work on the cross, as revealed in the authoritative
Scriptures. This designation would include most Protestants who are more or
less traditional in their theology. Some groups are organized into tighter coa-
litions or networks, are very conscious of being "evangelical," and sometimes
use that name. Others, such as most African-American Protestants, some
ethnic Protestant conservatives, and many smaller groups, have primarily
denominational loyalties and do not ordinarily call themselves "evangelical,"
even though they share basic evangelical beliefs. Evangelicalism is even more
diverse if it is considered as a rapidly growing, worldwide movement or set
of movements.

In the United States in 1960, despite the popularity of Billy Graham and
Oral Roberts, most analysts continued to write off evangelical Christianity as
left over from an earlier era rather than as a major force for the future. For
the past century, sociologists and other informed observers had been saying
that as modern industrial societies advance and modern scientific education
becomes universal, traditional, biblically based beliefs will fade away.

Traditional Christianity, in fact, had not been declining. Conservative
churches had long been growing, but as long as the mainline establishment
was dominant, few observers paid much attention. From 1940 to 1960, for
instance, the Southern Baptist Convention, a conservative (and overwhelmingly white) evangelical group that did not belong to the National Council
of Churches, doubled in membership from five to ten million. The fact,
however, was not much remarked on. In the decades after the mid-1960s,
however, conservative church membership growth was accompanied by de-
clines in the old mainline. By 1965, the Southern Baptists and the Methodist Church were virtually equal as the largest Protestant bodies, with about
eleven million members each. By 1985, the Southern Baptists were still
growing in all regions of the country and had reached fourteen and a half
million members. The Methodist Church, which was controlled by liberal
and moderate leadership, in the meantime declined to nine million. Just a
hundred years after Methodist Church Extension Society spokesman Charles
McCabe triumphantly proclaimed that the Methodists were starting a church
per day, the Methodists were losing well over a hundred members per day.[28]

Meanwhile, almost all conservative churches were growing. Pentecostalism was probably growing the fastest. For instance, the Assemblies of God, the largest of the many Pentecostal denominations, grew from a little over a half million members in 1965 to over two million by 1985.[29] A number of fundamentalist and Pentecostal individual congregations had also grown to memberships of five thousand to fifteen thousand.[30] Many conservative congregations within mainline churches were gaining members, as well. Most of these denominations also included vigorous evangelical renewal movements that were helping to combat liberal trends. By the 1970s and 1980s, pollsters were estimating that some thirty to fifty million Americans could be classified as "evangelical," the general term that now came to be used for conservative Protestant groups. That would likely be at least half of all Protestants, estimated at seventy-six million.[31]

Despite overall declining numbers in mainline churches, one source of the growth among them in the 1960s and 1970s was the wildfire spread of the charismatic movement. Charismatics differed from Pentecostals mainly in that they did not form separate denominations but, rather, worked within established congregations. Typically, the charismatic movement grew by means of networks of small-group Bible studies and personal contacts. Developing from the efforts of the Full Gospel Businessmen's Fellowship, the charismatic movement gained its first firm foothold in a mainline denomination when its teachings spread widely in an Episcopal congregation in Van Nuys, California, in 1960. From there, it spread to other mainline and evangelical groups and by the end of the decade was reaching many Catholics as well as Protestants. Though many millions were touched by the charismatic movement, it built little of an institutional base, and its long-term influence is difficult to measure.

"Born-Again" Politics

With the emergence of evangelicalism as a recognized cultural force in the 1970s, politics was initially not much of a factor. One reason was that evangelicalism was so diverse. White evangelicals stood on the opposite side of most political issues from black Bible-believers. White evangelicals also had long been divided among themselves, as between southern Democrats and northern Republicans. Most white evangelicals were conservative in their politics and, at least in the South, had favored segregation. Partly in reaction to liberal Protestants emphasizing politics so heavily, however, many evangelicals said that churches should distance themselves from politics. Although evangelical leaders and organizations did sometimes promote conservative agendas through personal influence, lobbying, and their publications, there was no considerable political mobilization on the national level. Locally, on school boards or regarding particular issues, conservative Christians might organize on the grassroots level. In southern California, for instance, white evangelicals, often transplanted from Arkansas, Oklahoma, and Texas, emerged as a force that helped elect Ronald Reagan as governor in 1966.[32]

The spark that touched off eventual mobilization of white evangelicals as a national political force was the election of Jimmy Carter to the presidency in 1976. During his campaign, Carter avowed that he was a born-again evangelical Christian. This sent secular reporters—who often lived in communities that long refused to take the evangelical part of America seriously—scurrying to find the meaning of *born again* and to find out whether it was a subversive opinion. Carter, in fact, was a moderate Southern Baptist, a tradition that included strong views on the separation of church and state. The public was satisfied that his religious views would not intrude unduly into his office. Carter received strong support from voters who also identified themselves as born-again Christians, and his candidacy led *Newsweek* to dub 1976 "the year of the evangelical."

Despite his evangelical credentials, Carter's liberal Democratic politics soon proved unpopular with many white evangelicals. Sociologically, many of them came from groups who had deep reactions against the liberalization and especially against the permissiveness that was prominent during the counterculture years. They were part of the backlash that President Richard Nixon had cultivated as the "silent majority." During the Vietnam War, this group deeply resented attacks on patriotism, and they feared that liberals and radicals were naively generous toward international communism.

The Nixon administration also proclaimed the need for American moral renewal; but when it turned out that the administration itself was deeply deceitful and scandal-ridden, and that the president's profane and vulgar private language seemed to belie his public intimations of piety, conservative religious people felt they had been co-opted by secular political forces.

One impact of the Nixon Watergate scandal, however, was that it convinced many Americans that morality and politics should not be separate. Religion and morality were obviously related already. Conservative church leaders who might have been reluctant to become involved in politics, therefore, now felt more free to actively campaign on moral questions that had political implications.[33]

Interestingly, some of the earliest evangelical voices calling for reclaiming a moral agenda for politics came from the political left. During the Nixon years, a vocal group of mostly younger, educated evangelicals began calling for applying biblical principles to issues such as racism, care for the poor, and the Vietnam War with its accompanying patriotic civil religion. A number of such evangelicals helped organize the evangelical Chicago Declaration on these issues in 1973. Eventually this "evangelical left" was eclipsed by the rise of the evangelical right later in the decade. Even if the politically progressive evangelicals were eventually "left behind," as one historian put it, the movement also produced long-term champions for greater justice and equality such as Ronald Sider or Jim Wallis of the *Sojourners* magazine and community. These progressives were also connected with international evangelical movements that supported liberation theology, as in Latin America. Even though after 1980 in the United States "evangelical" would often be identified as though it were primarily a group of white conservative voters, it is important to recall that the movement is much more diverse than that. As a worldwide movement it is unified not by any political stance but by shared religious beliefs and practices. And in the United States, most African-American Christians, for instance, are evangelicals in the sense of sharing the faith of this worldwide movement, even if, sadly, they have been divided socially, politically, and in church life from many of their white co-religionists, due to longstanding social antagonisms.

One of the early signs of political mobilization of white, conservative Christians was mounting reaction during the 1970s to the proposed Equal Rights Amendment (ERA) to the US Constitution, designed to prohibit public discrimination against women. Congressional passage of the ERA in 1972 and subsequent votes for state ratification, helped mobilize conservative religious opposition about issues regarding sexuality and the nature of the family. Opponents of the ERA, both Catholic and Protestant, succeeded in characterizing it as part of a government-sponsored program to promote a revolution in mores regarding family values. As a result, the amendment was not ratified.

Evangelical and related conservative religious groups, true to their diverse characters, were often divided within themselves, especially concerning issues that pertained to the roles of women. Particularly divisive was the question of women's ordination to the ministry, a practice resisted in many conservative and fundamentalist groups, although approved in many holiness and Pentecostal traditions and among moderate evangelicals, especially those who remained in mainline denominations.

Fundamentalist and conservative evangelical antifeminism was usually tied to the inerrancy of the Bible, a doctrine that emphasized both the historical reliability of Scripture and traditional interpretations. When fundamentalists and related groups had been battling theological modernism and higher criticism of the Bible earlier in the century, affirmations of biblical inerrancy had become increasingly important as tests of the faith. Similarly, in the latter decades of the century, conservatives in the Southern Baptist Convention, the nation's largest Protestant body, mobilized around the doctrine of biblical inerrancy. By the late 1970s, their conservative theological concerns coalesced with growing conservative political interests, including antifeminism, other issues of family and sexuality, conservative economics, militant patriotism, and a number of other issues. Promoters of this package of ideals mounted a wide-ranging campaign to wrest control of the denomination from moderates. By the 1990s, after some bitter controversies, conservatives gained dominance in the denomination and its seminaries.

While struggles between traditionalists and innovators in churches were a long-standing feature of modern religious life, what gave later twentieth-century controversies an additional political dimension was the perception that the federal government was becoming a major agent in promoting changes in social mores. Religious and political concerns had never been entirely separate. That was especially the case in the influential mainline Protestant denominations, which had often promoted progressive political causes, most notably the civil rights movement. Conservative Protestants, who often had support from big business interests that opposed government regulation, typically resisted such progressive political efforts while at the same time insisting, in opposition to mainline Protestant activism, that churches should stay away from direct political involvement.

The successes of the civil rights movement in the 1960s and 1970s left lingering resentments, especially in the states of the former Confederacy, against federal regulation. At the same time, the legal resolution concerning race discrimination helped pave the way for conservative-religious political mobilization. A new Christian conservative political movement now could avoid the stigma of having an overt anti-civil-rights agenda. Most importantly, the civil rights struggle had helped convince most white voters in southern states to move from the Democratic to the Republican Party and hence made possible a political alliance of northern and southern religious conservatives.

The Moral Majority

By 1980, alarm among conservatives in all sorts of religious groups was generating a notable new political coalition. Most significant was that these concerns brought together large numbers of conservative Protestants and Catholics, who united on issues of family and sexuality and on militant patriotism and anticommunism. These issues drew into a political coalition groups that had been rivals religiously. Mormons, for instance, shared these concerns, as did some conservative Jews. Also capitalizing on many of the same political and social resentments was the Reverend Sun Myung Moon, who raised remarkable amounts of money to help finance conservative political efforts. Politically conservative evangelical Protestants and Catholics, who in another era would have had nothing but disdain for Moon's claims to improve on the work of Jesus, now joined him in a common political effort.

One conspicuous issue that brought such people together was a widespread sense of outrage at the sexual permissiveness that had become characteristic of American life. Popular music, movies, pornography, and advertising all flaunted open sexuality, observing varying minimal standards of discretion. Television shows routinely made fun of anyone with antiquated ideas about sexuality and presented sexual permissiveness as a normal lifestyle. Such campaigns, to some degree, reflected a broadly based upheaval in attitudes toward sexuality. The percentage of Americans who said that premarital sex, for instance, was morally wrong dropped from nearly 80 percent in 1959 to less than 50 percent by 1973. Disapproval of divorce, according to one study, dropped from 43 to 18 percent.[34]

Early opposition to the Equal Rights Amendment fit into this context, for religious conservatives perceived that it was part of a more radical change in mores that the government now permitted or even condoned. Also included in these changes was a growing acceptance of gay and lesbian sexual practices and lifestyles. So, even during the presidency of the "born again" Jimmy Carter, the government seemed to be moving toward accepting sexual practices that traditional Judeo-Christian religions had always condemned. Since the government was seen as emerging as a principal promoter of changes in family values, political opposition increasingly came to be seen as a necessary means toward preserving more traditional values.

Religious conservatives could also point out that, in contrast to new governmental tolerance of open sexual expression, the courts had banned prayer in public schools. Even though that ban had occurred in the early 1960s, it continued to generate resentments. It also helped to convince many conservative Christians that they needed to establish their own schools or to provide home schooling in order to foster both their religious and political teachings. In the South the Christian school movement gained momentum after the ending of public school segregation. Although most of these Christian schools were not strictly segregated, they had overwhelmingly white constituencies. So race was at least implicitly a factor in their appeal. During the Carter administration, the IRS put pressure on such schools to demonstrate they were not racist if they were to keep their tax exemption. Proponents of the religious right, in turn, pointed to such pressure as evidence that conservative Christians must organize politically if they were to resist big government that might take away their freedoms.[35]

Most effective of the organizations bringing together the emerging politically conservative religious coalition was the Moral Majority, founded in 1979 by Jerry Falwell (1933–2007), pastor of a Baptist megachurch in Lynchburg, Virginia. He was an avowed fundamentalist. Fundamentalists, who formed the militant right wing of evangelicalism, had typically insisted, since the 1950s, on separation from mainline denominations and usually from other evangelicals. Falwell and many other fundamentalists also opposed church political involvement during the civil rights era. Now, however, Falwell took the lead in bringing large numbers of fundamentalists, as well as conservative evangelicals and some other conservatives, back into the political arena.

The fundamentalist tradition had long supported some avid anticommunist crusaders, but the addition of issues that had to do with family and sexuality brought it back to political prominence for the first time since the 1920s. Actually, the fundamentalist heritage contained two contradictory traditions regarding the church and politics. On the one hand, their dispensational premillennialist teaching that Jesus would return any day and set up his kingdom would seem to undermine political interest. In this view, America would be regarded as Babylon, and believers should simply be spiritual and wait for the coming kingdom. On the other hand, fundamentalists, like most white Protestants, shared in the Puritan heritage that believed America was a new Israel. So Falwell and other new religious right leaders typically talked about a covenant between God and the American people and advocated a return to a "Christian America." Despite their sectarian proclamations of the importance of Christians separating from the world, they were avid patriots.

The most compelling conservative religious narrative concerning what had happened to "Christian America" was that the Christian outlook that had once dominated the nation was being replaced by modern "secular humanism," which had taken over liberal culture and hence the nation's educational system and public life. Francis Schaeffer, an American evangelical, who had gained prominence as an evangelist to young intellectuals, was particularly influential in spreading this concern among the leaders of the religious right. In widely distributed films and books, Schaeffer described the seismic shifts that had taken place in Western culture and thought. He highlighted the eras when a Christian ethos had been prominent, and contrasted that with the soul-destroying alternatives of totalitarianism and relativism of the twentieth century.

For Schaeffer and for many of the Protestants, including Falwell, whom he influenced, the issue of abortion rather suddenly rose to the top among the list of reasons why concerned Christians should adopt a new stance of political activism. In 1973 the US Supreme Court in its *Roe v. Wade* decision legalized abortion as a right for women. In the years just before and after that decision, a number of prominent conservative Protestant groups, including the Southern Baptist Convention and the National Association of Evangelicals, took the stance that abortion might be morally permissible in some cases, but it was wrong if simply for the convenience of the mother. By the end of the 1970s, many militantly political evangelicals and fundamentalists, such as Schaeffer and the Moral Majority, had switched from this middle position to the traditional Catholic view that human personhood started at conception and hence abortion amounted to murder. In that view, the government's permissive stance toward abortion was allowing a "holocaust" in the killing of millions of unborn babies. Soon opposition to abortion became the most nonnegotiable issue in rallying conservative Christians to the Republican Party and to political action. It also helped build a new coalition of conservative Protestants and conservative Catholics.

The characteristic mentality of fundamentalists was to divide things into sharp either/or dichotomies that eliminated middle positions. One significant example was their views regarding creation and evolution. At the time of the Scopes trial, many evangelicals, including William Jennings Bryan himself, were open to the idea that the earth might be very old. Such firm Bible-believers typically would at least tolerate the view there could be God-directed evolution of lower species, but they insisted on God's special creation of humans. As the embattled fundamentalist movement developed during the next generations, such middle views that included limited acceptance of the mainstream science of origins became unacceptable in fundamentalist and many conservative evangelical circles. By the late 1970s, the prevailing view in such circles was that the earth was no more than some thousands of years old and that the geological and fossil evidence could be explained as the result of the great flood recorded in Genesis. So-called creation science provided arguments and evidence for this conclusion. Such views fit so well with the beliefs of many Bible-believers that two states, Arkansas and Louisiana, adopted laws requiring public schools to teach young-earth creation science views alongside secular evolutionary views as an exercise in balanced treatment. None of the middle positions were to be considered. These laws were struck down in the courts.

Even so, the growth during the twentieth century of the teaching that the biblical account of creation must be interpreted as literally as possible and therefore was incompatible with any view of evolution as a means of God's creation is a striking example of what was becoming an increasing tendency in American life. Positions were polarizing into incompatible either/or categories. That tendency (which, of course, can be found in many other cultural and religious conflicts throughout history) was heightened among fundamentalists as they defined a separatist movement after the 1920s. When, with the rise of the Moral Majority, fundamentalists became a conspicuous factor in mainstream political life, they helped encourage such polarizing tendencies among a wider coalition of religious and political people. Meanwhile, more liberal elements in the culture, especially since the 1960s, had been moving further from any deference to traditional Judeo-Christian mores and outlooks, thus also accentuating cultural polarization. So, while as late as the 1950s there had been widespread hopes to build an American consensus, built on shared humanistic ideals and the authority of science, by the end of the 1970s such dreams seemed a distant relic of the past.

In 1980, the Moral Majority claimed some credit for helping to elect Ronald Reagan to the presidency, although its influence likely was not decisive. Ronald Reagan himself was an ardent anticommunist and professed sympathy for the concerns regarding family questions and other symbolic issues favored by the religious right, such as allowing organized prayers in public schools. At one time, Reagan was influenced by conservative evangelical teachings, including dispensationalist interpretations of biblical prophecy, in a church in California. However, during his presidency, he was not a regular churchgoer and gave little more than rhetorical attention to most of the new Christian right concerns.

One politically significant aspect of the new religious right agenda was its unswerving support for the state of Israel. Because of the importance of Israel in dispensationalist interpretations of biblical prophecy, fundamentalist leaders were particularly concerned for the continued existence of Israel as an independent state. This added some political backing for the already established US policy of massive support for Israel. It also created some ambivalence in the attitude of the Jewish community toward fundamentalists. On the one hand, Jews generally were strongly opposed to any suggestion of a return to a "Christian America" and saw political fundamentalism as potentially a new American fascism. Moreover, they deeply resented fundamentalist efforts to convert Jews to Christianity. On the other hand, fundamentalist beliefs in the importance of Jews and of the nation of Israel to the fulfillment of prophecy gave Jews and fundamentalists an uneasy commonality on one important religious point.

Commercial Conservatism

The impact of the religious right in the 1970s and the 1980s was amplified by the emergence of extensive television ministries. How widespread was their influence is a matter of dispute. In the 1980s, the most modest estimate is that about thirteen million Americans watched such shows regularly, but other estimates claimed that up to sixty million Americans were at least occasional viewers. These audiences were disproportionately from the South and the Midwest and overwhelmingly of modest to poor means. Several of the largest ministries, nonetheless, raised well over a million dollars from their audiences every week.[36]

Most of the largest of these ministries, including Oral Roberts, Pat Robertson of the 700 Club, and Jim and Tammy Faye Bakker of the PTL ("Praise the Lord") Club, represented Pentecostal-charismatic traditions. They typically performed healings for innumerable small ailments among the viewing audiences, were upbeat, and promised health, wealth, and success to their supporters. Robert Schuller of the Crystal Cathedral in southern California, provided a similar success-oriented message for middle-class audiences. Schuller, from the mainline Reformed Church in America, stood in the tradition of Norman Vincent Peale, stressing the spiritual potential within everyone, rather than claiming special Pentecostal healing gifts. Jimmy Swaggart, the most popular of the television evangelists through much of the 1980s, though a Pentecostal, preached a simple fire-and-brimstone gospel of moral purity. Jerry Falwell, like most strict fundamentalists, did not believe in Pentecostal gifts and also preached a more traditional gospel as well as conservative politics. Falwell's, however, was the most politically oriented of the ministries, though during the 1980s, Robertson also moved in that direction. Ignoring the complexities and ambiguities of the role of Christianity in American history, politically oriented evangelists invoked nostalgia for simpler times when traditional Protestant values were the norm.

In 1987 and 1988, Robertson surpassed Falwell as the leading religious television figure in politics when he ran in the Republican presidential primaries. He gained considerable early attention by his ability to mobilize about 10 percent of the Republican vote in most states where he ran. Nonetheless, he also proved unable to move beyond that solid core of support and eventually dropped from the race.

Also in 1987 and 1988, the character of some of these ministries was revealed in a series of scandals that would have made a soap-opera writer envious. Early in 1987, Oral Roberts claimed that God personally told him that God would kill him if Roberts's supporters did not raise enough money by a specified date. About the same time, a scandal broke around Jim Bakker, who was alleged to have carried on illicit sexual relationships. Early in 1988, Jimmy Swaggart, who was particularly critical of Bakker, was forced to step down from his ministry because of sexual improprieties. Defying his denomination, the Assemblies of God, Swaggart soon returned to the air, now preaching more about forgiveness. Jim Bakker was sent to jail for financial fraud, bringing his PTL ministries to an end. Following these scandals, most television ministries continued but with much diminished influence.

The phenomenal early successes of television ministries evidenced the power of commercialism in a technological civilization. Although there were some very responsible ministries and often good intentions for others, the commercial pressures were high for doing whatever worked and for giving people what they wanted. Fundraising appeals, not regulated like commercial advertising, sometimes stretched the truth, used high-pressure scare techniques or implied extravagant benefits to donors. Some of the ministries constantly celebrated self and success. Although these ministries offered affirmations of many aspects of traditional Christianity and were valued for that by wide audiences, these commercial ministries also vividly illustrated some of the paradoxes found throughout American culture and religion.

Culture Wars

The often strident debates over moral and political issues that emerged in the late twentieth century came to be known as culture wars, and these would continue into the twenty-first century. Yet, despite their diametrically opposed stances on many issues, commonalities could also be found between the ideological left and the ideological right, even if neither side acknowledged these common traits. Both sides, for instance, were remarkably individualistic. Americans typically insisted on believing what they wanted and had a negative view of the authority of institutions. Many people on both sides talked of personal fulfillment and favored expressive individualism that valued intense personal experience. Both sides, despite professions to the contrary, tended toward materialism, often defining values in terms of availability of material comforts and security. Both sides were largely comfortable with the benefits and the pleasures of technological society, although ironically the religious right was often less critical of relying on technology than the left. Both sides were, in their own ways, moralistic, insisting that certain sorts of beliefs and behavior were unacceptable and hoping to legislate their standards for the whole society.

These outlooks, shared by wide varieties of Americans, point to a vast and often unrecognized revolution in what modern Americans expect from life. Whereas their forebears in the nineteenth century and throughout the Judeo-Christian era saw life and religion largely as learning to live with and accept adversity, contemporary Americans more typically presumed that the world owed them a living and that religion should be, at least in part, a means to self-fulfillment. Though there are many exceptions, the American characteristics that the Robert Bellah team identified in *Habits of the Heart* have influenced almost the whole spectrum of American religion.

The politicization of American culture, nonetheless, highlighted the extreme positions on many issues. Politics dominated what counted as news, and the more political conflict could be highlighted, the more entertaining was the news. The expansion of electronic media also brought almost everyone into the orbit of national debates. Cable television networks, which had fostered religious resurgence, also allowed expression of genuine political options that had not been present in the early days of TV, when three similar national networks had dominated TV news reporting. Especially important was the emergence of the Fox News Channel, founded in 1996, and soon to become the single most-watched news channel, as well as the favorite of both political and religious conservatives. Politically conservative talk radio also provided popular sources for highlighting differences with the liberal establishment that was seen as dominating mainstream media and education. Such politicized discourse, on the left as well as the right, intermixed with more specifically religious heritages in shaping many church-going Americans' cultural outlooks. This politicization, and hence the polarization of moral discourse, was also related to the vast expansion of government that had taken place during the twentieth century. Ever since the New Deal, the political left and the leadership of the progressive mainline Protestant churches that tended to support the political left had seen government as a principal agency for ensuring equitable welfare for all citizens. Since the civil rights era, the left had also emphasized government's role in ensuring nondiscrimination. In the latter decades of the century, campaigns for governmental protection expanded to include women and persons of various sexual preferences. At the same time, since the 1960s, the left had been critical of expansion of government when it came to the military and nuclear arms. Conservatives, in the meantime, had been consistently militant in opposition to international communism and hence in favor of increasing military strength. They also continued to see any expansion of the welfare rolls of the state as tinged with socialist implications. And, especially after the rise of the religious right, they countered the left's inclusivist moral agenda with standards based on traditional values regarding the family and sexuality that they hoped the government would support.[37]

During the 1990s, culture war rhetoric often dominated the intersections of American religion and culture, but the realities were much more mixed and often more moderate. Mainline Protestant churches had been continuing to decline in membership numbers since the 1960s. They also continued to move in a progressive direction that emphasized social concerns and inclusivism, including in matters regarding sexuality. But their constituents were often more conservative or moderate. Radical feminists sometimes sparked a conservative backlash, as happened after a well-attended mainline Re-Imagining conference in 1993 that emphasized inclusion of persons of all sexual orientations and celebrated God as Sophia, which critics alleged amounted to goddess worship. In a number of mainline denominations, the question of whether to ordain persons who were openly in gay or lesbian relationships became particularly divisive. Conservative minorities in a number of denominations eventually withdrew after long and painful controversies.

At the other extreme, the religious-political right continued in various guises to create a stir. In church life, its greatest triumph was the completion of a long campaign by theological and political conservatives to take over from moderates the control of the central agencies and theological seminaries of the Southern Baptist Convention, the nation's largest Protestant denomination. Politically, the religious right reached its greatest strength under the guidance of the Christian Coalition, headed by Pat Robertson and Ralph Reed. In 1994, conservative Christians played a discernible role in electing a strongly Republican House of Representatives led by the outspoken Speaker of the House, Newt Gingrich. While this "Republican Revolution" created a great stir and generated many heated exchanges with the Democratic administration of Bill Clinton, neither conservatives nor liberals made substantial gains in advancing their agendas. Clinton rather easily won re-election in 1996.

Searching for Sexual Standards in a Relativistic Era

The symbolic culmination of the rhetorical conflicts between right and left came in the 1998 through 1999 impeachment and trial of President Clinton. Clinton was a marvelous example of the mixture of the religious and the secular in American culture. Though he stood for the sort of progressive social agenda favored by mainline Protestant churches, he came from a Southern Baptist background, could point back to a born again experience, and was familiar with the language of evangelicals. As president he attended a United Methodist church along with his wife Hillary, a cradle Methodist. But there was a "Saturday night Bill" as well as a "Sunday morning Bill." When his sexual relationship with a young White House intern, Monica Lewinsky, was first revealed, much of the press believed it would bring down his presidency. Paradoxically, since the 1960s, the sexual revolution had helped make the private sexual behavior of politicians become a public concern. Prior to that, the press had politely ignored the sexual indiscretions of such public figures as Franklin D. Roosevelt and John F. Kennedy. Now sex was a matter for open mainstream discussion, and both the press and Clinton's political opponents could present the president's sexual infidelities as a major public issue. Clinton was alleged to have had many affairs, and he lied about the one with Lewinsky both to the American people and under oath. Still, despite the outcry, especially from religious conservatives, Clinton's behavior was not much different from that of some of the most popular sit-com TV characters of the era. More to the point, the Republicans lacked the two-thirds votes in the Senate required to remove the president from office. Clinton asked for forgiveness and promised to seek rehabilitation through evangelical religious counseling.

Many conservative Christians, in the meantime, had already been addressing the issues of the sexual revolution in a nonpolitical and less confrontational way. Most notable was the Promise Keepers organization for men. Under the leadership of football coach Bill McCartney, this group was able to fill stadiums all over the country, and in 1997 it held a Stand in the Gap rally that attracted hundreds of thousands of men to Washington, DC. Though largely evangelical, the group broke some stereotypes, avoiding politics and urging racial reconciliation. Its main emphasis was on spiritual renewal among men that would result in taking greater responsibilities for their families and sexual fidelity.

One general factor leading away from any simple polarization of the culture wars variety was the sheer religious diversity of America. No one group, whether evangelical, mainline Protestant, Catholic, Jewish, or other, could pretend to speak for even one side of an issue. One good illustration was the Million Man March that drew hundreds of thousands of black men to Washington, DC, in 1995. The march was a show of solidarity and, much like Promise Keepers, emphasized that men should take responsibility for their families. Its principal sponsors were not only Benjamin Chavis, a Protestant minister and former NAACP leader, but also Louis Farrakhan, a controversial leader of a splinter black Muslim group, the Nation of Islam.

Another symptom of the times related to the sexual revolution was that by the last decade of the century, allegations of sexual abuse of children by Roman Catholic priests were surfacing around the world. Thousands of these accusations, mostly from the latter decades of the twentieth century, would be confirmed in the United States and elsewhere. In this country, a *Boston Globe* investigation in 2001 was especially effective in uncovering the abuses and often their systematic cover-ups. A major 2015 film, *Spotlight*, directed by Tom McCarthy, dramatized that investigation and gave further publicity to the scandals, which by that time the church itself had been dealing with vigorously. Sexual abuse has been found in many other religious organizations and ministries, just as it is an ongoing problem whenever there is unequal power in human relationships—that is, almost always. Nonetheless, the Catholic instance was particularly striking because of the vast size of the organization, the complexities of the hierarchies' efforts to deal with it and/ or to cover it up, the tensions between forgiving sinners and protecting their victims, and the juxtaposition between the church's strict teachings on sexuality, its demands for clerical celibacy, and a culture where sexual expression was increasingly seen as essential to human identity.

New Styles of American Spirituality

In the United States, the Pentecostal and charismatic movements set the tone for a growing segment of churches. By the end of the century, Pentecostal denominations themselves numbered well over ten million, including more than five million African Americans.[38] The number of charismatics who belonged to other denominations is more difficult to estimate. Even many churches that did not engage in distinctive Pentecostal/charismatic practices, such as speaking in tongues, adopted what might be called a Pentecostal/charismatic style. Much of American worship became more informal, characterized by praise songs accompanied by bands, rather than hymns accompanied by organs. Contemporary congregations of many traditions increasingly emphasized spiritual experience and relationships more than any distinctive heritage of doctrine or worship. Some of the largest local congregations, attracting many thousands on a typical Sunday, offered seeker services that were upbeat, friendly, and non-confrontational.

In a larger perspective, one broad trend in American religious life was toward "a new spirituality of seeking."[39] Though Americans supported roughly the same set of denominations that had long been around, many did so with new attitudes. Rather than being strongly committed to particular traditions with distinctive doctrines, forms of worship, and sacred spaces, many religious people seemed to be seeking nonexclusivist spiritual experience. Participation in religious groups was increasingly a matter of personal choice. People chose religious affiliations as support groups in their personal quests to find meaning and community in a world of bewildering options. If they failed to find or sustain what they were looking for in one group or if they moved to a new location, they were ready to try something different. While many older traditions of doctrine and worship continued to attract adherents, members were less likely to hold to these traditions in strong or dogmatic ways.

Such trends toward spiritual seeking were among the factors that ran counter to a simple polarization of a culture wars variety. Those who were most militant on the side of religious-political conservatism typically came from more dogmatic religious traditions, most prominently conservative Catholicism and conservative evangelicalism or fundamentalism. These groups continued to sustain and attract loyal adherents. Nonetheless, nonconfrontational spirituality provided a popular alternative that pointed away from strong political and social engagement.

CHAPTER 9

The Twenty-First Century

Confident pluralism allows genuine difference to coexist without suppressing or minimizing our firmly held convictions.

John D. Inazu, *Confident Pluralism:*
Surviving and Thriving through Deep Difference (2016)

One lesson to learn from a study of the past is that we cannot reliably forecast the future. Though it is easy enough to spot and predict some trends, and we can also learn much from repeated patterns, human nature is so complex and filled with contradictions that collective behavior is not consistently predictable. Patterns that may seem steadily and surely developing may be thwarted by unexpectedly developing counter-trends. Often history is driven by reactions when a trend has gone too far. And sometimes unforeseen events such as natural catastrophes, wars, and revolutions jolt history toward a whole new direction.

The vicissitudes of the advance of secularism in the twentieth-century world provide some of the best examples of the dangers of simply projecting the trends of the recent past into the future. As late as 1970, many of the world's respected observers confidently predicted that the advances of modern science, technologies, and associated types of rationality, together with the attractions of modern individualism and materialism, would soon lead to secularization of most of the world. The great former colonial powers and cultural trend-setters, Great Britain and the nations of Western Europe, were rapidly secularizing. Marxists seemed to have routed traditional religion in other great swaths of territory and were among those most confident in predicting a secular millennium. The United States lagged behind in the pace of secularization, but it seemed plausible to assume that most of traditional American religiosity would fade with the advance of education and urbanization. The emerging nations of the rest of the world, it was also typically assumed, would become far less religious as they modernized.

The most dramatic event revealing how wrong were expectations that the twenty-first-century future would not be essentially an extension of twentieth-century trends was the unpredicted fall of the Soviet Union in 1989 and the accompanying rapid decline of Marxism as a world force. Once that had happened and the ominous clouds of the Cold War had finally lifted, a new world landscape appeared, one that looked very different from what might have been anticipated only a couple of decades earlier. Major traditional religions, especially Christianity and Islam, far from fading away, were rapidly growing.

Christianity's Center of Gravity Shifts to the Global South

One remarkable development of the twentieth century was that while Christianity diminished dramatically in the oldest parts of the former Christendom, including Western Europe and Great Britain, it spread like wildfire in many parts of the Global South. Such rapid growth, especially in former colonial areas such as Africa, went particularly against predictions of secularization theorists who had projected reactions against the religion of the colonizers once Western influences had withdrawn. Instead, the postcolonial era of the second half of the twentieth century saw some of the most rapid Christian growth of all time. Much of this growth, while overwhelmingly indigenous, had connections to American religious developments. The twentieth century had been truly "the American Century" in terms of international missions. American missions came to dominate the world missionary enterprise, and by the end of the century, roughly 90 percent of American foreign missionaries were evangelical.[1] These and other missionary efforts sowed seeds that often led to huge growth, often in new varieties on native soils. Protestant Christianity grew in Latin America, and Roman Catholic as well as various Protestant groups flourished in Africa and parts of East Asia. Chinese Christianity, planted by earlier multinational mission efforts, also blossomed remarkably despite long-standing government opposition. Most of worldwide Protestantism had a distinctly evangelical character. Smaller American sectarian movements, such as Mormonism, Jehovah's Witnesses, and Seventh-Day Adventism, also flourished on the world scene. Especially remarkable was the worldwide spread of Pentecostalism. It began as a tiny American movement in 1900, but by the end of the twentieth century Pentecostal and charismatic Christians numbered in the hundreds of millions worldwide.[2]

Historian Mark Noll, reflecting on this "new shape of world Christianity" in 2006, provided some striking illustrations of how dramatically the center of gravity of world Christianity had shifted in only a century. On any given Sunday at that time, he observed, there were more Anglicans attending church in any one of five African countries than all the Anglicans in Britain and Canada plus American Episcopalians combined. There were more Presbyterians in church in Ghana than in Scotland. The single largest Pentecostal church in Korea had more attending it than did the ten largest denominations in Canada. Possibly more Christians attended church in China than in all of "Christian" Europe. More Roman Catholics worshipped in the Philippines than in any single country of Europe, including historically Catholic Italy, Spain, and Poland.

Noll reflected on the extent to which such world Christianity, especially in its evangelical varieties, relates to the American religious experience. He concluded that, while there unquestionably have been direct American influences, a more helpful way to understand these developments is to see the United States as having provided an early model of how Christianity might flourish in a modernizing world. Nineteenth-century America provided an early instance of what the world would be like as it was transformed by new technologies, economic growth, unprecedented social and geographical mobility, and widely diverse populations. British and European Christianity transplanted into this American setting flourished by adopting new populist and enterprising forms that fit the free market. Such patterns, first modeled in the United States, later proved equally adaptable in many parts of the world where modernization similarly disrupted traditional and local cultures.[3]

World Religions in America

World religions in America were nothing new, but by the end of the twentieth century, Muslim prominence in American life was the most conspicuous example of increasing diversity. Estimates of numbers varied widely, but by the turn of the century the Muslim population was probably approaching at least three million.[4] Islam was thus coming to rival Judaism as the nation's second-largest religious grouping.

Asian immigration to the United States also increased the numbers of practitioners of Eastern religions, especially Buddhism. Buddhism and Hinduism both had long existed in America in many varieties, some of which attracted non-Asian adherents. In the late twentieth century the most popular Asian religious leader among Americans was the Dalai Lama, the exiled leader of the Tibetan form of Buddhism, who was widely regarded, even by many who did not share his exact faith, for his religious insight and pursuit of justice.

Despite its increasingly conspicuous religious diversity, the United States was still overwhelmingly Christian. A Gallup survey late in the twentieth century revealed that 85 percent of Americans identified themselves as Christian (including 58 percent Protestant and 25 percent Catholic), 2 percent identified as Jewish, and 5 percent identified with other religions. While many of these self-identified adherents may have seldom practiced their faith, only 8 percent of Americans expressed no religious preference.[5]

Far more than any other event, the terrorist attacks by Muslim extremists on September 11, 2001, brought home to most Americans the realities of living in a land of religious differences and in a world where religion sometimes remained a potent political force. Suddenly, everyone became aware of radical Islam. More broadly, the attacks brought to the fore a reality that had been emerging for decades: that one of the greatest challenges to American world influence was resurgent Islam. Religion had not faded away as a factor in international affairs, and Islam was growing almost as fast as Christianity. While American foreign policy had long been based on predominantly secular concerns, the United States was also the chief supporter of the State of Israel, a religious-political entity that was regarded as a standing source of grievance in the surrounding Arab world. Furthermore, Islam itself traditionally involved very close interrelations of religious and political power. Most Islamic countries had resisted Western-style secularization, though in varying degrees. Islam, like Christianity, came in many factions, and these were often feuding with each other. The great majority of Muslims did not condone terrorism. Nonetheless, a widespread resentment of the Western imperialism that in the early twentieth century had led to the partitioning of the once great Ottoman Empire continued to influence much of the Islamic world.

Early in 2003, under the leadership of President George W. Bush, the United States went to war with Iraq and the dictatorial regime of Saddam Hussein, an action that ensured that engagement with Islam would continue to play an increasing role in American foreign policy. American reactions to 9/11, as the 2001 attacks were called, had reawakened many expressions of civil religion. Furthermore, Bush was an evangelical Christian who could talk about being born again and who spoke of the war as a contest between the forces of righteousness and the forces of evil. While the war did bring the downfall of Saddam Hussein, it also helped to destabilize the region and to create a quagmire that immensely complicated American relationships with Islam and Islamic nations. The United States was also embroiled in a lengthy conflict in Afghanistan. And, beginning in 2011, a complex and devastating civil war developed in Syria, and ISIS (the "Islamic State") emerged as both a military force and one of the main sources for inspiring worldwide terrorist attacks.

After 9/11, awareness of the Muslim presence in the United States soared and became a matter of partisan debate. That debate was further complicated by increasing numbers of Islamic refugees from Middle Eastern wars. Some Americans feared that increasing immigration of Muslims would foster terrorism. Some criticized strict Muslim laws regarding how women dressed or women's roles as not fitting dominant American principles regarding women's rights. Others argued to the contrary, on religious grounds and on the premise that America should be an inclusive pluralistic society, that Muslims, and especially wartime refugees, should be welcomed.

Changing Religious Patterns

Meanwhile, one of the realities of the twenty-first century was that the percentage of self-identified Christians was dramatically receding. By the second decade of the century the number of Americans who said they were Christian was around 70 percent, still a large majority, but a significant drop from about 85 percent just two decades earlier. One notable factor contributing to that drop was the continuing dramatic decline in membership of mainline Protestant denominations. As recently as the early 1970s, these largely white major denominations could count almost 30 percent of the American population among their number. Forty years later that percentage had fallen by half, to under 15 percent. Meanwhile, especially in the early decades of the twenty-first century, the number of Americans who identified as "nones," or of no religious affiliation, rose sharply from around 8 percent in the 1990s to around 20 percent two decades later. These two notable trends were related. Denominational loyalties were fading and that meant that fewer people who had been reared in a denomination were likely to still identify with it after they had drifted away from it. The rise of the "nones," which was most pronounced among the younger generation, affected virtually all religious groups, but it was especially evident among mainline Protestants whose membership was graying conspicuously.[6] Being a "none" did not necessarily imply that one was irreligious. More than a third of Americans who had no formal religious affiliation would describe themselves as "spiritual but not religious."[7] Such religiousness might involve adaptations of Eastern or New Age religious practices or a more generalized private spirituality.

One implication of these changes, along with rising ethnic diversity, was that the dominance of white Protestantism was receding. Even though 70 percent of Americans identified as Christian, about 20 percent were Catholic. Roughly 6 percent were African American Protestant, and others were Asian, Latino, or other non-white Protestant or non-Protestant Christian such as Mormon or Eastern Orthodox. That left the number of traditional white Protestants at less than half of the Christian majority.

The implications of that numerical decline are difficult to measure. White Protestants had always been sharply divided among themselves— North versus South, for example, or liberal versus conservative. Only occasionally, as during Prohibition, or in opposition to the presidential candidacies of Al Smith and John F. Kennedy, had they been able to unite on much of anything. Nonetheless, in much of the country they had shaped the cultural ethos, as was evident in Sabbath legislation, prayers at public events, standards for public decency, and in laws governing marriage and divorce.

Most such influences had disappeared or were fast disappearing in the twenty-first century, but in the regions that remained most predominantly white Protestant, the changes in the national ethos and ethnicity produced a good bit of resentment and nostalgia for an early time. Sometimes such attitudes included some specifically religious concerns, but often religion was only a secondary factor for a population that saw itself as once having been culturally dominant but now as being left behind by an increasingly diverse national ethos.

Politics and Religion—Elusive Relationships

The "culture wars" mentality that had developed in the late twentieth century persisted into the twenty-first. Various organizations of the religious right continued to press for political mobilization. Such efforts gained some prominence, but never many tangible results, during the administration of George W. Bush. But with the election of Barack Obama in 2008, the religious right seemed to be left in disarray. Obama was an avowed Christian who regarded his progressive and inclusive political-social ideals as grounded in his faith. Once he was elected, the principal opposition to him, which included the Tea Party Movement and conservative media outlets, was based very largely on secular economic concerns, such as opposition to big government. Religious concerns nonetheless continued to play a subordinate supporting role to the agenda of the increasingly influential conservative wing of the Republican Party.

The inclusivist, multicultural social agenda of the Obama administration and of many secular institutions such as universities (which conservatives believed to be welcoming to everyone but them) contributed to an increasing political polarization. Conservative corporate interests opposed to big government and increased regulation of businesses found a populist base among those who resented being told how they should think and speak about persons differing from themselves. While Obama served as the first African American president, racial tensions seemed to grow.

But the issues that became the flashpoints for overt controversy between the new mores and the old most often had to do with sexual orientation and the campaigns for full acceptance of LGBT identities and lifestyles. The dominant public attitudes regarding such issues were changing with remarkable rapidity. In 1988, less than 15 percent of Americans approved of same-sex marriage. By 2001, that portion of the population had risen to a third. Attitudes were, as might be expected, changing most rapidly among the young. By about 2011, the majority of all Americans favored gay marriage. President Obama, who, like most progressive politicians, had been cautious on the issue, endorsed gay marriage in 2012. Soon a solid and growing majority of Americans approved the institution, and in 2015 the US Supreme Court followed suit by legalizing gay marriage. By 2017, support had risen to nearly two-thirds and was closer to three-fourths for those under forty years of age.[8]

In mainline Protestant denominations, many supported full LGBT inclusion and gay marriage as matters of religious principle. Typically, official denominational acceptance of such practices, including for ordained clergy, led to some strong conservative reactions, protracted controversies, and a few schisms. Tensions were especially strong in churches affiliated with significant majority-world populations, such as the Episcopal Church, part of the worldwide Anglican Communion that includes many African churches still very conservative on these issues.

More conservative Christians and others of traditionalist religious heritages, such as Muslims and Orthodox Jews, based their religious identities on the authority of ancient Scriptures and long-standing traditions that had condemned sexual practices outside of heterosexual wedlock. While some biblicist Protestants believed the Scriptures might be reinterpreted in the light of modern cultural norms, many traditionalists of various faiths did not see that as an option if they were to preserve the integrity of their faith and to have proper respect for authoritative teachings of their religious institutions. So, while they might be accepting of people with LGBT orientations, it did not seem an option to them to accept same-sex practices or marriages without giving up the authorities on which they based the rest of their faith and their most important identities.

Such issues (the question of the legality of abortion was the other most persistent one) kept some explicitly religious concerns within the mix of increasingly polarized American politics, but the exact role of religion remained ambiguous. The political polarization seemed to be driven largely by non-religious factors such as massive economic interests, social divisions, and long-standing attitudes toward government that sometimes became intertwined with the religious concerns of some of the constituents on each side. Race, ethnicity, and social and geographical location appeared to determine voting behavior more than specific religious teachings did. Nonetheless, as this history has repeatedly shown, religion often correlates with such other factors, and for some people it will provide decisive concerns.

The difficulty in measuring specifically religious influences in this mix of factors is best illustrated by the role of evangelicalism in recent American politics. For polling purposes, researchers have typically considered the term *evangelical* equivalent to *white evangelical*. So they have used a religious term that has a much larger worldwide application to designate a specific American ethno-religious group: the large group of older-stock, white people with strong concentrations in the South and in parts of the Midwest who retain some evangelical religious identification, however nominal. In the early twenty-first century, this group has voted overwhelmingly for Republican presidential candidates, with little apparent regard for the character of the candidate. Specific evangelical teachings doubtless play a significant role in the political behavior of some in this group, but ethnicity and social location seem more consistent indicators.[9] By contrast, churchgoing African Americans who subscribe to the same evangelical or "gospel" teachings as their white counterparts vote just as overwhelmingly Democratic. And if one adds Latino and Asian evangelicals into the mix, the patterns become even more complex.[10] And the point that ethnicity (combined with some other socioeconomic factors) more than religious teachings shapes most political behavior seems confirmed by looking at Catholic voting patterns. In 2016, close to 60 percent of white Catholics voted Republican, while only about one-fourth of Latino Catholics did so.[11] So Catholic teachings do not seem to be a major variable.

Such statistics do not negate the fact that for many pious religious individuals, specifically religious concerns determine their political behavior. But in large, aggregated religious populations that include many people who are loosely affiliated, only a minority is likely to be so motivated. Moreover, those for whom religious concerns are decisive may still be divided regarding how they vote. For instance, some of the deeply religious may see social justice issues as preeminent, while others may be more concerned to defend conservative standards regarding sexuality and traditional understandings of the family.

The Varieties of American Religious Faith and Practice

Such cautions against oversimplified generalizations regarding the impact of religious beliefs on American politics lead to a more general caution when we speak about the roles of religion in American culture. With such a wide spectrum of religions, with denominations and subgroups within each, it is important to be as specific as possible rather than lumping groups together and attributing to the whole traits that apply only to one part.

Once again, American evangelicalism provides some excellent examples. It is the largest American religious classification, including perhaps a quarter of the American population,[12] and the category that has received the most public attention in the twenty-first century. Recall that evangelicalism is an extraordinarily diverse, worldwide, multiethnic set of largely disconnected churches, movements, and organizations that are identifiable as evangelical because they share a set of gospel beliefs. These beliefs include the necessity of conversion based on the atoning work of Jesus Christ as recounted authoritatively in the Bible. In the United States, those who share these basic evangelical beliefs are divided not only by race and ethnicity; they are also divided into a bewilderingly complex world of denominations, independent churches, megachurches, and parachurch organizations. Some of the disparate groups who qualify as evangelical on the basis of affirming these gospel teachings seem to have almost nothing else in common.

For instance, one end of the evangelical spectrum generated one of the most influential developments of the late twentieth and early twenty-first centuries: the rise of the "prosperity gospel." Growing out of post–World War II Pentecostal healing revivals, and fostered by some of the giant TV ministries of the later twentieth century, the prosperity gospel promised believers not only healing but also wealth. Joel Osteen, bestselling author and pastor of a Houston megachurch with a large television ministry, became the most influential of a number of comparable figures who helped carry the prosperity message beyond strictly Pentecostal or charismatic circles. A *Time* magazine poll in 2006 found that 17 percent of American Christians said they identified with the movement, and 31 percent said that those who gave money to God would receive more money in return.[13] The message blended with America's long-standing gospel of success. More than forty of America's largest megachurches, each claiming 10,000 or more members, proclaimed this message of health and wealth.[14] The appeal of the prosperity gospel message was not simply that it fit with enduring American cultural motifs, but it also had a wide resonance as other parts of the world modernized. So the promise of health and wealth, as well as of eternal salvation, had some of its greatest successes in parts of Africa and Latin America, as well as in some South Korean churches.

But the evangelical label also applies to another, completely different theological movement: the resurgent Reformed movement. Tracing its specific roots to the Calvinist Reformation, this version of Christianity emphasized an elaborate set of biblically based doctrines as formulated in creeds long before the influences of modernity and America. Rather than stressing human abilities, the Reformed stress total dependence on God and Christ's sacrifice as a remedy for universal human sinfulness. In 2009, a *Time* magazine article cited "The New Calvinism" as one of "Ten Ideas That Are Changing the World Right Now."[15] The Reformed movement is not as large or as conspicuous as the prosperity gospel, but it is substantial. It is found in a number of primarily Presbyterian and Baptist denominations, and it includes some larger urban churches, of which Redeemer Presbyterian, founded by Timothy Keller (another bestselling evangelical author) in New York City, became the best known. While much of evangelicalism has tendencies toward anti-intellectualism, the Reformed have a long tradition of emphasizing high quality education and engagement with contemporary thought as substantial parts of their ministries. Their intellectual strengths are apparent in the faculties of a number of leading seminaries, universities, and colleges. The emphasis on "integrating faith and learning," developed primarily by Reformed thinkers, has become a major influence at many of more than a hundred schools in the Council for Christian Colleges and Universities. Their vital intellectual life is witnessed to by the hundreds of substantial books by Reformed authors published yearly, especially by Christian presses. Some other evangelical traditions have fostered healthy intellectual life as well, especially at their universities and seminaries, but the Reformed emphasis on relating faith and piety to intellect has been most integral to their mission.

The prosperity gospel and the Reformed faith are only two of the wide range of submovements that fall under the broad rubric of evangelical. Some are simply difficult to classify. Rick Warren, one of the best-known early twenty-first-century pastors in America, provides a significant example. His Saddleback Church in southern California is among the nation's largest megachurches, and his *The Purpose Driven Life*, published in 2002, sold over 30 million copies in just its first five years. Warren's theology is traditionalist evangelical with vaguely Reformed overtones. Although a Southern Baptist, he has played down denominational identity, and he has presented a more progressive profile regarding social issues. One of his major initiatives has been the PEACE program for mobilizing Christians as "servant leaders" in worldwide efforts to assist the poor and the sick, promote education, and provide reconciliation.

Some other evangelicals provide a more explicitly political emphasis in the conservative "culture wars." In the twentieth century, many of these might have been classified as fundamentalist to indicate their emphasis on militancy, usually on both doctrinal and political issues. During the early twenty-first century, the term *fundamentalist* fell from favor as a self-designation, probably because it had sometimes also been applied to Muslim extremists. Nonetheless, militant attitudes remained among a subset of evangelicals. Other evangelicals remained more open doctrinally and more progressive politically.

Mennonites, many of whom would fit the evangelical theological rubric, differ from any of the above on social stances. Like the Reformed, they represent an older Reformation tradition that has interacted with evangelicalism in recent centuries. Mennonites emphasize the authority of the Bible and lives radically changed by following Jesus and his teachings, but they see those teachings as requiring pacifism, and they place more emphasis on building community and lives of service to others, especially the poor, than do most other evangelicals. And to complicate the picture even more, Mennonites themselves are divided into many subgroups with distinct emphases.

One finds similar complexity among other evangelical groups and subgroups, such as in African American denominations, varieties of holiness groups, and Churches of Christ. A good many of those in these groups, like a good many of the Reformed and Mennonites, are reluctant to use the term *evangelical* to describe themselves. They may see themselves as simply traditionalist Christians of some sort. And one of the fastest-growing segments of American Protestantism has been nondenominational churches. The fact is that most Christians classed by researchers as evangelical do not use that name as a primary self-designation. So, although it is sometimes useful, as in histories that look at large patterns, to use the catchall term to designate groups that have some basic teachings in common, in most individual cases, it is better to identify people by their specific affiliation.

The diversity found among evangelicals has counterparts in varying degrees in most other major American religious groups. The Roman Catholic Church, the largest single religious organization, for instance, is by its very nature especially inclusive of a striking variety of points of view. Catholics who may celebrate the Mass together may also be poles apart regarding many of the particular implications of their faith. Very traditionalist Catholics may strongly oppose many of the doctrinal or social emphases progressive Catholics endorse. Catholics with conventionally conservative American political views may differ sharply from followers of Dorothy Day and the Catholic Workers Movement. Some Catholics emphasize a long tradition of high-level intellectual engagement, while others may look for charismatic gifts or stress the strict ascetic practices of various monastic traditions. Much the same variety can be found in most other larger denominations. If one learns that a new acquaintance is a member of the United Methodist Church or the Presbyterian Church (USA), that does not reveal much about the person's religious commitments until one learns what subtype of Methodist or Presbyterian the person is. And as in Christianity, so also in other major religious faiths, differences between subgroups and within each subgroup may be profound. Jewish identity, for instance, involves an especially wide range of outlooks, since being Jewish refers to an ethnicity that may or may not include religious practice, which in turn comes in a spectrum of varieties. Similarly, learning that someone is a Muslim tells you little until you know what variety of Islam that person practices and what subvariety of that tradition and how central the religious practice is to the person's identity.

One reason to look at specific religious behaviors rather than relying on stereotyped generalizations about various religious identities is that, even within subgroups of a particular faith, striking differences almost always appear between the core of dedicated followers and a broader group who make up the rest of a congregation or are occasional attenders. While the American population ranks high in religious profession for a highly industrialized country, much of that religiosity appears to be of low voltage. Close to 90 percent of early twenty-first-century Americans professed to believe in some sort of God; as many as 70 percent said they believe in such things as heaven or in angels.[16] Over a third claim to attend religious services weekly, and another third say they attend occasionally.[17] Yet actual church attendance on a given week is likely closer to one-quarter of the population.[18] And a late twentieth-century Gallup survey concluded that only about 13 percent of Americans had "what might be called a truly transforming faith, manifested in measurable and behavioral ways." That survey identified those who have "a truly transforming faith" as a set of believers who not only say their religious belief is highly important in their lives but also spend significant time helping those in need, "are less likely to be prejudiced against people of other races, and are more giving and more forgiving." They are those who "have bucked the trend of many in society toward narcissism and privatism."[19] There can be, of course, other standards for measuring "truly transforming faith." It is hard to gauge the degrees to which worship, prayers, redirected motivations, unrecorded acts of kindness and charity, self-disciplines, reshaped family relationships, consolations, and countless other immeasurable attitudes and behaviors to which religion may contribute are "transforming." But the 13 percent figure does provide a reminder that, however measured, levels of religious commitment differ greatly even among those who are active in the same congregations. Religious leaders themselves are typically the people most aware of such disparities between the core of parishioners whose commitments run deep and others for whom their faith seems to operate more as a sort of optional add-on to lives that are shaped far more by the characteristic beliefs and practices of contemporary American life.

One significant change from previous centuries is that, while in earlier times most religious communities provided some rigorous teachings for their young people, by the dawn of the more permissive twenty-first century, such provision had eroded, in most cases. Early in the century, sociologist Christian Smith conducted what became much-cited studies of the religious beliefs of American teenagers. He found that those reared in churches typically were not in rebellion against the religious teachings of their parents. Rather, they professed belief in their churches' teachings, but the vast majority of these young people were unable to provide more than the vaguest articulation of what those beliefs amounted to. Typically, they believed in a God who seemed to be something like a benevolent grand-parent on whom one could call in times of need, or for comfort in times of distress, or for something they wanted. Smith famously described the typical outlook of these churchgoing American young people as "moralistic therapeutic deism."[20] Though certain older church members could be much more articulate about their faith, many others might not be. As one observer put it, the effective creed of many American churchgoers is that God is nice and we should be nice also.[21] Many of the religions that flourish in American culture do so because they are so well adapted to the American environment. But as a downside, often a generalized American creed (as suggested in a church sign that read: "The last four letters in American are I CAN") tends to reshape the traditional faith.

Still, if something like a quarter to a third of the population is regularly involved in a religious community and perhaps another third is less regularly involved, that translates into a major cultural phenomenon, even if the varieties of faiths and degrees of commitment make the impacts difficult to measure.

One positive measurable effect of religious commitment is that people who have active religious affiliations typically contribute far more to charitable causes *and* even more to secular causes than their more secular neighbors typically do. The actively religious are also more likely to be active in civic life and to have done volunteer service or good deeds for others.[22] Moreover, America's religious and religious-charitable institutions provide an immense social infrastructure that touches almost everything in the culture. One late twentieth-century study estimated that faith-based organizations in Philadelphia alone provided social services that would cost government at least a billion dollars to replace.[23] The amount of charity generated by American religious faiths and the social services provided by many thousands of local congregations and larger religious charities are among the largely unsung dimensions of religion's cultural role. In response to natural disasters, religious agencies are almost always in the forefront of voluntary relief efforts.

Another factor that is culturally significant, even if hard to measure, is the degree to which America's many religious subcommunities have provided moral capital on which the larger American community is constantly drawing. All religious groups teach virtues such as honesty, justice, charity, mercy, thinking of the needs of others, honor to parents, and fidelity. Even if such lessons do not always get through, sometimes they do, and in those cases society benefits. Some religious prescriptions, of course, are arguably against the larger interest of the society. And sometimes the moral prescriptions of one group may contradict those of another. Sometimes religious groups or leaders violate their own higher standards. Often religious teachings fail to effectively counter their constituents' prejudices and moral blind spots. Yet even taking into account those exceptions, there seems little doubt that, on the whole, religious communities generate positive moral character from which everyone benefits.

Preserving a Pluralistic Society

In the face of increasing diversity, one concluding question is whether the United States can cultivate a pluralism that encourages so many varieties of religious and secular groups to live together in peace, despite some irreconcilable differences in what they most value and in some of their principles of morality. Such questions became accentuated in the twenty-first century with increased awareness of a Muslim presence in America, and to a lesser extent by the growth in numbers of Buddhists, Hindus, and others through immigration. At the same time, the ability to address such issues dispassionately has been thwarted to some degree by the inherited mentality of "culture wars" that has pitted conservative Christians and their allies against secular and religious progressives. Each side, in the tradition of promoting assimilation to one set of American ideals, has sometimes presented its moral principles as a set of absolutes to which everyone in public spheres should be required to conform.

One way to think about such issues would be to consider how a society might foster a pluralism of subcommunities that might both maintain their own distinctive institutions and be encouraged to participate in the free exchange of ideas in public spheres. Simply promoting diversity or inclusion in public spheres is a laudable ideal but one that is inherently limited by the fact that honoring one point of view may involve excluding the voices of those who strongly oppose that point of view. Public spheres are always liable to the tyranny of the majority, and that applies to questions of how to set limits to diversity and free speech. Cultivating a genuine pluralism would begin, by contrast, by considering what rules are necessary for public life within the framework of recognizing that a healthy national community ought to cultivate healthy subcommunities that are allowed to be genuinely diverse. The United States, because it has been a nation of immigrants, has always de facto had such strong subcommunities, most of which had a considerable religious basis. Yet because of the assimilationist ideal of the dominant white

Protestants and their secular allies, the nation never developed strong principles for cultivating such pluralism. The assumption was rather that eventually such subcommunities, or at least most of their distinctive outlooks and practices, should fade away, as many indeed have. Yet other subcommunities, especially those with a strong religious basis, have not faded away, even as their members participate as good citizens in the cultural mainstream as well. A genuine pluralism would encourage such real diversity, so far as that is possible. Some practices, including some religious practices, are inconsistent with the public welfare and need to be restricted. Nonetheless, those would be the exceptions to the general rule of being hospitable to the differences among religious subcultures. And encouraging such diversity would involve fostering diversity of institutions of learning, where the ideals of the subculture could be taught and propagated, rather than expecting everyone to eventually depend on public institutions and their necessarily more homogenous standards.

Such pluralism also fits with the American constitutional heritage that guarantees freedom for dissent and free expression, including religious dissent and free expression. As we have seen, however, the American heritage has never been entirely clear or consistent on these issues. The US Constitution, while protecting religious freedom, has allowed room for a continuing broadly Protestant informal establishment, and so also for later less-Protestant or secular informal establishments. Nonetheless, for those who wish to get beyond such cultural dominance coming from either the right or the left, encouraging subcommunities, including religious subcommunities and their distinctive institutions, seems a healthy direction in which to move. Cultivating a pluralism of subcommunities, in addition to cultivating shared principles for allowing peaceful diversity in the public domains, would be a way by which many people, both secular and religious, might constructively address the ongoing challenges of a society that is going to remain diverse.

This book is a history, and it is much easier to describe how the United States got to the point it has reached with respect to its secular and religious diversity than it is to prescribe exactly how its future with respect to those diversities might be improved. Still, we can safely say that there will be no improvement without historical understanding of how we got to be where we are. One lesson is sure. When it comes to religion, it will not do to resort to easy generalizations; evaluation of its roles must always be nuanced. Such nuance will help us to see that religion, even at what we may regard its best, appears in human affairs almost always as a mixed blessing.

Notes

Notes to the Introduction

1. http://www.pewforum.org/religious-landscape-study/belief-in-god/#social-and-politi cal-views.

2. Jon Butler, "Jack-in-the-Box Faith: The Religion Problem in Modern American History," *Journal of American History* 90 (March 2004): 1357–78.

3. John Tracy Ellis, "American Catholics and Intellectual Life," *Thought* 30 (1955): 24.

4. Both *religious* and *secular* are ambiguous terms. By *religion* or *religious* I mean things having to do with particular organized religions or faith in some higher power. *Secular* can mean something like *earthly*, in which case most religions want to engage the secular, or this present world. *Secularization* means the removal of some area of life from substantive religious reference, and so I often use *secular* in the descriptive sense of being disconnected from such substantive religion. That sense of *secular* does not imply evaluation. *Secularism* would be a belief that the removal of substantive religious reference is, as a rule, a good thing.

5. Blaise Pascal, *Thoughts,* Harvard Classics (New York: P. F. Collier & Son, 1910), 314. Original uses "men."

6. As a bishop in the Roman Empire at a time when Christianity was the official religion, Augustine's own applications of these theological insights were sometimes flawed, but the theological insights remain valuable.

Notes to Chapter 1

1. John Rolfe, *A Relation of the State of Virginia* (1616), 113, quoted in Perry Miller, "Religion and Society in the Early Literature of Virginia," in *Errand into the Wilderness* (New York: Harper and Row, 1956), 119.

2. Tracy McKenzie, *The First Thanksgiving: What the Real Story Tells Us about Loving*

God and Learning (Downers Grove, IL: InterVarsity Press, 2013), provides a valuable account of the real story and the mythology.

3. These observations are influenced in part by Reinhold Niebuhr, *The Irony of American History* (New York: Charles Scribner's Sons, 1962). See further discussion of Niebuhr's views in chapter 6 below.

4. Early Maryland, first settled in 1634, had genuine religious freedom at times, though clearly this was in the interest of the Catholic proprietors and settlers rather than a matter of principle. During most of Maryland's colonial history, however, Protestants dominated, and Catholic practice was officially outlawed, though it survived.

5. I have written on Edwards in more detail in *Jonathan Edwards: A Life* (New Haven: Yale University Press, 2003) and in *A Short Life of Jonathan Edwards* (Grand Rapids: Eerdmans, 2008).

6. From Phillis Wheatley, "On the Death of the Rev. Mr. George Whitefield. 1770," *Poems on Various Subjects* (1773).

Notes to Chapter 2

1. A classic statement of this interpretation is found in Gordon S. Wood, *The Creation of the American Republic, 1776–1787* (New York: W. W. Norton, 1969).

2. Nathan O. Hatch, *The Sacred Cause of Liberty: Republican Thought and the Millennium in Revolutionary New England* (New Haven: Yale University Press, 1977), 87.

3. Samuel Davies, "The Crisis," in *Sermons on Important Subjects* (Philadelphia, 1818), 5:257, 258, quoted in Mark A. Noll, Nathan O. Hatch, and George M. Marsden, *The Search for Christian America* (Westchester, IL: Crossway Books, 1983), 62.

4. Noll, Hatch, and Marsden, *Search for Christian America*, 64.

5. See Reinhold Niebuhr, *Moral Man and Immoral Society* (New York: Charles Scribner's Sons, 1932), and Reinhold Niebuhr, *The Irony of American History*, (New York: Charles Scribner's Sons, 1952).

6. Cf. Robert Bellah, "Civil Religion in America," *Daedalus* 96 (Winter 1967): 1–21.

7. John F. Wilson, "Religion, Government, and Power in the New American Nation" (paper presented at a conference on "Religion and American Politics," Institute for the Study of American Evangelicalism, Wheaton, IL, March 1988).

8. For a balanced view of these issues see John Fea, *Was America Founded as a Christian Nation? A Historical Introduction* (Louisville: Westminster John Knox Press, 2011).

9. I am indebted to the Rev. Ray McMillian, whose "Race to Unity" group sponsored a number of events emphasizing this question.

Notes to Chapter 3

1. Lyman Beecher, *The Autobiography of Lyman Beecher*, ed. Barbara M. Cross, 2 vols. (Cambridge, MA: Harvard University Press, 1961), 1:252–53.

2. C. C. Goen, *Broken Churches, Broken Nation* (Macon, GA: Mercer University Press, 1985), 55.

3. Alexis de Tocqueville, *Democracy in America*, trans. H. Reeve, vol. 1 (New York, 1955),

1:316, cited in John F. Wilson, *Public Religion in American Culture* (Philadelphia: Temple University Press, 1979), 11; cf. Goen, *Broken Churches*, 28–32.

4. Perry Miller, *The Life of the Mind in America: From the Revolution to the Civil War* (New York: Harcourt, Brace, and World, 1965), 6, 7.

5. William G. McLoughlin, ed., *The American Evangelicals, 1800–1900* (New York: Harper Torchbooks, 1968), 1.

6. Edmund S. Morgan, "The American Revolution Considered as an Intellectual Movement," in *Paths of American Thought*, ed. Morton White and Arthur M. Schlesinger Jr. (Boston: Houghton Mifflin, 1963), 11.

7. Nathan O. Hatch, *The Democratization of American Christianity* (New Haven: Yale University Press, 1989).

8. Erastus O. Haven, quoted in Kent Sagedorph, *Michigan: The Story of the University* (New York: E. P. Dutton, 1948), 115.

9. Quoted from *Second Reader* (1836 ed.), 136, in John H. Westerhoff III, *McGuffey and His Readers: Piety Morality, and Education in Nineteenth-Century America*, (Nashville: Abingdon, 1978), 78.

10. Lewis W. Green, *Lectures on the Evidence of Christianity* (New York: Richard Carter, 1854), 463, 464 (emphasis in original).

11. Francis Wayland, *Elements of Moral Science*, ed. Joseph Angus (London, 1860 [1835]), 219–20.

12. Theodore Dwight Bozeman, *Protestants in an Age of Science: The Baconian Ideal and Antebellum American Religious Thought* (Chapel Hill: University of North Carolina Press, 1977), 72.

13. *McGuffey's Fifth Eclectic Reader*, 1879 ed. (New York: New American Library, 1962).

14. The view that Jesus will set up a literal millennial kingdom is called premillennial since Jesus returns before the millennium. There are also amillennialists who say, essentially, that details about the last days are not precisely prophesied.

15. William R. Hutchison, *Errand to the World: American Protestant Thought and Foreign Missions* (Chicago: University of Chicago Press, 1987), 45.

16. Mark A. Noll, *The New Shape of World Christianity: How American Experience Reflects Global Faith* (Downers Grove, IL: IVP Academic, 2009), 41.

17. Kenneth Scott Latourette, *A History of Christianity* (New York: Harper and Brothers, 1953), 1,061.

18. Timothy L. Smith, *Revivalism and Social Reform: American Protestantism on the Eve of the Civil War* (New York: Harper Torchbooks, 1957), 20–21; Robert Baird, *Religion in America* (1844) in McLoughlin, *The American Evangelicals*, 33.

19. Mark A. Noll, *The Civil War as a Theological Crisis* (Chapel Hill: University of North Carolina Press, 2006).

20. Cf. Stanley M. Elkins, *Slavery: A Problem in American Institutional and Intellectual Life* (New York: Grosset and Dunlap, 1963), 37–52.

21. *Narrative of the Life of Frederick Douglass* (1845).

22. This is a point made by Donald Mathews, *Religion in the Old South* (Chicago: University of Chicago Press, 1977).

23. Lawrence W. Levine, *Black Culture and Black Consciousness: Afro-American Folk Thought from Slavery to Freedom* (New York: Oxford University Press, 1977), 17.

24. As Lawrence W. Levine observes in *Black Culture and Black Consciousness*, "If . . . historians have difficulty perceiving the sacred universe created by slaves as a serious alternative

to the societal system created by southern slaveholders, the problem may be the historians and not the slaves" (54).

25. Gregory Dowd, *A Spirited Resistance: The North American Indian Struggle for Unity, 1745–1815* (Baltimore: Johns Hopkins University Press, 1992).

26. Jay P. Dolan, *The American Catholic Experience: A History from Colonial Times to the Present* (Garden City, NY: Doubleday and Company, 1985); Debra Campbell, "Catholicism from Independence to World War I," in *Encyclopedia of the American Religious Experience*, ed. Charles H. Lippy and Peter W. Williams, 3 vols. (New York: Charles Scribner's Sons, 1988), 1:357–73.

27. Lewis O. Saum, *The Popular Mood of Pre-Civil War America* (Westport, CT: Greenwood Press, 1980), xxiii, 27, and 56.

28. Catherine A. Brekus, *Strangers and Pilgrims: Female Preaching in America, 1740–1845* (Chapel Hill: University of North Carolina Press, 1998).

29. Andrea Turpin, *A New Moral Vision: Gender, Religion, and the Changing Purposes of American Higher Education: 1837–1917* (Ithaca, NY: Cornell University Press, 2016).

30. Tocqueville, *Democracy in America*, 1:362.

31. Joel H. Silbey, Allan G. Bogue, and William H. Flanigan, eds., "Introduction to Part Three," *The History of American Electoral Behavior* (Princeton: Princeton University Press, 1978), 253–56.

32. For a balanced overview of the ways in which the many nonreligious factors, including prominently technological advance, mixed with religious forces and rationales in shaping the new republic, see Daniel Walker Howe's Pulitzer Prize-winning, *What Hath God Wrought: The Transformation of America, 1815–1848* (New York: Oxford University Press, 2007).

33. Robert Kelley, *Cultural Patterns in American Politics: The First Century* (New York: Alfred A. Knopf, 1979). A very detailed and convincing analysis of these typologies for a later period is offered in Philip R. VanderMeer, *The Hoosier Politician: Officeholding and Political Culture in Indiana: 1896–1920* (Urbana: University of Illinois Press, 1985), 96–120.

34. Daniel Walker Howe, *The Political Culture of the American Whigs* (Chicago: University of Chicago Press, 1979), 84.

35. Alice Felt Tyler, *Freedom's Ferment: Phases of American Social History to 1860* (Minneapolis: The University of Minnesota Press, 1944), 372.

36. Eugene D. Genovese, *The Slaveholders' Dilemma: Freedom and Progress in Southern Conservative Thought, 1820–1860* (Columbia: University of South Carolina Press, 1992). For a thoughtful Christian perspective on the topic, see Mark A. Noll, *The Civil War as a Theological Crisis*.

Notes to Chapter 4

1. See William R. Hutchison, *Errand to the World: American Protestant Thought and Foreign Missions* (Chicago: University of Chicago Press, 1987), 95.

2. Ferenc M. Szasz, *The Divided Mind of Protestant America, 1880–1930* (University, AL: University of Alabama Press, 1982).

3. George L. Prentiss, "The National Crisis," *American Theological Review* 1st ser., 4 (October 1862): 674–718.

4. Horace Bushnell, "Our Obligations to the Dead" (sermon preached in 1865), reprinted

in William G. McLoughlin, ed., *The American Evangelicals, 1800–1900* (New York: Harper Torchbooks, 1968), 141–57.

5. Mark Twain and Charles Dudley Warner, *The Gilded Age*, 2 vols. (New York: Harper and Brothers, 1915 [1873]), 2:215.

6. Henry Adams, *Democracy* (New York: Henry Holt and Co., 1908 [1880]), 353.

7. Winthrop Hudson, *American Protestantism* (Chicago: University of Chicago Press, 1961), 128; the preceding three quotations are all also from Hudson, 125–28.

8. See Martin Marty, *Three Paths to the Secular* (New York: Harper and Row, 1969).

9. Richard J. Jensen, *The Winning of the Midwest: Social and Political Conflict, 1888–1896* (Chicago: University of Chicago Press, 1971).

10. Paul Kleppner, *Who Voted? The Dynamics of Electoral Turnout, 1870–1980* (New York: Praeger, 1982), 77–78.

11. *Congregationalist*, May 13, 1886, 162, quoted in Henry F. May, *The Protestant Churches in Industrial America* (New York: Harper and Row, 1949), 101.

12. For this side of the story see Heath Carter, *Union Made: Working People and the Rise of Social Christianity in Chicago* (New York: Oxford University Press, 2015).

13. Francis Wayland, "The Elements of Political Economy" (1804), in McLoughlin, ed., *The American Evangelicals, 1800–1900*, 113–27.

14. Quoted in May, *Protestant Churches*, 69.

15. John H. Westerhoff III, *McGuffey and His Readers: Piety, Morality, and Education in Nineteenth-Century America* (Nashville: Abingdon, 1978), 98, cf. 15, and 94.

16. Russell H. Conwell, *Acres of Diamonds* (New York: Harper and Brothers, 1915), 18.

17. Quoted in Nancy A. Hardesty, *Women Called to Witness: Evangelical Feminism in the 19th Century* (Nashville: Abingdon Press, 1984), 152.

18. Hutchison, *Errand to the World*, 93.

19. Gerald H. Anderson, "American Protestants in Pursuit of Mission: 1886–1986," *International Bulletin of Missionary Research* 12, no. 3 (July 1988): 102.

20. Josiah Strong, *Our Country*, 160, quoted in Edwin S. Gaustad, "Our Country: One Century Later," in *Liberal Protestantism: Realities and Possibilities*, ed. Robert S. Michaelsen and Wade Clark Roof (New York: Pilgrim Press, 1986), 96.

21. Albert J. Beveridge, *The Meaning of the Times: and Other Speeches* (New York: Bobbs-Merrill Co., 1908), 85.

22. Winthrop S. Hudson, *Religion in America: An Historical Account of the Development of American Religious Life*, 3rd. ed. (New York: Charles Scribner's Sons, 1981), 320.

23. Grant Wacker, "A Plural World: The Protestant Awakening to World Religions," in *Between the Times: The Travail of the Protestant Establishment: 1900–1960*, ed. William R. Hutchison (New York: Cambridge University Press, 1989).

24. Richard Hofstadter, *The Age of Reform: From Bryan to FDR* (New York: Vintage Books, 1955), 320.

25. Oliver Wendell Holmes, "The Path of the Law, 1897," in *Sources of the American Mind*, ed. Loren Baritz (Hoboken, NJ: John Wiley and Sons, 1966), 2:102.

26. Robert W. Lynn, *Protestant Strategies in Education* (New York: Association Press, 1964), 57.

27. Stowe Persons, *American Minds: A History of Ideas* (New York: Holt, Rinehart and Winston, 1958), 245.

28. John Dewey, "The Scientific Factor in Reconstruction of Philosophy, 1920," in *Sources of the American Mind*, 2:159.

29. James Turner, *Without God, Without Creed: The Origins of Unbelief in America* (Baltimore: Johns Hopkins University Press, 1985).

30. David C. Lindberg and Ronald L. Numbers, "Beyond War and Peace: A Reappraisal of the Encounter between Christianity and Science," *Church History* 55 (September 1986): 338-54.

31. David N. Livingstone, *Darwin's Forgotten Defenders: The Encounter between Evangelical Theology and Evolutionary Thought* (Grand Rapids: Eerdmans and Scottish Academic Press, 1987).

32. Henry Ward Beecher, *Yale Lectures in Preaching* (New York, 1872), quoted in George M. Marsden, *Fundamentalism and American Culture: The Shaping of Twentieth Century Evangelicalism, 1870-1925* (New York: Oxford University Press, 1980), 25.

Notes to Chapter 5

1. Jay P. Dolan, *The American Catholic Experience: A History from Colonial Times to the Present* (Garden City, NY: Doubleday, 1985), 205-6.

2. Dolan, *American Catholic Experience*, 222.

3. Dolan, *American Catholic Experience*, 222-29.

4. Dolan, *American Catholic Experience*, 229-35.

5. Dolan, *American Catholic Experience*, 262-63; Rockne McCarthy, "Protestants and the Parochial School," in *Eerdmans' Handbook to Christianity in America*, ed. Mark A. Noll et al., (Grand Rapids: Eerdmans, 1983), 238-39.

6. Henry L. Feingold, *Zion in America: The Jewish Experience from Colonial Times to the Present* (New York: Hippocrene Books, 1974), 36-37, 158-78.

7. Feingold, *Zion in America*, 182-83.

8. Israel Zangwill, *The Melting Pot* (New York: Macmillan, 1909), 37, quoted in Sydney E. Ahlstrom, *A Religious History of the American People* (New Haven: Yale University Press, 1972), 3; cf. Feingold, *Zion in America*, 142-57.

9. Marcus L. Hansen, "The Problem of the Third Generation Immigrant," *Augustana Historical Society* (Rock Island, IL, 1938), quoted in Will Herberg, *Protestant-Catholic-Jew: An Essay in American Religious Sociology* (Garden City, NY: Doubleday, 1955), 218.

10. Feingold, *Zion in America*, 189; Nathan Glazer, *American Judaism* (Chicago: University of Chicago Press, 1957), 85; cf. Winthrop S. Hudson, *Religion in America: An Historical Account of the Development of American Religious Life*, 4th ed. (New York: Macmillan, 1987), 312.

11. Bertram Wyatt-Brown, *Honor and Violence in the Old South* (New York: Oxford University Press, 1986).

12. W. E. B. DuBois, "Of the Faith of the Fathers," in *Afro-American Religious History: A Documentary Witness*, ed. Milton C. Sernett (Durham, NC: Duke University Press, 1985), 312.

13. Lawrence N. Jones, "Black Churches: A New Agenda," in *Afro-American Religious History*, 492.

14. Evelyn Brooks Higginbotham, *Righteous Discontent: The Women's Movement in the Black Baptist Churches, 1880-1920* (Cambridge: Harvard University Press, 1993).

15. Lawrence W. Levine, *Black Culture and Black Consciousness* (New York: Oxford University Press, 1977), 158.

16. See Grant Wacker, "Pentecostalism," in *Encyclopedia of the American Religious Experience*, 2:933–45.

17. Ahlstrom, *A Religious History of the American People*, 1020–26; Stephen Gottschalk, "Christian Science and Harmonialism," in *Encyclopedia of the American Religious Experience*, 2:901–16; Stephen Gottschalk, *The Emergence of Christian Science in American Religious Life* (Berkeley: University of California Press, 1973).

Notes to Chapter 6

1. See John Shelton Reed, *The Enduring South: Subculture Persistence in Mass Society* (Chapel Hill: University of North Carolina, 1986), who suggested this.

2. Methodist Episcopal Church, South, General Conference, *Journal*, 1894, 34–35, quoted in Kenneth K. Bailey, *Southern White Protestantism in the Twentieth Century* (Gloucester, MA: Peter Smith, 1968 [1964]), 35.

3. W. J. Rorabaugh, *The Alcoholic Republic: An American Tradition* (New York: Oxford University Press, 1979).

4. Reprinted in *New World Metaphysics: Readings on the Religious Meaning of the American Experience*, ed. Giles Gunn (New York: Oxford University Press, 1981), 296.

5. C. Allyn Russell, *Voices of American Fundamentalism: Seven Biographical Studies* (Philadelphia: Westminster Press, 1976), 147–48; Robert Bolt, "American Involvement in World War I," in *The Wars of America: Christian Views*, ed. Ronald A. Wells (Grand Rapids: Eerdmans, 1981), 127–46.

6. Bolt, "American Involvement in World War I," 142.

7. Quoted in Douglas W. Frank, *Less Than Conquerors: How Evangelicals Entered the Twentieth Century* (Grand Rapids: Eerdmans, 1986), 179.

8. Heywood Broun, *The New York Tribune* (1915), quoted in *Eerdmans' Handbook to Christianity in America*, ed. Mark A. Noll et al. (Grand Rapids: Eerdmans, 1983), 369.

9. Ray H. Abrams, *Preachers Present Arms* (New York: Round Table Press, 1933), 79; William G. McLoughlin, *Billy Sunday Was His Real Name* (Chicago: University of Chicago Press, 1955); Frank, *Less Than Conquerors*, 173–95.

10. James R. Moore, *The Post-Darwinian Controversies: A Study of the Protestant Struggle to Come to Terms with Darwin in Great Britain and America, 1870–1900* (New York: Cambridge University Press, 1979), 73.

11. William Jennings Bryan, *In His Image* (New York: Fleming H. Revell, 1922), 93.

12. Ned B. Stonehouse, *J. Gresham Machen: A Biographical Memoir* (Grand Rapids: Eerdmans, 1954), 232.

13. J. Gresham Machen, *Christianity and Liberalism* (Grand Rapids: Eerdmans, 1923), 160.

14. Richard Hofstadter, *The Age of Reform* (New York: Vintage Books, 1955), 23.

15. Quoted in Henry May, *The Discontent of the Intellectuals: A Problem of the Twenties* (Chicago: Rand McNally, 1963), 26.

16. Quoted in May, *The Discontent of the Intellectuals*, 29.

17. James Hennesey, SJ, "Religion and American Politics: The Twentieth Century Roman Catholics" (paper presented at a conference on "Religion and American Politics," Institute for the Study of American Evangelicalism, Wheaton, IL, March 1988).

18. Hennesey, "Religion and American Politics."

19. Wilfred Parsons, SJ, "Are Protestants Americans?" *America* 36 (February 5, 1927): 404–6. I am indebted to Deborah Spears for her valuable paper that provides this reference and the basic information for much of this analysis.

20. Robert Anthony Orsi, *The Madonna of 115th Street: Faith and Community in Italian Harlem, 1880–1950* (New Haven: Yale University Press, 1985). On the importance of parish, see John McGreevy, *Parish Boundaries: The Catholic Encounter with Race in the Twentieth-Century Urban North* (Chicago: University of Chicago Press, 1996).

21. I am indebted for some of this discussion to Peter W. Williams, "Catholicism since World War I," in *Encyclopedia of the American Religious Experience*, ed. Charles H. Lippy and Peter W. Williams, 3 vols. (New York: Charles Scribner's Sons, 1988), 1:375–90.

22. Jay P. Dolan, *The American Catholic Experience: A History from Colonial Times to the Present* (Garden City, NY: Doubleday, 1985), 403.

23. Walter Lippmann, *A Preface to Morals* (New York: Macmillan, 1929), 12.

24. Ronald Steele, *Walter Lippmann and the American Century* (Boston: Atlantic-Little, Brown, 1980), 262.

25. Lippmann, *A Preface to Morals*, 31–32.

26. Quoted in Steele, *Walter Lippmann and the American Century*, 262.

27. Pitirim A. Sorokin, *The Crisis of Our Age* (New York: E. P. Dutton, 1941).

28. William E. Leuchtenburg, *The Perils of Prosperity, 1914–1932* (Chicago: University of Chicago Press, 1958), 168.

29. For all these examples, I am indebted to the fine discussion of William E. Leuchtenburg, *The Perils of Prosperity*, 168–71.

30. Frank, *Less than Conquerors*, 210. I am indebted to Frank's analysis on this point.

31. Sydney E. Ahlstrom, *A Religious History of the American People* (New Haven: Yale University Press, 1972), 905 (Luke 2:49 KJV).

32. Leuchtenburg, *Perils of Prosperity*, 142; 153, regarding Mencken's suggestion.

33. Daniel Pawley, "Ernest Hemingway: Tragedy of an Evangelical Family," *Christianity Today*, November 23, 1984, 20–27.

34. Joseph Wood Krutch, *The Modern Temper* (New York: Harcourt, Brace and World, 1929).

35. Carl Becker, *The Heavenly City of the Eighteenth-Century Philosophers* (New Haven: Yale University Press, 1932).

36. Becker, *The Heavenly City*, 14–15.

37. Henry Steele Commager, *The American Mind* (New Haven: Yale University Press, 1950), 100.

38. William James (quoting John Dewey), "What Pragmatism Means," in Perry Miller, *American Thought: Civil War to WWI* (New York: Holt, Rinehart and Winston, 1963 [1954]), 172.

39. John Dewey, *A Common Faith* (New Haven: Yale University Press, 1934).

40. Quoted in Sydney E. Ahlstrom, "Theology in America: A Historical Survey," in *The Shaping of American Religion*, ed. James Ward Smith and A. Leland Jameson, 2 vols. (Princeton: Princeton University Press, 1961), 1:287.

41. H. Richard Niebuhr, *The Church against the World* (1935), from excerpt in Sydney E. Ahlstrom, ed., *Theology in America: The Major Protestant Voices from Puritanism to Neo-Orthodoxy* (Indianapolis: Bobbs-Merrill, 1967), 616.

42. See Richard Wightman Fox, *Reinhold Niebuhr: A Biography* (New York: Pantheon Books, 1985) on these points.

43. See, for example, Reinhold Niebuhr, *The Nature and Destiny of Man* (New York: Charles Scribner's Sons, 1941) or *The Irony of American History* (New York: Charles Scribner's Sons, 1952).

44. Hofstadter, *Age of Reform*, 320.

Notes to Chapter 7

1. See Carl Becker, "What Is Still Living in the Political Philosophy of Thomas Jefferson?" *American Historical Review* 48 (July 1943): 705.

2. For examples of the serious academic discussion—during and after the war—of preserving Christian civilization, see C. T. McIntire, ed., *God, History, and Historians: Modern Christian Views of History* (New York: Oxford University Press, 1977).

3. Richard V. Pierard, "World War II," in *The Wars of America: Christian Views*, ed. Ronald A. Wells (Grand Rapids: Eerdmans, 1981), 147–74; Paul Johnson, *Modern Times: The World from the Twenties to the Eighties* (New York: Harper and Row, 1983), 404.

4. Reinhold Niebuhr, *The Irony of American History* (New York: Charles Scribner's Sons, 1952), 172 and passim.

5. Robert Wuthnow, *The Restructuring of American Religion: Society and Faith since World War II* (Princeton: Princeton University Press, 1988), 16–17.

6. Will Herberg, *Protestant-Catholic-Jew: An Essay in American Religious Sociology* (Garden City, NY: Doubleday, 1955), 14.

7. Martin Marty, *The New Shape of American Religion* (New York: Harper and Row, 1958), 15.

8. Marty, *The New Shape of American Religion*, 31–40.

9. William Lee Miller, *Piety along the Potomac: Notes on Politics and Morals in the Fifties* (Boston: Houghton Mifflin, 1964).

10. Herberg, *Protestant-Catholic-Jew*, 97, with Herberg's added italic.

11. Norman Vincent Peale, *The Power of Positive Thinking* (New York: Prentice-Hall, 1952), 1.

12. Herberg, *Protestant-Catholic-Jew*, 91–94.

13. Herberg, *Protestant-Catholic-Jew*, 86–90.

14. Herberg, *Protestant-Catholic-Jew*, 86.

15. See George M. Marsden, *Reforming Fundamentalism: Fuller Seminary and the New Fundamentalism* (Grand Rapids: Eerdmans, 1987), for a more complete discussion of these issues.

16. Winthrop S. Hudson, *American Protestantism* (Chicago: University of Chicago Press, 1961), 174.

17. See David Edwin Harrell Jr., *Oral Roberts: An American Life* (Bloomington: Indiana University Press, 1985).

18. David O. Levine, *The American College and the Culture of Aspiration, 1915–1940* (Ithaca, NY: Cornell University Press, 1986), 146–50.

19. Dan A. Oren, *Joining the Club: A History of Jews at Yale* (New Haven: Yale University Press, 1985).

20. Neal Gabler, *An Empire of Their Own: How the Jews Invented Hollywood* (New York: Crown Publishers, 1988).

21. Jacob Neusner, "Judaism in Contemporary America," in *Encyclopedia of the American Religious Experience*, ed. Charles H. Lippy and Peter W. Williams, 3 vols. (New York: Charles Scribner's Sons, 1988), 1:321.

22. H. Paul Chalfant, Robert E. Beckley, and C. Eddie Palmer, *Religion in Contemporary Society*, 2nd ed. (Palo Alto, CA: Mayfield Publishing, 1987), 164.

23. Edward L. Queen II, "Judaism," in *The Encyclopedia of American Religious History*, ed. Edward L. Queen II et al. (New York: Facts on File, 1996), 1:333–41; Chalfant, Beckley, and Palmer, *Religion in Contemporary Society*, 164–66; cf. Herberg, *Protestant-Catholic-Jew*, 210.

24. John Dart, "Woody Allen, Theologian," *The Christian Century*, June 22–29, 1977, 585–88.

25. Wuthnow, *The Restructuring of American Religion*, 74.

26. I am indebted to Robert Moats Miller for this quotation in his unpublished essay, "Catholic-Protestant Tensions in Post–World War II America: The Experience of Methodist Bishop G. Bromley Oxnam" (1987).

27. Quoted from *Presbyterian Tribune*, January 1946, 9–10, in Wuthnow, *The Restructuring of American Religion*, 73.

28. Wuthnow, *The Restructuring of American Religion*, 73.

29. Herberg, *Protestant-Catholic-Jew*, 168, 174.

30. Jay P. Dolan, *American Catholic Experience: A History from Colonial Times to the Present* (Garden City, NY: Doubleday, 1985), 385–86.

31. Richard Fox, *Reinhold Niebuhr: A Biography* (New York: Pantheon, 1985), 276.

32. John Courtney Murray, SJ, *We Hold These Truths: Catholic Reflections on the American Proposition* (New York: Sheed and Ward, 1960), 21–22.

33. Marty, *New Shape of American Religion*, 76, 79.

34. See, for example, Sidney E. Mead, *The Lively Experiment: The Shaping of Christianity in America* (New York: Harper and Row, 1963), 68.

35. David L. Chappell, *A Stone of Hope: Prophetic Religion and the Death of Jim Crow* (Chapel Hill: University of North Carolina Press, 2004), suggests the importance of the combination of Niebuhrian realism with peaceful protests and the revival fervor of the African-American heritage.

36. From *Ebony*, August 1965, 7, quoted in James H. Cone, "Black Religious Thought," in *Encyclopedia of the American Religious Experience*, 2:1, 181. I am indebted to this article for its insights on King. Also valuable is Richard Lischer, *The Preacher King: Martin Luther King, Jr., and the Word That Moved America* (New York: Oxford University Press, 1995).

37. Stephen B. Oates, *Let the Trumpet Sound: The Life of Martin Luther King, Jr.* (New York: New American Library, 1985 [1981]), 84–85.

38. Milton C. Sernett, ed., *Afro-American Religious History* (Durham: Duke University Press, 1985), 423.

39. Oates, *Let the Trumpet Sound*, 87.

40. https://www.aol.com/article/news/2017/01/16/dr-martin-luther-kings-i-have -a-dream-speech-full-text/21655947/.

41. National Conference of Black Churchmen, "Black Power Statement, July 31, 1966 and Black Theology Statement, June 13, 1969," in *Afro-American Religious History*, 465–88.

Notes to Chapter 8

1. See Theodore Roszak, *The Making of a Counter Culture: Reflections on the Technocratic Society and Its Youthful Opposition* (Garden City, NY: Doubleday, 1969), 8.

2. Roszak, *The Making of a Counter Culture*, 8.

3. See Steven M. Tipton, *Getting Saved from the Sixties* (Berkeley: University of California Press, 1982), 15 and passim.

4. Harvey Cox, *The Secular City: Secularization and Urbanization in Theological Perspective*, rev. ed. (New York: Macmillan, 1966 [1965]), 4, 10, 109.

5. Leonard Sweet, "The 1960s: The Crisis of Liberal Christianity and the Public Emergence of Evangelicalism," in *Evangelicalism and Modern America*, ed. George Marsden (Grand Rapids: Eerdmans, 1984), 33.

6. Cf. Sweet, "The 1960s: The Crisis of Liberal Christianity"; Tipton, *Getting Saved from the Sixties*; Robert N. Bellah et al., *Habits of the Heart: Individualism and Commitment in American Life* (Berkeley: University of California Press, 1985).

7. Statement from Stanley Hauerwas to the author.

8. John McGreevy, *Parish Boundaries: The Catholic Encounter with Race in the Twentieth-Century Urban North* (Chicago: University of Chicago Press, 1996).

9. Jay P. Dolan, *The American Catholic Experience: A History from Colonial Times to the Present* (Garden City, NY: Doubleday, 1985), 424.

10. I am grateful for the valuable discussions of Jay P. Dolan, *American Catholic Experience*, 425–30, which I follow closely in this section.

11. Dolan, *American Catholic Experience*, 433–37.

12. Peter W. Williams, "Catholicism Since World War I," in *Encyclopedia of the American Religious Experience*, ed. Charles H. Lippy and Peter W. Williams, 3 vols. (New York: Charles Scribner's Sons, 1988), 1:384–86.

13. Dolan, *American Catholic Experience*, 442; Williams, "Catholicism since World War I," 387.

14. Margaret Bendroth, "The Search for Women's Role in American Evangelicalism, 1930–1980," in *Evangelicalism and Modern America*, 122–34; Rosemary Skinner Keller, "Women and Religion," in *Encyclopedia of the American Religious Experience*, 3:1547–62. See also Mark Chaves, *Ordaining Women: Culture and Conflict in Religious Organizations* (Cambridge: Harvard University Press, 1997).

15. Jack Drescher, "Out of DSM: Depathologizing Homosexuality," *Behavioral Science*, Dec. 2015, 565–75. https://www.ncbi.nlm.nih.gov/pmc/articles/PMC4695779/.

16. Charles S. Prebish, "Buddhism," 2:669–82; John Y. Fenton, "Hinduism," 2:683–98; C. Carlyle Haaland, "Shinto and Indigenous Chinese Religion," 2:699–709; Newell S. Booth Jr., "Islam in North America," 2:723–29, all in *Encyclopedia of the American Religious Experience*. Thomas A. Tweed, *The American Encounter with Buddhism, 1844–1912: Victorian Culture and the Limits of Dissent* (Bloomington: Indiana University Press, 1992).

17. Thomas Robbins and Dick Anthony, "Cults in the Late Twentieth Century," in *Encyclopedia of the American Religious Experience*, 2:747–48.

18. See Prebish, "Buddhism", 2:669–82; Fenton, "Hinduism", 2:683–98; Robert S. Ellwood, "Occult Movements in America," 2:699–710; and Thomas Robbins and Dick Anthony, "Cults in the Late Twentieth Century," 2:741–54, all in *Encyclopedia of the American Religious Experience*.

19. Robert S. Ellwood, *Alternative Altars: Unconventional and Eastern Spirituality in America* (Chicago: University of Chicago Press, 1979), 21.

20. Ellwood, *Alternative Altars*, 34.

21. Tipton, *Getting Saved from the Sixties*, 1–24.

22. Bellah et al., *Habits of the Heart*, 43–48.

23. Bellah, *Habits of the Heart*, 72.

24. Bellah, *Habits of the Heart*, 228; from a 1978 Gallup poll.

25. Bellah, *Habits of the Heart*, 221.

26. Christopher Lasch, *The Culture of Narcissism* (New York: Norton, 1991 [1979]), 57, 59.

27. For instance, Wilfred M. McClay, *The Masterless: Self and Society in Modern America* (Chapel Hill: University of North Carolina Press, 1994); David Brooks, *Bobos in Paradise: The New Upper Class and How It Got There* (New York: Simon and Schuster, 2000).

28. Constant H. Jacquet, ed., "Church Membership Statistics, 1940–1985, for selected U.S. Denominations," *Yearbook of American and Canadian Churches* (Nashville: Abingdon Press, 1987), 254–55.

29. Jacquet, ed., "Church Membership Statistics, 1940–1985," 254–55.

30. See Jerry Falwell, ed., *The Fundamentalist Phenomenon* (Garden City, NY: Doubleday, 1981), 18.

31. Paul Chalfant, Robert E. Beckley, and C. Eddie Palmer, *Religion in Contemporary Society*, 2nd ed. (Palo Alto, CA: Mayfield, 1987), 157. This book lists 52.5 million Catholics, 39 million mainline Protestants, 37 million conservative Protestants (nonmembers of the National Council of Churches), and 5.5 million Jews for 1985.

32. Darren Dochuk, *From Bible Belt to Sun Belt: Plain-Folk Religion, Grassroots Politics, and the Rise of Evangelical Conservatism* (New York: Norton, 2011).

33. Robert Wuthnow, *The Restructuring of American Religion: Society and Faith Since World War II* (Princeton: Princeton University Press, 1988), 200–205.

34. Wuthnow, *The Restructuring of American Religion*, 156.

35. Randall Balmer, *Redeemer: The Life of Jimmy Carter* (New York: Basic Books, 2014), 103–8.

36. William Martin, "Mass Communications," in *Encyclopedia of the American Religious Experience*, 3:1719–23.

37. I am indebted to Robert Wuthnow, *Restructuring of American Religion*, 314–22, for his valuable insights on these points.

38. The Web site www.adherents.com lists the Church of God in Christ, the largest black denomination and fourth largest of all American denominations, as having five and a half million adherents in 1991.

39. This is based on Robert Wuthnow, *After Heaven: Spirituality in America since the 1950s* (Berkeley: University of California Press, 1998).

Notes to Chapter 9

1. Joel Carpenter and Wilbert Shenk, *Earthen Vessels: American Evangelicals and Foreign Missions, 1880–1980* (Grand Rapids: Wm. B. Eerdmans, 1990), xii.

2. These estimates, like most such statistics, vary widely. The Web site www.adherents

.com in 1999 listed 105 million Pentecostals. *1998 Britannica Book of the Year* reported 540 million Pentecostals *and* charismatics worldwide.

3. Mark Noll, *The New Shape of World Christianity* (Downers Grove, IL: IVP Academic, 2006), 20–21, 189–200.

4. Number of Muslims in the United States, http://www.adherents.com/largecom/com_islam_usa.html.

5. George H. Gallup Jr., *Religion in America 1996* (Princeton: Princeton Religion Research Center, 1996), 4–5.

6. Robert D. Putnam and David E. Campbell, *American Grace: How Religion Divides and Unites Us* (New York: Simon and Schuster, 2010), 104–5.

7. Cary Funk and Greg Smith, "Nones on the Rise: One-in-Five Adults Have No Religious Affiliation," Pew Forum on Religion and Public Life, October 9, 2012.

8. Putnam and Campbell, *American Grace,* 403. "Changing Attitudes on Gay Marriage," Pew Research Center: Religion and Public Life, http://www.pewforum.org/fact-sheet/changing-attitudes-on-gay-marriage/.

9. One of the more telling evidences for this conclusion is that in a 2011 survey only 30 percent of white evangelicals agreed with the statement that "an elected official who commits an immoral act in their personal life can still behave ethically and fulfill their duties in their public and professional life." In 2016, when Donald Trump was the Republican candidate for president, approval of the same statement skyrocketed to 72 percent, moving "evangelicals" from being the most judgmental group surveyed on that issue, to the least judgmental. From Public Religion Research polls cited in Thomas B. Edsall, "Trump Says Jump. His Supporters Say, How High?" *New York Times,* Sept. 14, 2017.

10. Stephen V. Monsma, "What Is an Evangelical? And Does It Matter?" *Christian Scholar's Review* 46:4 (Summer 2017): 323–40, provides excellent insights on this issue.

11. Pew Research Center, "How the Faithful Voted: A Preliminary Analysis," November 2016. These groups differed in voting patterns in similar degrees in the preceding elections.

12. Pew Research Center, "America's Changing Religious Landscape," Pew Forum on Religious and Public Life, May 12, 2015. These numbers include a good many whose evangelical affiliation may be loose. They are mostly based on denominational affiliation and do not include people who identify with what Pew labels as "historically black Protestantism," and they also exclude Catholics who self-apply the term "born again."

13. David Van Biema and Jeff Chu, "Does God Want You to Be Rich?" *Time,* September 10, 2006.

14. Kate Bowler, *Blessed* (New York: Oxford University Press, 2013), 239–42.

15. David Van Biema, "Ten Ideas That Are Changing the World Right Now" and "The New Calvinism," *Time,* March 12, 2009.

16. Gallup, "Most Americans Still Believe in God," 2016 poll.

17. Pew Research Forum, "Attendance at Religious Services," Pew Landscape Study, 2014.

18. C. Kirk Hadaway and Penny Long Marler, "How Many Americans Attend Worship Each Week? An Alternative Approach to Measurement," *Journal for the Scientific Study of Religion* 44:3 (2005): 307–22.

19. George Gallup Jr. and Timothy Jones, *The Saints Among Us* (Richfield, CT: Morehouse Publishing, 1992), 14–15. At that time, the 13 percent accounted for only about one-third of

those who reported regular church attendance (43 percent)(p. 19). And that was at a time when reported attendance rates were somewhat higher than in twenty-first-century surveys.

20. Christian Smith, *Soul Searching: The Religious and Spiritual Lives of American Teenagers* (New York: Oxford University Press, 2005), esp. 162–70.

21. Paraphrase of Stanley Hauerwas.

22. Putnam and Campbell, *American Grace*, 444–54. These figures, which vary little across religious traditions, are compatible with the 13 percent of the earlier survey if, as is likely, a strong core of regular churchgoers give disproportionately higher amounts of their time and money.

23. D. W. Miller, "Measuring the Role of 'the Faith Factor' in Social Change," reporting on estimate by Ram A. Cnaan, *Chronicle of Higher Education,* November 26, 1999, A21.

Index

Index

Index

English Civil War. *See* Civil War (England)

English Reformation, 14–15

Enlightenment, 38–41, 45, 50, 54–55, 63, 65, 71, 81–82, 103, 108, 137, 158, 219

Episcopalians, 90, 104, 254. *See also* Anglicanism

equality; spiritual sources of, 23–24; for women, 68, 86, 88, 112. *See also* feminism

Equal Rights Amendment, 239, 241

Erhard Seminars Training (EST), 233

established churches, establishment of churches, 8, 21, 24, 27–28, 33, 37, 41–42, 50–53, 55, 131, 163; antidisestablishmentarianism, 55

ethnic groups: Catholic, 77, 126–30, 131–32; Eastern Orthodox churches and, 134–35; Jewish, 135–39; Protestant, 130. *See also* immigration

evangelicals and evangelicalism, 29, 33, 59–68, 235–46; and Billy Graham, 198–200; and Billy Sunday, 168–69; Catholic, 179–80; divisions within, 68–69, 235–39; evangelical left, 239; millennialism and, 67–68; white evangelicals, 259–60. *See also* revivalism

evolution, 170–71; Scopes Trial and, 173–74. *See also* Darwin, Charles

Falwell, Jerry, 200, 242–43, 245–46

Farrakhan, Louis, 250

Father Divine, 214

Federal Council of Churches, 125, 165, 195, 199

feminism, 228–30

Fillmore, Millard, 92

Finney, Charles G., 58–61, 63–64, 68, 88, 91, 146, 168. *See also* Oberlin College

First Amendment, 50, 52

First Great Awakening. *See* Great Awakening

First World War. *See* World War I

Fletcher, Joseph, 223

Folklore of Capitalism, The (Arnold), 190

Ford, Henry, 202

Fosdick, Harry Emerson, 172, 189, 199

Fox, George, 26, 71

Fox News, 247

France, New World missionaries and, 14

Franklin, Benjamin, 39

free individual, evangelicalism and, 60–61

Free Masonry. *See* Masons

Free Methodist Church, 146

French and Indian Wars, 46

Freud, Sigmund, 120, 182

Fuller, Charles E., 198–99

Fuller, Margaret, 81

Full Gospel Businessmen's Fellowship International, 201, 237

fundamentalists, 91, 158–59, 171–72, 175–76, 237; election of 1928 and, 176–77; Falwell and, 200, 242–43; Graham and, 198–200; modernists and, 167–69; Scopes Trial and, 173–76, 243

Fundamentals, The (books), 168

Gallup surveys, 255, 264

Gandhi, Mahatma, 211

Garvey, Marcus, 214

gay and lesbian movement, 230, 258–59

German immigrants, 78, 132–34; World War I and, 165–66

Germany: Jews from, 137–38. *See also* German immigrants; Hitler, Adolf; Nazis

Gibbons, James Cardinal, 115, 130–31

Gilded Age, 99–100, 106

Gilded Age, The (Twain and Warner), 100

Gingrich, Newt, 249

Gladden, Washington, 116

Global South, 251–52, 258

Glorious Revolution, 25

"God is Dead" movement, 222

Grace, Sweet Daddy, 214

Graham, Billy, 198–200, 236

Graham, Sylvester, 83

Great Awakening, 29–32, 45–46; missions and, 31–32; Second, 57; slaves and, 33–34; women and, 34–35, 88. *See also* Whitefield, George

Great Britain, 252–53

Great War. *See* World War I

Guyana, 232

Habits of the Heart (Bellah), 234–35, 247

Hamilton, Alexander, 57

Hansen, Marcus, 139

Index